CW01657868

P

The Home Book of German Cookery

The Home Book of GERMAN COOKERY

Hanne Lambley

FABER AND FABER
London Boston

First published in 1979
by Faber and Faber Limited
3 Queen Square London WC1N 3AU
Typeset by
Latimer Trend & Company Ltd Plymouth
Printed in Great Britain by
Redwood Burn Ltd, Trowbridge & Esher
All rights reserved

© *Hanne Lambley 1979*

CONDITIONS OF SALE

This book is sold subject to the condition that it shall not, by way of trade or otherwise, be lent, re-sold, hired out or otherwise circulated without the publisher's prior consent in any form of binding or cover other than that in which it is published and without a similar condition including this condition being imposed on the subsequent purchaser

British Library Cataloguing in Publication Data

Lambley, Hanne
The home book of German cookery.
1. Cookery, German
I. Title
641.5′943 TX721

ISBN 0-571-11394-X
ISBN 0-571-11419-9 Pbk

In memory of my Mother Elsbeth Mangold
and with love and gratitude to my Husband Donald

Contents

Acknowledgements

My thanks are due to:

Familie Heute and *Bäckerpost,* publishers Dr Holm, Köln; Hotel- and Gaststätten-Verbände in Germany; Fremdenverkehrsverbände in Germany; Pott Rumhandelshaus, Flensburg; Eckes Stammhaus, Nieder-Olm; Centrale Marketinggesellschaft der Deutschen Agrarwirtschaft, Bonn; Weinkellerei Gerhard Stratmann, Nierstein; Alfred Schladerer, Schwarzwälder Brennerei, Staufen im Breisgau; W. Mast Spirituosenfabrik, Wolfenbüttel; Deinhard Wine and Champagne Company, Koblenz; G. Vetter-Liqueur, Wunsiedel; Stadtverwaltung Wuppertal; Landkreis Harburg and Frau Röhrs, Wesel; Verbraucher—Zentrale Niedersachsen, Hannover; Verein Naturschutzpark, Hamburg; Statistisches Bundesamt, Wiesbaden; Bundesausschuss für Volkswirtschaftliche Aufklärung e.V., Köln; and all my friends and relations in Germany.

Introduction

The climate and geography of a country have a considerable influence on the life-style of its inhabitants. Over the years, people in different parts of the world have developed different traditional ways of living. These differences are very clearly reflected in dietary habits. Every country has its own traditions and specialities as far as food and drink are concerned. One path towards an understanding of a foreign country and its population leads through the stomach.

What do Germans eat and drink? 'Sauerkraut, sausages and beer' seems to be the general opinion, when German food is mentioned. German cooking has a reputation of being substantial, simple and fattening and is by no means as famous as the French cuisine. Visitors to Germany, however, will have discovered that the German kitchen has a wide culinary range and that there are also regional differences within the country. If one were to question German people on their traditional ways of eating, different specialities would be named by those in the south of the country from those in the north. This is due partly to geographical factors and partly to political development. East Germany, which includes large agricultural areas, is now under a separate administration. West Germany, being a federal republic, consists of eleven states, each with a certain measure of autonomy. Geographically, the country is flat in the north, hilly and wooded in the centre and alpine in the south. It is surrounded by ten other countries which have also influenced German cooking across the borders. The Bavarian kitchen reflects the proximity of Austria in eating habits whilst the adjacent Scandinavian countries have influenced the cuisine of North Germany.

A number of recipes in this book refer to the region from which they originate and how they were created. An attempt is made to present a general picture of the German cooking and eating pattern and also to take the reader on a culinary journey through the kitchens of the various regions.

The German working day sees an early start, and the people have developed the practice of taking a first and second breakfast. The early breakfast usually consists of fresh bread rolls, one or two kinds of bread served with unsalted butter, boiled egg, jam, cheese and a freshly made pot of coffee. Most people have to take their second breakfast—also called Vesper or Brotzeit—between 10 and 11 o'clock at their place of work: a sausage or cheese sandwich brought from home accompanied by a drink of coffee, milk or beer. Children usually take a sandwich and an apple or other fruit to school. On Sundays, the first breakfast is taken later with the family, and slices of fruit loaf or plain cake are served in addition to the usual fare. Instead of the second breakfast, the Frühschoppen between 11 o'clock and 12 noon is popular when a clear soup or other appetizer and a glass of beer or wine is taken. The main cooked meal of the day is lunch, usually consisting of soup, main course and dessert.

Between 4 and 5 o'clock is the time for a pot of coffee and some home-made cake, or a visit to one of the many pleasant cafés which are found even in villages and in greater number in towns and cities. Cafés in Germany are quite different from those in present-day England. They bear more similarity to the earlier coffee houses. Only cakes, gateaux, coffee, cocoa, tea, liqueurs and ice creams are served. The coffee hour is often the meeting and 'chatting' time, particularly for women. The saying 'coffee parties are gatherings where the best is eaten and drunk and the worst is talked' seems to describe the event quite well.

On Sundays or birthdays, it is at coffee time that family friends and relations are invited. Cakes and gateaux are usually home made, but it is also possible to purchase them at the numerous bakeries and Konditoreien (patisseries), where they are usually prepared on the premises.

The evening meal consists of soups or light casserole dishes followed by salads and open sandwiches served with a drink of beer or sometimes tea. Restaurants and public houses also serve sandwich 'platters' with drinks at almost any time of the day.

Germans are always prepared to have a bread snack (Brotzeit), consisting of bread or fresh rolls with cold or roast meat, sausages or cheese. This explains the many sausage rotisseries in towns and cities where sausages are roasted or fried and sold with bread rolls.

There is no official supper in the evening, but most Germans settle down for the evening with a bottle of beer or invite friends to a glass of wine or 'Bowle', when also salt or cheese biscuits and open sandwiches are served.

Since the end of the Second World War, several million people from the East have moved to live in West Germany and have brought with them their ways of eating and cooking. The habit of serving fruit with meat and other savoury food is an acquired *East German* taste. Carp from the Mecklenburg lakes, roast herb sausage from Thüringen, poultry and potato dumplings are familiar items on the East German menu. Their agricultural areas present opportunities for the collection of berries and herbs for the production of delicious spirits and liqueurs.

Well known are cakes from *Saxony,* of which the Dresden Christstollen (Christmas Cake) is regarded as the king. From this area originates the expression 'flower coffee' which is a coffee best avoided, being so thin as to allow the flower pattern in the bottom of the cup to be seen.

Also in Saxony the first European porcelain (Meissner) was manufactured by Friedrich Böttger in 1710, setting an attractive frame for a well-presented coffee table. To this day, great emphasis is placed on a well-laid table by the German housewife, with crisp table-cloths, tasteful crockery and cutlery. Coffee tables are usually set with a vase of flowers in the centre.

The inhabitants of *Berlin* have a special affinity for sour and salty food, the development of which can be traced back to the Emperor Frederick the Great and his salt monopoly. The same emperor is also responsible for the Berliners' liking for potatoes. Sauerkraut, Kasseler, Berliner pancakes (doughnuts) and tree cake (Baumkuchen) have their origin in Berlin.

In the *North German* diet, fish dishes play an important part. The agricultural state of Schleswig-Holstein with its extensive pig-farming provides for the production of the well-known smoked ham (Schinken). The area around Hamburg and Bremen provides a large part of Germany's poultry. Lower Saxony is Germany's main potato growing area. The cold winds from the sea make warming drinks a necessity. The North Germans, particularly the East Fresians, like tea and grog—a hot rum and water drink. Spirits from cereals, berries and herbs are distilled in different parts of North Germany, one of which—Kümmel from Hamburg—is very popular.

Although not in a wine growing area, the Ratskeller of Bremen offers the longest wine-list of all German wine restaurants, a choice of six hundred different wines being available.

Westphalians like substantial food. Apart from the industrial area around the Ruhr district, the land is used for farming. Pumpernickel, sausages, ham and beer are the specialities. A visitor to Westphalia will admire the appetite its inhabitants develop around the well-known coffee table in the afternoon (Bergische Kaffeetafel). Together with a large pot of coffee, the following selection is served: freshly baked waffles, dark rye bread, raisin bread, milk rice, apple syrup, jam, honey, unsalted butter, curd cheese, sliced hard cheese, fresh fruit and whipped cream.

People from the *Rhineland* are said to be of a particularly happy nature and this is often ascribed to the growing of wine in the area. The Rhinelanders enjoy celebrating and, with Munich, this is the area where Karneval—before the beginning of Lent—is celebrated, with Cologne and Mainz as the centres. The autumn witnesses a series of wine festivals in almost all the villages and towns where wine is grown. A number of wine festivals take place along the so-called 'German Wine Street' which stretches for eighty kilometres through the south of the Rhineland Palatinate, the best known being the Dürkheimer Wurstmarkt. Speyrer Bretzel are eaten with the wine. People in the Rhineland have such a liking for potatoes that they have even created recipes for main meals consisting of potatoes only.

During the last few years the very old way of cooking meat, roasts and vegetables in clay pots has been revived. The Römertopf is manufactured in the Westerwald from local clay and is certainly effective in retaining the full flavour of the food.

Hessen's most widely known speciality, the Frankfurter sausage, can look back on a long tradition, having been first produced in 1280. Hessen apple cider, Frankfurt 'green sauce' and 'hand cheese with music' (the hand-shaped sour cheese with onions) also enjoy great popularity.

In *South Germany* dumplings and noodles are preferred with meals instead of potatoes. The consumption of farinaceous food is a habit shared by Austrian and Italian neighbours. Noodles called Spätzle are also cooked in soups, which accompany almost every meal in Baden-Württemberg. Rolls, cakes and the savoury onion cake are just as much a speciality as the sausages, the wines and the famous fruit brandies, one of which led to the famous recipe for the Black Forest Gateau.

In *Bavaria* many kinds of dumplings are available, together with the well-known range of strudels. In Bavaria or Baden-Württemberg, strudel is regarded not as a dessert but as a main course dish, only preceded by a vegetable or potato soup. Consumption of meat takes place here in large quantities and game is available from the forests. Specialities such as Leberkäse, Weisswurst and liver balls are also very much appreciated by visitors to Bavaria.

An attraction for tourists is the Munich October festival which was introduced 160 years ago as a public festival for a sovereign's wedding. During its sixteen days, many a Mass (1 litre) or Halbe ($\frac{1}{2}$ litre) of beer are consumed. In between drinks the Bavarians 'assist' their thirst by eating salted Radi (radish), cheese and bretzel. The city of Nuremberg is famous for its spicy cakes and marzipan.

The recipes in this book have been chosen as being typical of German cooking. From the wealth of available material, it has not always been easy to decide which of the typical German dishes might appeal to the foreign palate. It is, however, hoped that the book will revive happy memories for those who have already visited Germany and sampled the country's food, whilst introducing the German way of eating to those who have not yet toured the country. Where possible, appropriate background information has been given to make the book more than just a collection of recipes. It is hoped that the book will encourage readers to try German specialities at home.

Through the German Cooking Year

1. New Year's Day is a well-established holiday in Germany when it is common to write cards with good wishes to friends and relations. Bakeries and patisseries sell 'New Year's circles' (Neujahrskränze) of varying sizes, consisting of plaited rings made from yeast dough. For afternoon coffee-time, a New Year's Gateau (Neujahrstorte) is often served which is a buttercream gateau, decorated as a clock face or a page of the calendar.

2. Karneval, Fastnacht or Fasching is the time between 7 January and Ash Wednesday, although officially it begins on 11 November. Cologne, Mainz and Munich are the centres for the carnival's activities, with the four days before Ash Wednesday being the main time. Particularly on the Monday (Rosenmontag), processions, fancy-dress parties and balls accompanied by much drinking are held in towns and cities decorated with confetti and streamers. Carnival is the time to bake Cologne Muzen. Plenty of rollmops, pickled gherkins and pickled beetroot are prepared for the morning of Ash Wednesday when they are consumed with beer at the 'hangover breakfast' (Katerfrühstück).

3. Easter, the first large festival of the year, comes with the beginning of spring when the custom of giving Easter eggs is widespread. Some chocolate eggs are presented but more usually hens' eggs, these having been hard boiled and then coloured and decorated. For children it is a very important and enjoyable Easter activity to collect eggs which the Easter rabbit has hidden for them in the house and garden. Carefully painted eggshells are also used for decorations in the house; with cotton threads they are suspended from birch circles or branches arranged in a vase. In Bavarian villages it is the custom to decorate the fountain in the market square with painted eggshells and flowers during the night of Easter Saturday.

At Easter the food on the breakfast and evening-meal table is usually dominated by hard-boiled Easter eggs. The traditional Easter roast for lunch is leg of lamb. For coffee-time in the afternoon families have either sponge cake baked in the shape of an Easter lamb and dusted with icing sugar or an Easter gateau which is a basic gateau filled and covered with whipped cream and decorated with chocolate Easter rabbits and small sugar eggs.

4. *Whitsuntide* marks the beginning of the summer. It is the time of the first woodruff Bowle (Waldmeisterbowle) and fresh strawberry cake.

5. *The Christmas Period* begins with the first Sunday in Advent. This is the time for the housewife to start her Christmas baking, beginning with the Christmas bread (Stollen). Then tin after tin is filled with Christmas biscuits. Spekulatius, cinnamon stars, peppernuts, Printen and marzipan. Most of these are kept for Christmas although some are used to fill the children's shoes on St Nikolaus day (6 December). In Swabia, Hutzelbrot is prepared during Christmas time. Many mothers bake Nuremberg honey-cakes and construct a honey-cake house which is given to the children on Christmas Eve. The traditional Advent circle with four candles and vases with fir branches decorate the house during the four weeks before Christmas; the Christmas tree is only put in place on Christmas Eve. It is an old tradition to decorate it with red apples, home-baked biscuits, nuts, hand-made straw stars and beeswax candles. Among the presents which are exchanged on Christ-

mas Eve, everybody receives a plate with biscuits, nuts and marzipan. Carp in beer or goose are traditional for Christmas dinner.

6. *On New Year's Eve* (Silvester) parties are held throughout the land. Rooms are decorated with paper streamers. A Feuerzangenbowle helps to pass the time before midnight when church bells and fireworks greet the New Year. Then champagne and a light meal or open sandwiches and salads are served. In most parts of Germany carp in wine is the traditional New Year's Eve meal.

Herbs and Spices

The taste and scent of herbs and spices are often inseparable from certain dishes. They should, however, integrate with the food rather than dominate it.

Aniseed (Anis) The seeds are used in baking, especially for Christmas baking.

Basil (Basilikum) This herb originated from Mediterranean areas. The leaves are used in sauces, soups and with fish.

Bay-leaves (Lorbeer) Dried evergreen leaves from the bay-tree; they grow in the Mediterranean area. They are used in the preparation of soups, vegetables, meat, fish and preserves.

Bean Herb (Bohnenkraut) This originated from the Black Sea area and grows well in the European climate. It has an aromatic, peppery taste. The plants are cut and dried before the flowers develop. The herb should be added whilst cooking beans and then removed.

Caraway Seeds (Kümmel) Originally growing wild, they are now cultivated. The spicy seeds are used in cheese, bread, preserves, sausage and brandy.

Cardamom (Kardamom) A pea-sized dried fruit from Ceylon and India. The spicy ground seeds are used in Christmas baking and sausage preparation.

Chervil (Kerbel) A sweet aromatic herb belonging to the parsley family; used in soups, omelettes and sauces.

Cinnamon (Zimt) This is the bark of the evergreen cinnamon tree. Ceylon cinnamon is particularly good in quality. It is light, thin and rolls up into shape. The originally 40 cm (16 in) long cinnamon bark bars are cut into 10 cm (4 in) lengths before being sold in Europe. Cinnamon powder is produced from ground bark. It is used for sweet soups and sauces, stewed fruit, cakes, Christmas baking and punches. Cinnamon bark and powder should be kept in a dark airtight container.

Cloves (Nelken) These are the dried flower buds of trees which grow in Madagascar. The scent is similar to that of garden carnations. They are used when cooking red cabbage, in marinades, preserves, stewed fruit, game and Christmas baking.

Garlic (Knoblauch) An onion type of plant from Asia, although it is possible to grow it in an English garden. It is used in sauces, dressings, meat and sausages.

Juniper (Wachholder) The dark berries take two years to ripen. They usually come from Italy. They are used in marinades and in the preparation of sauerkraut, sour roast, game and brandy.

Marjoram (Majoran) An aromatic herb, originally from southern Europe, it will grow in the British climate. It is used in salads, dressings, meat and sausages.

Mustard Seeds (Senfkörner) The white mustard seeds are an aromatic spice used in marinades and in the preparation of preserves and sausages.

Nutmeg (Muskatnuss) These are seeds from nutmeg trees which grow in Brazil and Africa. Ground nutmeg is used as flavouring in baking, potato dishes, cereal dishes and sausages.

Thyme (Thymian) Originating from southern Europe, it is an aromatic herb used in salads, dressings, sauces, meat and sausages. It is often combined with marjoram.

Vanilla (Vanille) The pod of a Mexican orchid plant, its mild aromatic flavouring is used in milk and cream dishes, fruits and cakes. Vanilla sugar is commercially produced by mixing pulverized vanilla pods with sugar. It can also be obtained by keeping 3–4 vanilla pods in a tightly closed sugar-filled jar.

Shopping for German Provisions in England

The availability of German provisions in this country has increased considerably in recent years and now most supermarket chains carry a reasonable selection. The choice is, however, sometimes limited and a fuller range is normally available among the department stores and more particularly the specialist delicatessen shops which are found in all the major cities.

Firms which are known to market German provisions in their supermarkets and hypermarkets are:

Budgen Food Shops
Cater Bros (Provisions) Ltd
W. H. Cullen
Mac Fisheries
Marks & Spencer Ltd
Oakeshotts Ltd
Safeway Food Stores Ltd
J. Sainsbury Ltd
Tesco Stores Ltd
Waitrose Supermarkets
F. W. Woolworth & Co. Ltd

Department stores to be found in London (with, in some cases, branches elsewhere in the country) are Fortnum and Mason Ltd, Harrods Ltd, John Lewis Partnership and Selfridges.

Mention must also be made of The German Food Centre Ltd, 44 Knightsbridge, London SW1 (which carries a wide range of German grocery), Joseph Burton & Sons, Smithy Row, Nottingham, and the branches of Lewis's Ltd.

USEFUL ADDRESSES

The following are not retailers but may be approached for information on retailers in your area.

'Schladerer' spirits, e.g. Schwarzwälder Kirschwasser:
Messrs. Walter S. Siegel Ltd.
43/44 Albemarle Street
London W1X 3FE

Wine and champagne:
Deinhard & Co. Ltd
29 Addington Street
London SE1 7XT

Herb liqueur:
'Underberg' Ltd
8 The Mall
Ealing
London W5 2PJ

'Apollinaris' natural springwater:
Britvic Ltd
West House
Broomfield Road
Chelmsford CM1 1TU

German bread mixture:
German and International Food Imports Ltd
Stour Street
Manningtree
Essex

'Römertopf'—U.K. distributors:
Ideal Home Household Equipment London Ltd
Endeavour House
North Circular Road
Brent Cross
London NW2 1JT

Frenzli (Sauerkraut):
Robert A. Jewison Ltd
Mandrell Road
London SW2

Weights and Measures

Metric weights and measures are used for the recipes with imperial quantities in brackets. You should stick to one or the other system for each recipe. The conversions are not exact equivalents but are intended to produce the same proportions of ingredients. The imperial recipes will produce slightly larger quantities than the metric.

The Germans tend to eat larger portions of a particular dish than are served in this country, but with less variety in a meal. The majority of the recipes would cater for four to six people depending on their appetites, but some should be prepared in larger quantities to do the recipe justice (e.g. Labskaus).

Soups

(*Suppen*)

Savoury Soups	**Herzhafte Suppen**
Clear Meat Broth	Fleischbrühe
Clear Broth from Bones	Knochenbrühe
Clear Chicken Broth	Hühnerbrühe
Creamy Chicken Soup	Hühnercremesuppe
Accompaniments for Clear Soups:	Suppeneinlagen:
Clotted Egg	Eierstich
Baked Flour 'Peas'	Backerbsen
Riebele	Riebele
Sliced Pancakes	Flädle
Swabian Noodles	Spätzle
Meat Balls	Fleischklösschen
Marrow Dumplings	Markklösschen
Cheese Balls	Käseklösschen
Hamburg Eel Soup	Hamburger Aalsuppe
Sausage Soup	Wurstsuppe
Goulash Soup	Gulaschsuppe
Potato Soup	Kartoffelsuppe
Pea Soup	Erbsensuppe
Lentil Soup	Linsensuppe
Dried Bean Soup	Bohnensuppe

Green Bean Soup	Grüne Bohnensuppe
Hunters' Soup	Jägersuppe
Mixed Vegetable Soup	Gemüsesuppe
Fresh Asparagus Soup	Spargelsuppe
Cheese Soup	Käsesuppe
Bread Soup	Brotsuppe

Sweet Soups	**Süsse Suppen**
Beer Soup	Biersuppe
Wine Soup	Weinsuppe
Fruit Soup	Obstsuppe
Elderberry Soup	Holunderbeersuppe
Soured Cream Soup	Schmandsuppe
Rose-hip Soup	Hagebuttensuppe
Rusk Soup	Zwiebacksuppe
Milk Soup	Milchsuppe
Buttermilk Soup	Buttermilchsuppe
Chocolate Soup	Schokoladensuppe
Cold Gooseberry Soup	Stachelbeerkaltschale
Cherry Soup	Kirschsuppe

The Germans like their home-made soups. The quality of a cook or housewife is believed to show in the ability to prepare a tasty soup—be it as a starter or as a heavy main course soup. Clear meat soups are popular all over the country, but especially liked in Württemberg, the 'soup land' where they are served with different garnishes and where a meal is felt to be incomplete without soup. North Germany specializes in fish soups and fruit soups whilst the Bavarians like sweet soups.

Soups are served in bowls or cups. The word 'Suppe' originates from the old German word 'supen' which means 'to sip noisily'. Nowadays this habit is not greatly appreciated. For certain types of soup served in a cup, however, it is still permitted to lead the cup to the mouth, holding it with the right hand only, after half the cup has been emptied by spoon. It is also regarded as bad manners to blow soup if it is too hot. It should be stirred slowly and gently with the spoon.

The versatility of German soups makes it possible to serve them on almost any occasion: for a second breakfast on a Sunday between 10 o'clock and midday (usually a clear soup or oxtail soup served in a cup); for a business breakfast; in between meals; as a TV snack; as a midnight snack during a party. The soup eating habit has also influenced some German customs for its symbolical value. It is the custom in some parts of East Germany for the bride and bridegroom to empty a bowl of soup together before going to church. For good luck both have to start and finish spooning the soup together.

SAVOURY SOUPS *(Herzhafte Suppen)*

Clear soups are the most popular first course for a meal in Germany and are varied by the use of different garnishes. It is important to start the soup by putting the meat or bones into cold water, as this makes a richer soup.

Clear Meat Broth *(Fleischbrühe)*

250g (9 oz) beef bones
400 g (14 oz) cheap stewing beef
2 slices of liver, heart or kidney if available
2 l ($3\frac{3}{4}$ pt) cold water
1 large onion
2 leeks
2 or 3 leaves from a celery plant
1 tomato
1 bay-leaf
parsley
1 medium carrot
salt

This soup can be prepared a day in advance. Put the bones, meat and water into a covered saucepan, bring to the boil and simmer for 1 hour. Add the herbs, seasoning and vegetables and simmer for another $1\frac{1}{2}$–2 hours. Strain through a fine sieve and keep the meat separate. If the soup is felt to be too fat, skim. Try letting it cool down, when the fat will form at the top, and in this way superfluous fat can easily be removed. Reheat the meat and soup together.

Dice the meat and place into soup bowls. Pour over the hot soup sprinkled with freshly chopped chives and parsley or with one of the accompaniments on pages 33–6.

Clear Broth from Bones (*Knochenbrühe*)

750 g (1¾ lb) beef bones
2 l (3¾ pt) water
pieces of liver, heart or kidney if available
salt and pepper
2 leeks
2–3 leaves from a celery plant
1 sprig of thyme
1 carrot
1 tomato
1 onion

Place the bones into cold water, heat and simmer for 3 hours. Add the vegetables and seasoning, and simmer for another hour. Prepare in the same way as Clear Meat Broth (above).

Clear Chicken Broth (*Hühnerbrühe*)

1 chicken or chicken portions or giblets (liver, heart, neck)
2 l (3¾ pt) water
vegetables as for Clear Meat Broth (page 31)
salt, pepper
2 bay-leaves
2 tablespoons white wine

Place the chicken or giblets into a saucepan with cold water. Bring to the boil and simmer for 1½–2 hours. Then add the vegetables, bay-leaves and seasoning and boil for another 30 minutes. Skim, strain through a fine sieve, add the wine and serve with some of the chicken meat.

If a whole chicken has been cooked, use the rest of the meat for chicken salad, Queen's Pastries (page 52) or fricassee.

Creamy Chicken Soup *(Hühnercremesuppe)*

1½ l (3 pt) Clear Chicken Broth (previous recipe)
50 g (2 oz) flour
50 g (2 oz) butter
pinch of ground nutmeg
3 tablespoons single cream
2–3 tablespoons white wine
salt

Melt the butter, stir in the flour to a smooth paste. Gradually add the chicken broth stirring all the time. Simmer for 10 minutes. Add the salt, nutmeg and wine. Serve in cups with the finely cut chicken meat.

ACCOMPANIMENTS FOR CLEAR SOUPS
(*Suppeneinlagen*)

Soups can be made more complete and also more nourishing by adding different kinds of garnishes. The most usual are small noodles in various shapes, rice or sago, which are sprinkled into the soup 15–20 minutes before serving. Not more than 100 g (4 oz) should be used for 1½ l (3 pt) of soup. It is more interesting to prepare one of the following home-made garnishes to accompany German soups.

Clotted Egg *(Eierstich)*

2 eggs
2 tablespoons milk
1 teaspoon finely chopped chives and parsley
pinch of salt and nutmeg

Beat the eggs and milk together, then add the other ingredients. Pour into a buttered fireproof dish and stand in boiling water for 15–20 minutes until the mixture is firm. Leave to cool, cut in strips or cubes and add to the soup when serving.

Baked Flour 'Peas' *(Backerbsen—South Germany)*

125 g (4½ oz) flour
2 eggs
1 teaspoon oil
⅛ l (¼ pt) milk
pinch of salt and nutmeg
fat for frying

Mix the ingredients to a thick dough. Fry small drops of the mixture in deep fat until golden brown and crisp. Dry on kitchen paper and serve floating on clear soup.

Riebele *(Bavarian)*

1 egg
100 g (4 oz) flour
pinch of salt

Work the ingredients to a dough. Grate on a coarse grater; leave to dry for 2 hours. Sprinkle into the soup and simmer for 10 minutes until floating to the top.

Sliced Pancakes *(Flädle—South Germany)*

1 egg
125 g (4½ oz) flour
¼ l (½ pt) milk
pinch of salt and nutmeg
fat

Mix the flour and cold milk to a smooth consistency; add the egg, salt and nutmeg. Bake thin pancakes in the fat. Cut into thin strips; distribute into bowls and add hot soup.

Swabian Noodles *(Spätzle-Schwaben)*

150 g (5 oz) flour
1 egg
salt
some water

Mix the ingredients and add just enough water to work a not too stiff dough. Roll out flat on a board. Cut into thin short strips and push into the boiling soup. Simmer for about 8 minutes until the Spätzle float to the top.

Meat Balls (*Fleischklösschen*)

125 g (4½ oz) minced meat
1 small chopped onion
1 egg
3 tablespoons breadcrumbs
pinch of salt and pepper
1 teaspoon chopped parsley

Put all ingredients into a dish and knead together. If the mixture is too soft, add more breadcrumbs. Form small dumplings of about 3 cm (1¼ in) diameter. Simmer for 10 minutes in the soup until cooked.

Marrow Dumplings (*Markklösschen—Rhineland*)

100 g (4 oz) marrow from a beef marrow bone
1 egg
100 g (4 oz) breadcrumbs
¼ teaspoon salt
pinch of pepper and nutmeg
1 teaspoon chopped parsley

Melt the marrow. Pour it over the breadcrumbs. Mix in the egg, salt, pepper, nutmeg and parsley and leave for 15 minutes. Form small dumplings of about 2 cm (¾ in) diameter adding more breadcrumbs if necessary. Immerse in the soup and simmer for about 10 minutes.

Cheese Balls (*Käseklösschen*)

These very tasty dumplings can be served in the soup or separately with it.

20 g (¾ oz) butter
⅛ l (¼ pt) milk
pinch of salt
60 g (2½ oz) flour
2 eggs
2 tablespoons grated hard cheese (Parmesan)
pinch of nutmeg
fat

Put the milk, butter and salt into a saucepan and bring to the boil. At once add all the flour and stir over a low heat until a dumpling is formed and comes away from the sides of the pan. Now mix one egg into the dough. Then add the second egg, the nutmeg and finally the cheese. With a wet teaspoon, scoop little dumplings from the dough and deep fry them until golden brown.

Hamburg Eel Soup *(Hamburger Aalsuppe)*

Fish soups are popular in the whole of North Germany. Particularly well known as a delicacy is the Hamburg Eel Soup which is of a sweet-sour taste. Very important in the preparation is the special eel herb mixture which consists of dill, rosemary, chervil, thyme, borage, sage, parsley, chives and celery leaves.

1000 g (2¼ lb) ham on the bone (preferably smoked)
2 l (3¾ pt) water
250 g (9 oz) prunes
250 g (9 oz) pears (dried or fresh)
150 g (5 oz) peas
150 g (5 oz) diced carrots
200 g (7 oz) diced potatoes
¼ l (½ pt) white wine
salt, sugar, pepper, eel herbs
1 bay-leaf
juice of 1 lemon
1 dessertspoon sugar
400 g (14 oz) fresh eel
2 small onions

Soak the prunes on the previous night. On the next day wash the ham on the bone; put into a saucepan with the water (use all the prune water) and simmer for 1½ hours. When the meat is cooked, lift on to a plate and boil the vegetables, fruit and potatoes in the broth for 30 minutes. Wash and clean the eel, sprinkle with lemon juice, then cook in the wine together with the herbs and onions until tender. Cut the eel into small pieces and add with the broth to the soup. Cut the ham off the bone, dice and add to soup. Season to taste with salt, pepper and sugar. If necessary, thicken the soup with some cornflour.

Sausage Soup *(Wurstsuppe)*

Long before refrigerators and freezers were available, farms and country households used to slaughter their fat stock during autumn and prepare a store of meats and sausages for the following months. To preserve the meat it was salted, smoked, or made into sausages. The whole household was involved in the preparations and the slaughter of an animal became a real feast. The custom of Schlachtfest (slaughter feast) is still alive in German country areas and one of the main attractions served to visitors is the Wurstsuppe in which the meat and sausages have been boiled. Quite often some sausages burst and their contents pour into the soup enriching its taste.

The following recipe is a way of creating a Wurstsuppe without a Schlachtfest.

2 l (3¾ pt) water
250 g (9 oz) liver sausage
250 g (9 oz) black pudding (Blutwurst)
1 small onion
1 carrot
2 celery leaves
1 garlic clove
500 g (1 lb 2 oz) pig's trotter
½ teaspoon marjoram
½ teaspoon thyme
pinch of pepper, salt and ground cloves

Bring the pig's trotter, vegetables and herbs to the boil in the water. Simmer for 1 hour, until the meat is tender and can be removed from the bone and diced. Return the cut meat to the soup. Open the sausages and empty their contents into the soup. Add herbs and all other spices and simmer for another 10 minutes. Serve with dark rye bread and butter.

Goulash Soup (*Gulaschsuppe*)

This is a very tasty soup for between meals, being less than a main course soup and more than a first course soup.

500 g (1 lb 2 oz) beef cut into small pieces
1 l (2 pt) water
4 sliced onions
60 g (2½ oz) butter
20 g (¾ oz) flour
3 sliced tomatoes
4 tablespoons tomato purée
salt, sweet paprika, caraway, thyme and marjoram to taste
2 tablespoons single cream
2 tablespoons wine

Fry the meat and onions in the fat until brown. Sprinkle with flour. Add the tomatoes and cover with a lid. Leave for 5 minutes over low heat. Add the water, bring to the boil and simmer until the meat is tender (approx. 1 hour). Add the seasoning, herbs, tomato purée and wine. Heat. Remove from the stove and add the cream. Serve with fresh bread rolls.

Potato Soup (*Kartoffelsuppe*)

Many regional recipes exist for this main course soup in Germany. The following preparation is served with Frankfurter sausages or Fleischwurst and fresh rolls. A piece of smoked lean bacon (durchwachsener Speck) boiled with the soup produces a particularly rich taste.

750 g (1¾ lb) potatoes
1½ l (3 pt) water
2 carrots
2 tomatoes
1 leek
2 pieces of celery, finely chopped
100 g (4 oz) smoked bacon
1 large onion
1 dessertspoon chopped parsley
1 dessertspoon chopped chives
4 tablespoons soured cream
salt, pepper

Wash the peeled potatoes, carrots, leek, celery and tomatoes; cut into small pieces. Put with the water into a large saucepan. Cover, bring to the boil and simmer for 45 minutes or until potatoes start to fall apart. Whisk until a smooth, thick texture is achieved. Season to taste with salt and pepper. Add the cream. Cut the smoked bacon into small cubes and heat until crisp in a frying pan. Then add the finely chopped onion and fry until golden. Pour the mixture over the soup. Ten minutes before serving, heat the Frankfurters in the soup (do not boil). Serve sprinkled with parsley and chives.

Pea Soup *(Erbsensuppe)*

Pea soup is favoured just as much in Berlin as in the Rhineland or in Bavaria. It is served as a main course soup with the meat from pig's trotters, Frankfurters or Bockwurst. To improve the taste of the soup, 250 g (9 oz) smoked pork belly, trotters or Kasseler can be cooked with the peas.

500 g (1 lb 2 oz) dried peas
150 g (5 oz) potatoes
2 l (3¾ pt) water
2 sliced onions
1 leek
2 pieces of celery with leaves
pinch of marjoram and pepper
1 teaspoon salt
50 g (2 oz) smoked bacon
1 onion

Wash and soak the peas the night before. The next day bring them to the boil in the water in which they have soaked. Cover and simmer for 1½ hours. Then add the pork belly (optional) and the sliced vegetables. Simmer for another hour. Season to taste with salt, pepper and marjoram. Add the sausages 15 minutes before serving but do not let the soup boil any more. Heat the smoked, diced bacon in a frying pan until golden and crisp; add the diced onion and fry until golden brown.

Place the soup, the sausages and boiled meat in a tureen, pouring the fried bacon and onion mixture over the top. Serve with fresh rolls.

Lentil Soup (*Linsensuppe*)

This is also a main course soup and served with much the same accompaniments as potato and pea soup.

250 g (9 oz) lentils
1½ l (3 pt) water
1 piece of celery
2 carrots
2 leeks
1 chopped onion
1 bay-leaf
pinch of pepper and salt
pinch of marjoram
1 tablespoon vinegar
50 g (2 oz) butter
30 g (1¼ oz) flour

Wash the lentils and soak overnight. The next day bring them to the boil in the water in which they have soaked; cover and simmer for 1 hour. Add the sliced celery, carrots and leeks, the marjoram and bay-leaf and simmer for another hour. Fry the chopped onion in the melted butter until golden. Mix in the flour gradually. Add some of the soup broth, stirring to a thick smooth consistency. Stir this mixture into the soup. Leave to simmer for 15 minutes. Season to taste with salt, pepper and vinegar.

If served with sausages, they can be sliced into the soup.

Dried Bean Soup (*Bohnensuppe*)

200 g (7 oz) white dried beans
2½ l (4½ pt) water
1 piece of celery
2 carrots
200 g (7 oz) boiling beef
200 g (7 oz) smoked belly pork, Kasseler or pig's trotters
200 g (7 oz) diced potatoes
pinch of salt, pepper, nutmeg
2 sprigs of bean herb
1 tablespoon vinegar

Soak the beans in 1 l (1½ pt) water overnight. Heat to boiling the next day. Pour away the boiling water. Place the meat into a saucepan with 1½ l (3 pt) of cold water. Bring to the boil; add the beans and simmer for about 1½ hours. Add the cut vegetables and bean herb and simmer for another 40 minutes or until beans are tender. Season with salt, pepper, nutmeg and vinegar. Remove the bean herb before serving.

For accompaniments, see Pea and Potato Soup (pages 38–9).

Green Bean Soup *(Grüne Bohnensuppe)*

This is a main course soup popular on summer Saturdays.

300 g (11 oz) sliced french or runner beans
200 g (7 oz) potatoes
300 g (11 oz) boiling beef
1½ l (3 pt) water
1 leek
1 piece of celery
salt, pepper
50 g (2 oz) butter
30 g (1¼ oz) flour

Place the meat and cold water into a saucepan; cover, bring to the boil and simmer for 1½ hours. Add the sliced beans and vegetables. Simmer for another 30–40 minutes. Melt the butter, mix in the flour. Mix over heat to a smooth consistency with some of the soup. Stir the mixture into the soup. Add seasoning.

People in the Pfalz and Hessen eat plum cake with this soup.

Hunters' Soup *(Jägersuppe)*

400 g (14 oz) mushrooms
1–2 tablespoons of oil
50 g (2 oz) diced smoked bacon
1 chopped onion
50 g (2 oz) flour
1 l (2 pt) broth
salt, pepper
1 dessertspoon chopped chives or parsley
4 tablespoons single cream
3 tablespoons wine

Chop the mushrooms finely. Heat the oil. Add the bacon and onion. Cover with a lid and fry over medium heat until the onions are a golden colour. Add the mushrooms. After 5 minutes dust over with the flour. Stir in the broth. Bring to the boil and simmer for 20 minutes. Before serving, add the cream, wine, seasoning and herbs.

Mixed Vegetable Soup *(Gemüsesuppe)*

Vegetable soups are so popular in Germany that the food industry found it worth while to produce freezer packs with the ingredients for a family mixed vegetable soup.

500 g (1 lb 2 oz) mixed vegetables (cauliflower, fresh beans, tomatoes, carrots, leeks, peas, brussels sprouts, cabbage)
2 large potatoes
1½ l (3 pt) water
50 g (2 oz) butter
50 g (2 oz) flour
1 meat cube
100 g (4 oz) smoked ham (diced)
1 tablespoon parsley

Wash and slice the vegetables and fry in the melted butter, stirring frequently. Sprinkle in the flour. Dissolve the meat cube in the water and pour over the vegetables. Add the ham. Boil for 30–40 minutes. Season. Serve with Frankfurter sausages or Bockwurst and slices of brown rye bread.

In some areas in South Germany, fresh yeast fruit cakes (Blechkuchen, page 229) or waffles (page 240) are served with this soup.

Fresh Asparagus Soup *(Spargelsuppe)*

The upper Rhine valley south of Mainz is a particularly fertile area with a mild climate suitable for high-class fruit and vegetables. The well-known Ingelheim and Schwetzingen asparagus grow in this area. German asparagus is white with blue tips. Asparagus time is supposed to last for the seven weeks starting in the middle of April. One of the specialities offered during May and June is fresh asparagus soup.

500 g (1 lb 2 oz) fresh asparagus
½ l (1 pt) water
½ l (1 pt) chicken broth
50 g (2 oz) butter
50 g (2 oz) flour
1 egg yolk
3–4 tablespoons single cream
pinch of salt, sugar, pepper
1 dessertspoon chopped parsley

Wash and peel the asparagus and cut into 2–3 cm (¾–1¼ in) long pieces, separating the tips. Bring the water to the boil, add tips; simmer for 15 minutes and remove the tips. Then boil the remaining asparagus in the water for 30 minutes. Pass the asparagus, apart from the tips, through a sieve or liquidizer with the water. Add the chicken broth. In another saucepan melt the butter. Mix in the flour and stir over heat until yellow. Add some of the liquid and mix over heat to a smooth consistency. Gradually stir in the rest of the liquid and boil for 10 minutes. Season to taste. Mix the yolk with the cream and a little soup. Carefully blend the mixture into the soup. Add tips and parsley; heat the soup but do not boil. Serve.

Cheese Soup *(Käsesuppe)*

This is a quickly prepared nourishing soup which can easily be made from cheese left-overs. The recipe comes from the Allgäu which is well known for its milk and cheese products.

60 g (2½ oz) butter
60 g (2½ oz) flour
¾ l (1½ pt) broth
¼ l (½ pt) milk
150 g (5 oz) grated cheese
salt, pepper, nutmeg

Melt the butter; mix in the flour. Add the broth and milk gradually, stirring well. Leave to boil for 10 minutes. Stir in the cheese; season to taste and serve with fried bread cubes in a rustic bowl.

Bread Soup (*Brotsuppe*)

200 g (7 oz) rye bread
30 g (1¼ oz) butter
1 piece celery
1 leek
1 dessertspoon flour
1 onion
1 l (2 pt) broth
1 egg yolk
salt, pepper
1 tablespoon soured cream
chopped parsley

Slice the bread, toast it and cut into small squares. Fry the finely chopped onion in the melted butter; add the sliced leek and celery; dust with the flour. Add the broth and the bread. Boil for 20 minutes. Pass through a sieve or liquidizer. Heat again. Season to taste. Whisk the yolk with the soured cream and a little hot soup. Stir this mixture into the soup. Serve garnished with parsley.

SWEET SOUPS (*Süsse Suppen*)

Sweet soups are a popular first course during the summer and often represent the more substantial part of a simple evening meal followed by a course of open cheese and sausage sandwiches (Käse- und Wurstbrote).

Beer Soup (*Biersuppe*)

This type of soup is rather an acquired taste to a non-German. Try the following example as being typical of the many known varieties in Germany.

30 g (1¼ oz) butter
50 g (2 oz) flour
1 tablespoon sugar
1 l (2 pt) beer
50 g (2 oz) sugar
pinch of salt
½ cinnamon bar
2 cloves
grated rind of ¼ lemon
bread cubes fried in butter

Melt the butter in a saucepan, add the flour, stir in the tablespoon of sugar. Brown the mixture over medium heat stirring all the time. Add the beer gradually. Add the 50 g (2 oz) sugar, cinnamon and lemon rind, cloves and salt. Bring to the boil. Serve hot with fried bread cubes, or cold.

This soup can be refined by adding 2 or 3 tablespoons of cream before serving but do not boil after the cream has been added.

Wine Soup *(Weinsuppe—Rhineland)*

Use one of the cheaper dry wines, red or white. It is also possible to use cider or apple juice instead of wine.

½ l (1 pt) wine
½ l (1 pt) water
grated rind of 1 lemon
25 g (1 oz) cornflour
100 g (4 oz) sugar
2 egg yolks
¼ l (½ pt) single cream
pinch of cinnamon to taste
1 egg white
pinch of salt
20 g (¾ oz) castor sugar

Mix the wine and water and bring ¾ of the liquid with the lemon rind to the boil. Add the cornflour to ¼ l (½ pt) of the cold liquid. Stir into the boiling mixture. Add the sugar. Beat the egg yolks and cream; add the hot soup gradually. Return to the hot plate but do not boil the soup again. Add the cinnamon.

Beat the egg white with the salt and sugar. Serve the soup hot in bowls dotted with small 'icebergs' of beaten egg whites.

Fruit Soup *(Obstsuppe)*

In Bavaria fruit soups are served for a light evening meal, followed by open sandwiches with sliced sausage or ham.

500 g (1 lb 2 oz) fruit (apples, plums, pears, cherries, berries)
water according to fruit
lemon juice
lemon rind and sugar to taste
50 g (2 oz) semolina, rice or oats or 25 g (1 oz) cornflour

Wash the fruit, cut into small pieces, boil in the water until soft. Pass through a sieve or liquidizer. Make up with water to 1½ l (3 pt). Add the lemon juice, rind, sugar and semolina (or rice or oats). Bring to the boil and simmer until the semolina is soft. If cornflour is used, mix with cold water and add.

For a more creamy soup, breadcrumbs or flour mixed in a little water should be added. 2–3 tablespoons of wine will improve the soup.

Elderberry Soup *(Holunderbeersuppe)*

500 g (1 lb 2 oz) elderberries
175 g (6 oz) plums or apples
100 g (4 oz) sugar
¼ l (½ pt) wine
1 tablespoon lemon juice
pinch of ground cloves
1 tablespoon cornflour

Pull the elderberries off the twigs with a fork, wash them and put them with the other fruit, lemon juice, sugar and cloves, into a saucepan. Bring to the boil and simmer for 15 minutes. Stir the cornflour into the cold wine and add to the elderberry mixture. Boil for another 5 minutes. Serve hot.

Soured Cream Soup *(Schmandsuppe—East Germany)*

This soup originates from Prussia.

2 l (3¾ pt) water
400 g (14 oz) prunes (stoned)
2 tablespoons golden syrup
¼ l (½ pt) soured cream
1 tablespoon flour
grated lemon rind
pinch of cinnamon

Soak the prunes in the water overnight. Next day bring to the boil with the water and simmer 15–20 minutes. Remove the prunes from the water. Add the syrup to the water. Mix the flour into the soured cream and stir into the soup; add lemon rind and cinnamon and bring back to boil carefully. Add the prunes.

Serve hot or cold.

Rose-hip Soup *(Hagebuttensuppe—East Germany)*

This soup is popular as a first course for the harvest supper. It originates from Pommern in North-East Germany where it is eaten topped with whipped cream and biscuits.

1 l (2 pt) water
500 g (1 lb 2 oz) rose-hips
50 g (2 oz) butter
25 g (1 oz) flour
1 tablespoon sugar
2 tablespoons red wine
1 tablespoon lemon juice
salt
1 pinch cinnamon
3–4 tablespoons whipped cream

Remove stem, crown and seeds from freshly collected rose-hips and wash them well. Bring to the boil in 1 l (2 pt) water; boil for 30 minutes. Take the rose-hips out of the water and pass through a sieve.

Brown the flour in the melted butter, stirring all the time. Gradually add enough of the rose-hip water to make a smooth mixture. Stir in the rose-hip purée; simmer for a few minutes; season to taste with salt, sugar, cinnamon, lemon juice and wine, and serve hot topped with whipped cream.

Rusk Soup *(Zwiebacksuppe)*

This soup is particularly liked by children. It appeals more to adults if instead of the milk, ½ l (1 pt) of water and ¼ l (½ pt) white wine are used.

100 g (4 oz) grated rusks (Zwieback) or dry toast
$\frac{3}{4}$ l ($1\frac{1}{2}$ pt) milk
40 g ($1\frac{3}{4}$ oz) butter
2 tablespoons sugar
4 tablespoons single cream
2 egg yolks
grated rind of $\frac{1}{2}$ lemon
pinch of salt
cinnamon to taste

Put the rusks, butter and salt with the milk in a saucepan. Simmer for 5 minutes stirring well. Add the sugar, cinnamon and the yolks mixed with the cream. Serve hot but avoid boiling the soup again.

Milk Soup ***(Milchsuppe)***

1 l (2 pt) milk
2 egg yolks
grated rind of $\frac{1}{2}$ lemon
pinch of salt
30 g ($1\frac{1}{4}$ oz) cornflour
40 g ($1\frac{3}{4}$ oz) sugar
some bitter almond essence or 2 finely ground bitter almonds

Boil the milk in a saucepan. Meanwhile, mix the yolks, sugar, salt, cornflour, lemon rind and almond with a little cold milk to a smooth mixture. Remove the saucepan from hot plate, stir in the cornflour mixture. Return to hot plate and bring to boil, continuously stirring.

Milk soup is nourishing and very popular with children. It can be served in different ways:

(a) with biscuits or rusks;
(b) with fruit juice;
(c) with egg-white dumplings
(1 egg white beaten with a pinch of salt; scoop soupspoonfuls on to the soup, cover with a lid and leave for 5 minutes);
(d) poured over buttered toast in bowls.

Buttermilk Soup ***(Buttermilchsuppe)***

1 l (2 pt) buttermilk
40 g ($1\frac{3}{4}$ oz) custard powder
50 g (2 oz) sugar
pinch of salt
50 g (2 oz) raisins

Mix the buttermilk and custard powder. Heat in a saucepan stirring continuously until boiling point is reached. Add the salt, sugar and raisins. Serve hot or cold.

This is an easily digestible soup for a light evening meal.

Chocolate Soup (*Schokoladensuppe*)

60 g (2½ oz) chocolate
30 g (1¼ oz) cornflour
30 g (1¼ oz) sugar
1 l (2 pt) milk
1 teaspoon vanilla sugar
pinch of cinnamon
1 egg yolk

Put the milk into a saucepan keeping back half a cup. Crumble the chocolate into the milk. Heat the milk. Meanwhile mix the sugar, cornflour and ½ a cup of cold milk. Remove the boiling milk from the hot plate and add the mixture. Add the cinnamon and bring to the boil again. Beat the egg yolk whilst gradually adding some of the hot soup. Return the egg mixture to the remaining soup and serve with toast or biscuits.

Serving suggestion: decorate with balls of beaten egg white.

Cold Gooseberry Soup (*Stachelbeerkaltschale*)

This very refreshing soup is enjoyed on a hot day.

500 g (1 lb 2 oz) gooseberries
¾ l (1½ pt) water
175 g (6 oz) sugar
juice and grated rind of ½ lemon
½ l (1 pt) wine
4 rusks (french toast) or biscuits

Cut the stems and crowns from the gooseberries; wash them and boil with the sugar, water and lemon until soft. Pour over the crumbled rusks; lastly add the wine. Serve refrigerated.

Cherry Soup *(Kirschsuppe)*

July is cherry time in Germany. Whilst sweet black and red cherries are eaten fresh, the sweet-sour (morello) type is preferred for any cooked dishes. The following recipe is particularly tasty if for half the amount of cherries the sweet-sour kind is used.

500 g (1 lb 2 oz) cherries
juice of 1 lemon
2 teaspoons vanilla sugar
120 g (4½ oz) sugar
2 tablespoons icing sugar
4 cloves
2 eggs
pinch of cinnamon
1 l (2 pt) water

Heat the stoned cherries with the lemon juice, water, sugar, cloves and cinnamon in a saucepan. Simmer for 15 minutes. Separate the eggs. Beat the two yolks adding a cup of the hot soup gradually. Then pour into the soup stirring generously. Take off the hot plate immediately. Beat the egg whites with icing sugar until stiff. Serve the soup hot, dotted with 'icebergs' of beaten egg white.

Appetizers and Light Dishes

(*Vorspeisen und Zwischengerichte*)

Queen's Pastries	Königin Pasteten
Holstein Shrimps	Holsteiner Krabben
Ham and Cheese Toast	Schinken-Käse Toast
Stuffed Tomatoes	Gefüllte Tomaten
Westphalian Open Sandwiches	Westfälische Stammtischschnitten
Potatoes on Skewers	Kartoffelspiesse
Filled Bread Rolls	Gefüllte Brötchen
Asparagus Toast	Spargeltoast
Salted Almonds	Salzmandeln
Ham Melon	Schinken-Melone
Onion Flan	Zwiebelkuchen
Egg Dishes	**Eierspeisen**
Egg Cheese	Eierkäse
Egg Asparagus	Eierspargel
Farmer's Omelette	Bauernomelette
Meat Filled Pancakes	Gefüllte Flädle
Hunter's Pancakes	Jägerpfannkuchen
Green Pancakes	Grüne Pfannkuchen
Boiled Eggs in Brine	Soleier
Mustard Eggs	Senfeier
Eggs in Sour Sauce	Saure Eier

Cheese Dishes	**Käsegerichte**
Cooking with Sour Milk Cheese	Kochen mit Sauermilchkäse
Savoury Curd Cheese	Herzhafter Quark
Sour Cheese	Korbkäse
Curd Cheese Pancakes	Quarkpfannkuchen
Curd Cheese Dumplings	Quarkknödel
Cooking with Hard Cheese	Kochen mit Hartkäse
Cheese Soufflé	Käseauflauf
Individual Cheese Soufflés	Käsesoufflés
Cheese Fondue	Käsefondue

The recipes in this chapter are suitable to precede a main course. The dishes can also be served as a light supper or an in-between meal or snack.

Queen's Pastries *(Königin Pasteten)*

6–8 baked puff pastry cases (6–7 cm (2¼–2¾ in) diameter)
250 g (9 oz) cooked chicken meat
125 g (4½ oz) cooked and sliced mushrooms
50 g (2 oz) butter
50 g (2 oz) flour
¼ l (½ pt) chicken broth
⅛ l (¼ pt) white wine
2 egg yolks
1 tablespoon soured cream
salt, pepper
1 dessertspoon lemon juice
2–3 tablespoons grated cheese

Cut the chicken meat into small pieces. Melt the butter, mix in the flour; gradually blend in the chicken broth and stir to a smooth thick consistency. Add the wine, the lemon juice, the meat and the mushrooms. The sauce must not be too thin. Season to taste. Take the saucepan off the hot plate. Whisk the egg yolks with soured cream and pour into the mixture.

Heat the oven to 210 °C (400 °F, gas mark 6). Place the pastry cases on a tray and warm in the oven for 5 minutes. Then fill with the prepared mixture; sprinkle with grated cheese and bake for another 5–10 minutes. Serve with lemon segments and Worcester sauce.

Instead of puff pastry cases, individual fireproof dishes can be used.

Holstein Shrimps (*Holsteiner Krabben*)

175 g (6 oz) washed shrimps
125 g (4½ oz) sliced mushrooms
30 g (1¼ oz) butter
30 g (1¼ oz) flour
⅛ l (¼ pt) meat or vegetable broth
2 tablespoons white wine
1 egg yolk
2 tablespoons grated cheese
salt, pepper
lemon juice

Melt the butter, stir into it the flour, then the broth a little at a time. Boil well. Add the salt, pepper and wine. Take the sauce off the hot plate; blend in the yolk. Add the shrimps (sprinkled with lemon juice) and mushrooms. Fill into buttered individual fireproof dishes; sprinkle with grated cheese and bake in a pre-heated oven, 210 °C (400 °F, gas mark 6), for 10–15 minutes. Serve at once.

Ham and Cheese Toast (*Schinken-Käse Toast*)

4 slices of toasted white bread
20 g (¾ oz) butter
4 slices smoked ham
4 slices cheese
2 eggs
salt, pepper, nutmeg
1 tablespoon chopped chives

Butter the toast. Cover each with a slice of smoked ham. Put slices of cheese on top of the ham. Beat the egg whites with salt, pepper and nutmeg to a firm consistency. Cover each slice with beaten egg white. Make a hollow in the egg white on each slice and fill with yolk. Sprinkle with chives and bake on the top shelf in a pre-heated oven, 230 °C (450 °F, gas mark 8), for 5–10 minutes.

Serve hot with lettuce leaves and tomato slices.

Stuffed Tomatoes (*Gefüllte Tomaten*)

4 good-sized tomatoes
4 eggs
salt, pepper

Cut the lid off the tomatoes. Scoop out most of the inside. Sprinkle with salt and pepper. Break an egg into each tomato. Season. Bake in an ovenproof dish in a pre-heated oven, 230 °C (450 °F, gas mark 8), until the eggs are set. Serve with buttered bread.

Westphalian Open Sandwiches (*Westfälische Stammtischschnitten*)

4 slices of rye bread
20 g ($\frac{3}{4}$ oz) butter
4 tablespoons sauerkraut
4 sausages (Knackwurst)
4 slices of cheese

Butter the bread. Put on a layer of sauerkraut and a slice of cheese. Skin and halve the sausages lengthwise and place on top of the cheese. Bake in a pre-heated oven, 210 °C (400 °F, gas mark 6) for 15–20 minutes. Serve with tomato slices.

Potatoes on Skewers (*Kartoffelspiesse*)

1000 g ($2\frac{1}{4}$ lb) medium-sized potatoes
500 g (1 lb 2 oz) medium-sized onions
250 g (9 oz) lean smoked bacon
salt, pepper
caraway seeds
75 g (3 oz) melted butter

Wash and slice the potatoes ($\frac{1}{2}$ to 1 cm ($\frac{1}{4}$ to $\frac{1}{2}$ in) thick); peel and slice the onions. Slice the bacon.

Alternately, spike potato, onion and bacon on to a wooden or metal skewer. Brush with melted butter; sprinkle with caraway seeds, salt and pepper and bake on a baking tray in a pre-heated oven, 220 °C (425 °F, gas mark 7), for 35–40 minutes.

Filled Bread Rolls (*Gefüllte Brötchen*)

4 bread rolls
400 g (14 oz) lean minced beef
1 chopped onion
1 egg
1 dessertspoon vegetable oil
1–2 tablespoons breadcrumbs
salt, pepper, thyme, marjoram
8 slices of cheese (size of bread rolls)

Halve the bread rolls and scoop out some of the inside. Mix the minced beef, onion, egg, oil, breadcrumbs, herbs and seasoning. Divide the filling between the 8 bread roll halves. Place them on a greased baking tray. Bake in a pre-heated oven, 230 °C (450 °F, gas mark 8), for 15 minutes. Place a slice of cheese on top of each and bake for another 5 minutes until the cheese starts to melt. Serve with slices of tomato and cucumber.

Asparagus Toast (*Spargeltoast*)

4 slices of toast
250 g (9 oz) cooked asparagus (or tinned)
4 slices cooked ham or tongue
30 g (1¼ oz) butter
1 egg yolk
2 tablespoons grated cheese

Place the ham or tongue on buttered toast. Top with asparagus. Brush with melted butter. Mix the egg yolk and cheese and spread over the asparagus. Grill until set and golden. Serve with lettuce and tomatoes.

Salted Almonds (*Salzmandeln*)

This provides a welcome nibble with beer or wine.

250 g (9 oz) blanched almonds
2 tablespoons vegetable oil

Heat the oil in a frying pan. Add the almonds and stir until golden brown. Turn first on to a sieve, then on to some greaseproof paper and sprinkle with salt.

Ham Melon (Schinken-Melone)

1 melon

125 g (4½ oz) thinly sliced smoked ham or smoked beef

Halve the melon, remove seeds and cut into segments. Wrap two slices of ham around each melon segment and serve with buttered pumpernickel or thin toast.

Onion Flan (Zwiebelkuchen—Hessen and Württemberg)

Dough

250 g (9 oz) plain flour
10 g (½ oz) fresh yeast
3–4 tablespoons milk (lukewarm)
60 g (2½ oz) soft butter or lard
1 egg
pinch of salt

Filling

600 g (1 lb 6 oz) sliced onions
30 g (1¼ oz) butter
100 g (4 oz) diced smoked bacon
1 egg
3–4 tablespoons soured cream
1 level teaspoon salt
¼ teaspoon pepper
1 teaspoon caraway seeds

Dissolve the yeast in the milk. Sieve the flour into a bowl, mixing in the salt. Make a well, pour in the yeast/milk mixture and mix with a little flour. Leave to rise in a warm, draught-proof place. Mix with the rest of the flour, butter, and egg to a soft dough. Line the bottom of a round cake tin or flan case (24 cm (10 in) diameter). Leave to rise again.

Meanwhile heat the butter and the bacon. Add the onions and cook them in the fat over low heat. Do not let them become brown. Take off the heat. Stir in salt, pepper, caraway seeds, egg and cream. Do not let the egg set. Spread the mixture on to the risen flan and bake in a pre-heated oven, 210 °C (400 °F, gas mark 6), for 30–40 minutes. Serve warm with cider, wine or beer.

EGG DISHES *(Eierspeisen)*

'Boiled egg for breakfast' is still a popular German eating habit. For the English breakfast taste this seems to lack imagination. There are, however, some German egg recipes which show more originality and might also appear appetizing to English palates.

Egg dishes are nutritious and time-saving and therefore particularly suitable for a light meal or when unexpected visitors arrive.

In Germany the marketing of eggs is carried out according to strict rules. Eggs are packed in cartons of six specifying freshness (A, B, C), week when packed, weight class (1, 2, 3) and country of origin.

When preparing egg dishes it is important not to apply too high a heat as the egg white becomes firm at a temperature of 60 °C (140 °F).

Egg Cheese *(Eierkäse)*

Egg cheese is an old Westerwald recipe. It is the custom in this area to serve it at meals at weddings as well as funerals. The Westerwald is the district of the potter's trade and over the years a special earthenware 'egg-cheese' dish has been developed. It is a round pottery dish with a ribbed perforated bottom used instead of a sieve.

4 eggs
1 tablespoon sugar
pinch of salt
½ l (1 pt) milk

Beat the eggs, sugar and salt well before gradually stirring in the milk. Pour the mixture into a basin and stand in boiling water for 20 minutes or until set. Spoon into a muslin coated sieve or an egg-cheese dish and leave to clear away the whey. When dry turn out and serve with sugar and on buttered white bread or currant bread.

Egg Asparagus *(Eierspargel)*

4 eggs
4 cooked asparagus stalks cut into small pieces
2 tablespoons milk
20 g (¾ oz) melted butter
salt, pepper, sweet paprika
chopped parsley

Place the asparagus into 4 greased individual fireproof dishes. Mix the eggs, milk and seasoning and pour into the dishes. Spread melted butter over the top. Place the dishes into a pan with boiling water and cover with a lid. Leave for 30 minutes until set in the pan in the hot (not boiling) water. Sprinkle with parsley and serve immediately.

Farmer's Omelette *(Bauernomelette—Schleswig Holstein)*

This very popular North German dish is often served for a second breakfast and therefore also carries the name Farmer's Breakfast (Bauernfrühstück). It can also be served as a light lunch or for supper and is a good way of using up left-overs.

100 g (4 oz) diced smoked bacon
2 small cooked potatoes (sliced)
2 tablespoons left-over vegetables (preferably asparagus, cauliflower, peas)
3 eggs
40 g (1¾ oz) butter
pinch of pepper, nutmeg, marjoram
1 dessertspoon cut chives

In a pan fry the bacon and potatoes, finally adding the vegetables. Cover with a lid and keep warm. Heat the butter in another pan.

Meanwhile, beat the eggs and seasoning well with a whisk. Pour the egg mixture into the butter. Frequently shake the pan. When the bottom of the omelette starts to set, place the ham and vegetables on top. Cover with a lid and leave to set completely. With a spatula glide on to a hot plate and serve sprinkled with chives.

Meat Filled Pancakes

(Gefüllte Flädle—South Germany)

The following ingredients should be sufficient for 5–6 Flädle:

125 g (4½ oz) plain flour
¼ l (½ pt) milk
2 eggs
salt
½ tablespoon vegetable oil

Mix the flour and cold milk to a smooth consistency; add the eggs and salt. Make thin pancakes using as little fat as possible. Leave to cool.

Filling
250 g (9 oz) lean minced beef
1 small chopped onion
2 tablespoons tomato purée
1 tablespoon cider
salt, pepper, marjoram, thyme
1 tablespoon oil

Heat the oil. Fry the onions and the meat. After 10 minutes add the tomato purée, cider, herbs and seasoning. Spread the filling over each pancake; roll them up. Cut each rolled pancake into 3 pieces and fry again over medium heat for 10–12 minutes, turning once.

Serve with crisp lettuce or tomato salad.

Hunter's Pancakes

(Jägerpfannkuchen)

This is a useful and tasty way of using up game left-overs. Instead of game, it is possible to use chicken or other meat.

250 g (9 oz) plain flour
½ l (1 pt) cold water
3 eggs
pinch of salt

Filling
200 g (7 oz) cooked game
3–5 tablespoons gravy
salt, pepper
30 g (1¼ oz) butter
1 small chopped onion

Blend the flour, water, eggs and salt to a smooth mixture. Heat a little fat in a frying pan, bake pancakes and keep warm.

For the filling, fry the onion in the butter. Add the meat, gravy and seasoning. Place some meat on one half of the pancake; fold over the other half. Serve garnished with parsley and tomato slices.

Green Pancakes *(Grüne Pfannkuchen—Hessen)*

One of the characteristics of Hessian cooking is a preference for the colour green, which expresses their particular liking of herbs. Green Pancakes are possibly not as famous as the Hessian green sauce. They are, however, a nourishing dish of inviting appearance.

2 eggs
1 teaspoon salt
250 g (9 oz) plain flour
½ l (1 pt) milk
1 tablespoon vegetable oil
4 tablespoons chopped chives
1 sliced leek

Beat the eggs with the salt; gradually add the flour and milk and stir to a smooth consistency. Finally add the oil, chives and leek.

Make 3–4 pancakes and serve immediately with dressed lettuce.

Boiled Eggs in Brine *(Soleier—Berlin)*

This is one of the recipes which reflects the Berlin taste for salty food. This taste originated from the time of Frederick the Great and his salt monopoly. He forced his subjects to buy more salt than they normally needed. The Berlin people made a virtue of necessity.

Eggs in brine are served with beer in public houses. They can be offered as a snack or with sandwiches for a cold evening meal.

eggs (number which will be covered by 1 l (2 pt) water)	*1 l (2 pt) water*
	100 g (4 oz) salt

Boil the eggs for 10 minutes and leave to cool. Crack the shells all around without removing them. Prepare the brine by boiling the water, adding the salt and leaving it to cool.

Immerse the cold eggs in the cold brine. Leave for at least 24 hours. The eggs will keep for a week in the brine provided they are stored in a cool place. After the eggs are peeled, they are eaten in the following way: Cut off the head of the egg. Remove the yolk. Sprinkle oil, salt and pepper into the cavity. Replace the yolk and eat.

Mustard Eggs *(Senfeier)*

Halve hard-boiled eggs lengthwise. Remove the yolk and mix it with made mustard, salt, sweet paprika, pepper and chives according to taste. A little cream or soured cream and oil may also be added. Replace the yolk mixture in the eggs.

Serve with open sandwiches or on their own with beer.

Eggs in Sour Sauce *(Saure Eier)*

6–8 hard-boiled eggs	*1 bay-leaf*
40 g (1¾ oz) butter	*1 dessertspoon sugar*
40 g (1¾ oz) plain flour	*1 teaspoon made mustard*
1 finely chopped onion	*2–3 tablespoons wine vinegar*
pinch of salt and pepper	*½ l (1 pt) broth*

Melt the butter; mix in the flour and onion. Gradually stir in the broth. Bring to the boil. Add remaining ingredients for the sauce. Simmer for 10 minutes.

Immerse the eggs in the sauce; keep for another 5 minutes on the hot plate, but do not allow to boil. Serve with potatoes boiled in their jackets and tomato or cucumber salad.

CHEESE DISHES *(Käsegerichte)*

The German palate has a liking for cheese: cheese rolls at breakfast time, cheese sandwiches for second breakfast, at evening meal time, cheese cubes with wine or beer as a snack at night. Germany produces six hundred different cheeses. According to the process of manufacture, they can be separated into two main groups—sour milk cheese and sweet milk cheese. All cheeses belonging to the first group are produced when the milk is curdled by the presence of an acid. For the second group, curdling is achieved by the addition of an enzyme, obtained from calves' stomachs. Nearly half the cheese consumed in Germany is sour milk cheese, such as curd cheese (Quark) and Mainzer cheese. Sweet milk cheeses are the hard types such as 'butter' cheese (Emmentaler), the latter being a Bavarian speciality made from raw unpasteurized milk. German shops normally provide hard cheese already sliced.

Schleswig-Holstein in North Germany and Bavaria in South Germany are important milk and cheese producing areas where a cheese platter (Käseplatte) ordered in a restaurant will provide a worthwhile meal. A variety of sliced cheeses are served on a wooden plate accompanied by tomatoes, sweet-sour gherkins, onions, radishes, grapes and other fruit. Bread is not essential with cheese. In Bavaria where many village and district fairs take place, the many glasses of beer which are drunk are normally accompanied by the regular consumption of sliced cheese sprinkled with salt and pepper, rolled up and eaten with the large sliced radishes which are also a speciality of the area.

With the help of cheese a number of tasty recipes can be prepared. The following selection is divided according to the two basic groups previously mentioned.

COOKING WITH SOUR MILK CHEESE

(Kochen mit Sauermilchkäse)

Curd cheese (Quark) is also called 'white cheese' (Weisskäse) or Topfen. It can be prepared as a savoury dish, or used in desserts (pages 199–201). For its use in baking see page 249–56.

Savoury Curd Cheese *(Herzhafter Quark)*

In Hessen and the Rhineland savoury curd cheese is eaten with potatoes boiled in their skins (Pellkartoffeln). It also tastes good when thickly spread on dark rye bread and pumpernickel and is favoured for breakfast or evening meal.

250 g (9 oz) curd cheese
1/8 l (1/4 pt) milk (approximately, depending on the dryness of the curd cheese)
3 tablespoons double cream
1/2 teaspoon salt
pinch of pepper

Mix the curd cheese with the milk, cream, salt and pepper. Beat until creamy. According to taste, add one or more of the following:

2 medium-sized finely chopped or grated onions
1 tablespoon caraway seeds
1 teaspoon paprika powder
1 tablespoon horse-radish
1 teaspoon curry powder
2–3 tablespoons finely chopped fresh chives
2–3 tablespoons finely chopped fresh parsley
1–2 tablespoons finely cut fresh dill leaves
1–2 tablespoons finely chopped marjoram

Sour Cheese *(Korbkäse—Mainz, Hessen, Harz)*

When curd cheese is left to ripen a new type of cheese develops called basket (Korb-), peasant (Bauern-), or hand cheese (Handkäse). These small and rindless cheeses in the shape of discs (about 2 cm (¾ in) thick, 4–5 cm (1½–2 in) diameter) are favoured in the areas around Mainz, in Hessen and the Harz, where they are served with cider and 'music'—a marinade made from oil, vinegar and onion. They have a strong taste, a high protein and low fat content (about 1%) Basket cheese can be bought commercially produced in packets with four discs and is also imported into the United Kingdom. It is, however, possible to produce basket cheese from curd cheese at home according to the following recipe:

500 g (1 lb 2 oz) curd cheese
1 teaspoon salt
3–4 teaspoons caraway seeds (according to taste)

Knead the curd cheese with the salt and caraway seeds. Form round cheeses of about 5 cm (2 in) diameter. Place on a wooden board and leave to dry for a few days, turning them daily. When the cheeses are dry outside but still soft inside, arrange them in an earthenware dish and leave until covered with mould. This should take about 8 days. Then wash them with salt water, wine or beer and return them to the cleaned earthenware dish. Repeat the process every 3 or 4 days until the cheeses have ripened. This takes several weeks. When starting to mature, wrap in a cloth and keep in a cool damp place (cellar). When ready to be eaten, they should be yellow and moist outside. Some people like them yellow and moist inside whilst others prefer the centre to be white. Serve sliced with 'music' and dark rye bread.

'Music'
Make a marinade with:

2 tablespoons wine vinegar
1 tablespoon water
1 tablespoon vegetable oil
1 medium-sized finely chopped onion

Curd Cheese Pancakes *(Quarkpfannkuchen)*

100 g (4 oz) curd cheese
a few tablespoons milk
90 g (3½ oz) plain flour
pinch of salt
3 eggs
butter for frying

Mix the curd cheese and milk to a creamy consistency, the amount of milk depending on the dryness of the cheese. Add the flour, salt and eggs. Fry 4 pancakes in the hot butter.

Curd Cheese Dumplings *(Quarkknödel—East Germany)*

500 g (1 lb 2 oz) curd cheese
80 g (3½ oz) sugar
2 teaspoons vanilla sugar
3 eggs
75 g (3 oz) unsalted butter
180 g (6½ oz) semolina
50 g (2 oz) fine breadcrumbs
grated rind of 1 lemon
2 level teaspoons baking powder
pinch of salt
100 g (4 oz) raisins
50 g (2 oz) chopped hazel-nuts
2 l (3¾ pt) water with 1 teaspoon salt

Cream butter and sugar; gradually stir in curd cheese and eggs. Add lemon rind. Mix semolina, baking powder, salt and breadcrumbs and stir into the dough. Add raisins and hazel-nuts. Bring the water to the boil. Reduce heat. Form dumplings and simmer for about 15 minutes. Serve with stewed fruit for an evening meal preceding cheese, sausage and ham sandwiches.

COOKING WITH HARD CHEESE

(*Kochen mit Hartkäse*)

This refers to the group of cheeses produced from unpasteurized sweet milk, one of the best known being the Allgäuer Emmentaler produced in the Bavarian Alps.

Cheese Soufflé *(Käseauflauf)*

100 g (4 oz) butter
150 g (5 oz) plain flour
½ l (1 pt) milk
150 g (5 oz) grated Emmental cheese
4 egg yolks
pinch of salt and nutmeg
4 beaten egg whites
1 level teaspoon baking powder

Melt the butter over a low heat and mix in the flour. Gradually add the milk and bring to the boil, stirring all the time until a smooth mixture is obtained. Leave to cool. Then add egg yolks, grated cheese, seasoning and baking powder. Stir well. Fold in the beaten egg whites. Pour the mixture into a well-greased soufflé dish and bake at 200 °C (400 °F, gas mark 6), for about 60 minutes.

Individual Cheese Soufflés *(Käsesoufflés)*

150 g (5 oz) grated (Emmental) cheese
100 g (4 oz) butter
4 eggs
30 g (1¼ oz) flour
⅛ l (¼ pt) soured cream
salt, pepper, sweet paprika
breadcrumbs

Whisk the soft butter with salt, pepper and paprika. Blend in the egg yolks gradually. Add the cheese, cream and flour. Beat the egg whites to a stiff consistency and carefully lift on to the mixture and fold in. Do not stir unnecessarily.

Butter individual fireproof party dishes and sprinkle with breadcrumbs. Fill with the soufflé mixture and bake at once in a preheated oven, 230 °C (450 °F, gas mark 8), for 10–15 minutes.

Serve with fresh bread rolls and a glass of red Ahr wine.

Cheese Fondue *(Käsefondue)*

Although originally a Swiss dish, Cheese Fondue is very popular in Germany. It is usually prepared in a shallow earthenware, cast-iron or stainless steel réchaud-dish and provides much entertainment as well as being a good-tasting snack.

500 g (1 lb 2 oz) Allgäuer Emmentaler cut into small cubes
1 garlic clove
½ l (1 pt) dry white wine
pinch of pepper and nutmeg
1 tablespoon Black Forest kirsch-water (a fruit brandy, not *a liqueur)*
1 teaspoon potato flour
1 tablespoon mixed finely chopped herbs (parsley, chives, chervil)
600 g (1 lb 6 oz) white bread or bread rolls cut into small pieces

Rub the inside of the fondue dish with the garlic clove. Place the cheese cubes into the dish and pour the wine over them. With the réchaud heat the dish, stirring with a wooden spoon in the same direction until all the cheese is melted. Mix the kirsch-water and potato flour and add to the bubbling cheese/wine mixture. Stir in the herbs and seasoning.

Serve the fondue in the dish on the réchaud, as it must be kept bubbling all the time. Set out the bread pieces in 2–3 baskets on the table. It is customary for everybody to eat out of the *one* fondue dish by piercing a bread cube on to the two-pronged fondue fork and dipping it into the hot cheese mixture. Special fondue forks have a long, slim, round handle which makes it easy to twirl the fork after having dipped it into the cheese. Dry white wine or hot tea, sweet-sour mixed pickles and tender vegetable salads are served as accompaniments.

The rule for a fondue party is that any male participant who loses his bread cube in the fondue has to pay for the next round of wine, whilst women have to pay with a kiss to their male neighbour.

Fish

(*Fisch*)

Eel in Beer Sauce	Aal in Biersosse
Mosel Eel in White Wine Sauce	Mosel Aal in Weissweinsosse
Freshwater Fish in Wine Sauce	Flussfisch in Weinsosse
Carp in Beer	Karpfen in Bier
Fish Ragout	Fischragout
Fish Fillet in Dill Sauce	Fischfilet in Dillsosse
Blue Trout	Forelle Blau
Salt Water Fish	Seefisch
Prawn Pie	Krabbentorte
Herring Dishes	**Heringsgerichte**
Rollmops	Rollmops
Bismarck Herring	Bismarckheringe
Herring Salad	Heringssalat
Smoked Fish	**Geräucherter Fisch**
Smoked Herring with Scrambled Egg	Gebratene Bücklinge mit Rührei
Smoked Fish with Fried Potatoes	Räucherfisch mit Bratkartoffeln
Smoked Fish on Sauerkraut	Räucherfisch auf Sauerkraut
Smoked Fish with Rice	Räucherfisch mit Reis

Eel in Beer Sauce *(Aal in Biersosse)*

750 g ($1\frac{3}{4}$ lb) eel
$\frac{3}{4}$ l ($1\frac{1}{2}$ pt) beer
2 chopped onions
1 sliced carrot
1 piece celery
1 bay-leaf
3 peppercorns
50 g (2 oz) butter
40 g ($1\frac{3}{4}$ oz) plain flour
1 tablespoon chopped parsley

Bring the beer with the vegetables and spices to the boil and simmer for 20–30 minutes. Skin and wash the eel and cut into 5 cm (2 in) pieces. Add to the simmering beer-broth for 15–20 minutes. Take out the eel pieces and keep warm. Pass the broth through a sieve and thicken in the following way: mix the flour into the melted butter; gradually add the broth, stirring all the time. Pour this sauce over the eel pieces; sprinkle with parsley and serve immediately with boiled potatoes.

Mosel Eel in White Wine Sauce *(Mosel Aal in Weissweinsosse—Rhineland)*

Young eel from the Mosel is a delicacy which is often prepared unskinned and left whole. The following recipe is very popular and can be employed in the preparation of young eel generally.

500 g (1 lb 2 oz) eel
1 tablespoon chopped onion
50 g (2 oz) butter
40 g ($1\frac{3}{4}$ oz) plain flour
1 sprig fresh dill herb or $\frac{1}{2}$ teaspoon dill seeds
$\frac{1}{4}$ l ($\frac{1}{2}$ pt) white wine (Mosel Riesling)
$\frac{1}{4}$ l ($\frac{1}{2}$ pt) meat broth (not chicken)
pinch of salt and pepper
1 teaspoon lemon juice
1 tablespoon chopped parsley to garnish

Wash and clean the eel. Fry the onion in the butter. Add the eel; dust with flour. Pour in the broth and wine. Add the dill, lemon juice and seasoning. Simmer for 20–30 minutes according to the size of the eel or until cooked. Serve sprinkled with parsley.

Freshwater Fish in Wine Sauce

(Flussfisch in Weinsosse—Rhineland)

Salmon from the Rhine, eel and pike from the Mosel, trout from the many clear water tributaries, all enjoy great popularity in Germany. Most of these rivers flow through a countryside of vineyards which surely has had its influence on the following recipe:

500 g (1 lb 2 oz) freshwater fish
¼ l (½ pt) water
¼ l (½ pt) white wine
pinch of salt and pepper
1 sprig of chervil
1 sprig of dill
2 teaspoons lemon juice

Sauce
50 g (2 oz) butter
30 g (1¼ oz) plain flour
2 egg yolks
¼ l (½ pt) single cream
1 tablespoon chopped parsley
4 lemon slices

Bring the wine and water, with the herbs, lemon juice, pepper and salt, to the boil. Add the prepared fish and simmer over low heat for 20–30 minutes or until cooked (according to size of fish).

Prepare the sauce by mixing the flour with the melted butter over low heat. Gradually add enough of the fish stock to obtain a smooth thick sauce. Leave to simmer for 5–10 minutes. Remove from the hot plate. Whisk the yolks with the cream. Carefully add 1 cup of sauce whisking all the time. Pour this mixture into the sauce, reheat, but do not boil.

Arrange the fish on a warm dish. Pour over the sauce. Garnish with parsley and lemon slices and serve with mashed potatoes and fresh dressed salad.

Carp in Beer ***(Karpfen in Bier—East Germany)***

Carp ponds are found in all parts of Germany. East Germany and the Schleswig-Holstein lakes in the north are, however, well known for their wealth of carp. Carp in red wine is the traditional New Year's Eve dish in many parts of Germany. In all parts of East

Germany it is customary to have carp cooked in beer for Christmas Eve.

For Carp in Wine use the same recipe but replace the ale and water with ½ l (1 pt) wine and ½ l (1 pt) water.

1000–1500 g (2¼–3½ lb) carp
¾ l (1½ pt) brown ale (must not be bitter)
¼ l (½ pt) water
1 chopped onion
2 small diced carrots
1 diced piece of celery
1 chopped parsley root
1 teaspoon lemon juice
2 tablespoons vinegar
1 bay-leaf
5 peppercorns
3 cloves
60 g (2½ oz) butter
30 g (1¼ oz) plain flour
1 dessertspoon sugar
1 teaspoon salt
60 g (2½ oz) soft crumbled gingerbread (Pfefferkuchen)
100 g (4 oz) blanched chopped almonds
100 g (4 oz) raisins

Prepare and wash the carp; leave whole or cut into portions. Place in a fish casserole. Put the beer, water, lemon juice, vinegar, vegetables and spices into a saucepan. Bring to the boil and simmer for 10 minutes. Melt the butter, mix in the flour; gradually stir in the prepared stock. Add the gingerbread, sugar, salt, almonds and raisins. Pour this sauce over the carp in the casserole dish. Put into a pre-heated oven, 195 °C (375 °F, gas mark 5), and stew for 30–45 minutes (according to size). The carp is cooked when the back fin comes away easily. Lift the carp on to a hot serving dish. Pass the sauce through a fine sieve. Taste for seasoning. If necessary, thicken with a little flour and water. Pour the sauce over the fish and serve. East Germans like bread-roll dumplings with this meal.

Fish Ragout *(Fischragout)*

750–1000 g (1¾–2¼ lb) cooked fish fillet
50 g (2 oz) cooked button mushrooms
50 g (2 oz) shrimps
1 medium chopped onion
50 g (2 oz) butter
40 g (1¾ oz) plain flour

juice of ½ lemon
salt, pepper
1 tablespoon capers
¼ l (½ pt) fish stock or meat broth
¼ l (½ pt) white wine
2 egg yolks

Fry the onion in the butter until just yellow. Mix in the flour. Stir until golden brown. Gradually pour in the stock and wine. Bring to the boil and simmer for 10 minutes. Add the lemon juice, salt, pepper and capers. Remove from the hot plate. Beat the egg yolks with some of the hot sauce before pouring it into the sauce. Add the cooked fish, mushrooms and shrimps. Reheat but do not boil. Serve with boiled or mashed potatoes.

Fish Fillet in Dill Sauce *(Fischfilet in Dillsosse)*

This dish is best prepared with fresh dill herbs from the garden. If they are not available, it is also possible to use dried dill seeds and leaves.

500 g (1 lb 2 oz) fish fillet
½ l (1 pt) water
1 bay-leaf
2 tablespoons chopped fresh dill (1¼ tablespoons if dried dill is used)
1 medium sliced onion
60 g (2½ oz) butter
30 g (1¼ oz) plain flour
2 tablespoons soured cream
1 teaspoon salt

Place the water, onion, bay-leaf and salt into a saucepan and bring to the boil. Immerse the fish fillet and simmer for 10 minutes. Remove the fish from the pan and keep on a warm plate. Mix the flour with the melted butter; gradually add about ¼ l (½ pt) fish stock. Simmer for 10 minutes. Remove from the hot plate. Add the dill and soured cream. Pour the sauce over the fish and serve with boiled or mashed potatoes.

Blue Trout *(Forelle Blau)*

Blue trout is a very popular dish along the tributaries of the Rhine. Along the Ahr valley, for example, thousands of trout are bred every summer. They enjoy the clear, fast flowing water of the smaller rivers. It is important that the trout is very fresh. During the cooking process, the skin of the trout turns blue. It is therefore important to handle the fish with care. Do not scale or scrub.

4 young trout
1 l (2 pt) water
1 tablespoon salt
4 tablespoons vinegar
4 tablespoons white wine
2 small sliced onions
1 bay-leaf
3 peppercorns
1 clove
½ teaspoon basil

Clean and wash the trout under cold running water. Fasten each into a circle by tying the head to the tail. Bring the water with the vinegar, wine, onions, herbs and spices to the boil. Immerse trout and leave covered simmering over low heat for 10–20 minutes. They are cooked when the fins can be pulled off easily.

Serve with knobs of butter or herb butter, lemon discs and new potatoes (sprinkled with parsley).

Salt Water Fish *(Seefisch)*

Salt water fish can be either fried in butter or steamed and served hot or cold. Apart from the usual white sauces with capers, chives, onions, parsley and cheese, German cookery offers a number of appetizing sauces, particularly suitable to accompany salt water fish:

Brandy Sauce (page 177)
Bacon Sauce (page 179)
Saxony Fish Sauce (page 179)
Soured Cream Sauce (page 182)
Horse-radish Cream (page 183)

Prawn Pie *(Krabbentorte—North Germany)*

Pastry
180 g (6½ oz) plain flour
1 level teaspoon baking powder
pinch of salt and pepper
120 g (4½ oz) butter or margarine
3–4 tablespoons water

Filling
50 g (2 oz) butter
200 g (7 oz) prawns or shrimps
100 g (4 oz) mild grated cheese
100 g (4 oz) boiled ham (diced)
1 sprig of thyme
1 finely chopped onion
3 eggs
¼ l (½ pt) milk
salt, pepper

Make the pastry from the ingredients and line a tin of 25 cm (10 in) diameter. Form a 3-cm (1¼-in) high rim around the edge. Bake for 15 minutes at 200 °C (400 °F, gas mark 6).

Prepare the filling by melting the butter and mixing with the other ingredients. Spread the filling on to the pastry case and bake for 30–40 minutes at 200 °C (400 °F, gas mark 6). Serve hot with dressed lettuce or tomato salad.

HERRING DISHES *(Heringsgerichte)*

For variety in method of preparation, no other fish can compare with the herring. There are recipes for fresh, salted, smoked and marinaded herrings. The term Matjeshering is used for the fatter, but more tender, unspawned fish, whilst a Vollhering is the one filled with milk or roe. The females are called Rogener, the males Milchner.

Herring was originally regarded as a very simple food and was mainly eaten during the period of Lent. These days the sour herring or rollmops (collared herring) is still regarded as the main dish for breakfast on Ash Wednesday, the first day of Lent, the morning after carnival celebrations. In particular, people with a hangover seem to welcome a sour and spicy herring for their breakfast. From a medical standpoint this is considered to be a sensible idea. Excessive intake of alcohol is known to reduce the salt content in the body and this needs to be rectified by the consumption of salty food. Apart from the salt, herring also provides much needed protein.

The following recipes offer a variety of sour/salty herring dishes. If the herrings cannot be obtained ready salted, they can be salted by leaving them for a few hours in brine (½ l (1 pt) water plus 120 g (4½ oz) salt).

Rollmops *(preferably Milchner)*

6 salted herrings
¼ l (½ pt) wine vinegar
⅛ l (¼ pt) water
6–8 tablespoons milk
2 bay-leaves
4 peppercorns
½ teaspoon mustard seeds
1 dessertspoon sweet-sour mustard
2 chopped onions
1 diced apple
4 diced pickled gherkins
1 tablespoon lemon juice

Put the vinegar, water, bay-leaves, mustard seeds and peppercorns into a saucepan. Bring to the boil; leave to cool. Bone, clean, halve lengthwise and wash the herrings, preserving the herrings' milk. Spread some mustard on the inside of the herring halves; spread with apple, onion and gherkin cubes. Roll them up and secure with a wooden toothpick or cocktail stick. Place these Rollmöpse into an earthenware dish. Pass the herrings' milk through a sieve and add with the milk and lemon juice to the cooled pickling sauce. Pour this marinade over the Rollmöpse and leave for 8 days in an earthenware dish.

In the Rhineland—particularly in the area of the Eifel—Rollmöpse and potatoes boiled in their skins are a very popular evening meal.

Bismarck Herring *(Bismarckheringe)*

Bismarck herring is another term for pickled herring fillets which are left for 24 hours in a marinade of vinegar, onions, salt and pepper. The dish is called after the German statesman who declared the herring to be a delicacy which due to its comparative cheapness failed to be recognized as such.

There are a number of refined variations of the basic pickled herring recipe as for example the following:

1000 g (2¼ lb) salt herrings
1½ l (3 pt) water
3–4 medium-sized sliced onions
3–4 bay-leaves
10 peppercorns
1 teaspoon mustard seeds
3 juniper berries
½ teaspoon sugar
¼ l (½ pt) wine vinegar
⅛ l (¼ pt) milk
⅛ l (¼ pt) double cream or soured cream

Soak the salted herrings in the water for 24 hours, changing the water several times. Wash the herrings, cut off heads and tails, skin, bone and clean.

Meanwhile, bring the vinegar with the sugar, bay-leaves, peppercorns, mustard seeds and juniper berries to the boil. Leave to cool. Then mix with the milk and cream. Arrange layers of the herring fillets and onion rings in an earthenware dish. Over each layer pour some of the marinade. The herring must be covered with marinade. Leave in a cool place for 2–3 days. Germans like this dish with hot potatoes boiled in their skins and dressed lettuce.

Herring Salad *(Heringssalat—Rhineland)*

Herring salad is particularly liked in the Rhineland and is usually served for the evening meal with buttered dark bread. It is also an attractive feature in a cold buffet.

4 salted matjes fillets (watered for 24 hours and diced)
100 g (4 oz) cooked diced chicken meat
500 g (1 lb 2 oz) boiled diced potatoes
200 g (7 oz) peeled diced apples
5 sweet-sour pickled gherkins (diced)
1 medium-sized finely chopped onion
1 dessertspoon sugar

½ teaspoon pepper
1 teaspoon sweet-sour mustard
3–5 tablespoons mayonnaise
⅛ l (¼ pt) soured cream
1 dessertspoon lemon juice
salt to taste
1 level teaspoon black pepper
1 hard-boiled egg (diced)
2 tablespoons chopped walnuts
⅛ l (¼ pt) single cream

Mix the mayonnaise, cream, mustard, lemon juice, sugar and pepper to a smooth sauce. Put all the ingredients into a large bowl and pour the sauce over them. Mix well and place for 4–5 hours in the refrigerator.

Sometimes, 250 g (9 oz) boiled diced beetroot is added to the herring salad which gives it a pink colouring. The salad can be garnished with slices of egg and is served with fresh bread rolls, pumpernickel, or thinly sliced dark rye bread.

SMOKED FISH *(Geräucherter Fisch)*

The Germans have a particular liking for smoked foods. The most suitable fish for this kind of food preparation are salmon, eel, trout and herring. Smoked Black Forest trout fillet is a well-known delicacy. The North German area along the Baltic and North Sea is famous for smoked fish. Kieler Sprotten (Kiel sprats) in their typical wooden boxes are sent all over the country. They are eaten by holding them at head and tail and biting into the middle of the little fish which is a small brother of the herring. Bücklinge are whole herring which have been hot-smoked at a temperature of 60 °C (140 °F) or more. And from Schleswig-Holstein comes the smoked Baltic Sea salmon, usually served with black bread, herb butter and beer. Salmon is usually salted for improved preservation and is subsequently only cold-smoked at a maximum temperature of 30 °C (86 °F). Hot-smoked eel is a delicacy which can be found throughout the whole of North Germany and along the Rhine and Mosel. Smoked eel is best when young—not too thick and not too long.

The area around Oldenburg has developed a traditional way of eating smoked eel. Hold the eel with the left hand just below its head. Break off the head and pull away the skin with the right hand. Then holding the eel with both hands, bite your way through. To aid digestion of this rather greasy fish, it is customary to take a local clear Schnaps (corn brandy) before, during and after eating eel. It is the so-called 'spoon drink' as the Schnaps is drunk from a tin spoon held in the left hand. After the eel meal a little corn brandy offered by the waiter straight from the bottle is poured into the palm of the hand and rubbed over both hands to take away the fish smell.

Smoked fish is mostly eaten cold with black rye bread. The following are, however, a number of recipes with warm smoked fish.

Smoked Herring with Scrambled Egg

(Gebratene Bücklinge mit Rührei)

Open the herrings, clean and bone. Fry in butter. Whisk 2 eggs with a pinch of pepper and paprika. Pour over the fried herrings and stir until the scrambled egg mixture is set.

Smoked Fish with Fried Potatoes

(Räucherfisch mit Bratkartoffeln)

Fry the sliced potatoes in a frying pan. When nearly ready add pieces of smoked fish. Fry with the potatoes for a short period. Serve with dressed lettuce (page 160).

Smoked Fish on Sauerkraut

(Räucherfisch auf Sauerkraut)

Cook the sauerkraut as suggested on page 142. Put into a fireproof dish. Place the smoked fish on top of the hot sauerkraut. Cover with aluminium foil and cook for 10–20 minutes in a pre-heated oven.

Smoked Fish with Rice *(Räucherfisch mit Reis)*

Tear the fish to pieces and fry in butter with chopped onion or parsley. Mix with boiled rice and season with salt and pepper to taste. Serve with tomato or cucumber salad (page 161).

Meat, Poultry and Game

(*Fleisch, Geflügel und Wild*)

Pork	**Schweinefleisch**
Slaughter Plate	Schlachtplatte
Roast Sucking Pig	Gebratenes Spanferkel
Westerwald Barbecue	Westerwälder Spiessbraten
Stuffed Pig's Belly	Gefüllte Schweinebrust
Pork Pot-roast	Schweinebraten
Smoked Pork Rib	Kasseler Rippenspeer
White Cabbage and Pork	Weisskohl mit Schweinefleisch
Pig's Trotters	Eisbein
Holstein Cutlet	Holsteiner Schnitzel
Neck of Pork in Beer	Schweinenacken in Bier
Sour Pork	Schweinesauer
Pork Goulash	Schweinegulasch
Shoemaker's Pan	Schusterpfanne
Tenderloin	Schweinefilet
Marinaded Pork	Schweinepfeffer
Fried or Grilled Pork Sausage	Bratwurst
Beef	**Rindfleisch**
Stewed Pickled Beef	Sauerbraten
Lindau Wedding Braised Beef	Lindauer Hochzeitsbraten
Beef Pot-roast	Schmorbraten

Beef Olives	Rouladen
Beef Steaks in Red Wine	Rindersteaks in Rotwein
Meat Fondue	Fleischfondue
Westphalian Goulash	Westfälischer Pfefferpotthast
Boiled Beef	Gekochtes Rindfleisch
Savoy Cabbage with Beef	Wirsing mit Rindfleisch
Beef Stewed in Beer	Gedämpftes Rindfleisch in Bier
Wine Goulash	Weingulasch
Cured Meat and Fish Hot-pot	Labskaus
Veal	**Kalbfleisch**
Viennese Cutlet	Wiener Schnitzel
Veal Cutlet à la Holstein	Kalbschnitzel à la Holstein
Hunter's Cutlet	Jägerschnitzel
Cutlet in Cream Sauce	Rahmschnitzel
Paprika Cutlet	Paprikaschnitzel
Meat Cushions	Fleischpolster
Birds' Nests	Vogelnester
Veal and Kidney Roast	Kalbsnierenbraten
Braised Knuckle of Veal	Kalbshaxe
Stuffed Breast of Veal	Gefüllte Kalbsbrust
Veal Fricassee	Kalbsfrikassee
Lamb	**Lamm**
Marinaded Leg of Lamb	Gebeizte Lammkeule
Mixed Meat Dishes	**Fleischspeisen**
Fried Meat Balls	Frikadellen
Königsberg Meat Balls	Königsberger Klopse
Stuffed Green Peppers	Gefüllte Paprikaschoten
Cabbage Meat Rolls	Kohlrouladen
Liver Cheese	Leberkäse
Mixed Goulash	Gulasch von dreierlei Fleisch
Pichelstein Hot-pot	Pichelsteiner Topf
Liver, Kidneys, Tongue	**Leber, Nieren, Zunge**
Liver—Berlin Style	Leber auf Berliner Art

Liver in Wine	Leber in Wein
Liver Dumplings	Leberknödel
Meat on Skewers	Fleischspiesse
Sour Kidneys	Saure Nieren
Boiled Tongue	Gekochte Zunge
Poultry	**Geflügel**
Bremen Chicken Ragout	Bremer Kükenragout
Roasted Goose	Gänsebraten
Neuenahr Goose Breast	Neuenahrer Gänsebrust
Roast Duck	Entenbraten
Game	**Wild**
Roast Pheasant	Fasanbraten
Saddle of Venison	Rehrücken
Game Ragout	Wildragout
Roast Wild Boar	Wildschweinbraten
Roast Hare	Hasenbraten
Braised Leg of Moorland Lamb	Heidschnucken Lammkeule

'Eating and drinking keeps body and soul together.' This proverb seems to describe very well the German attitude to eating, and meat dishes rank high in their order of preference. In 1974/75 for example, the average lean meat consumed in West Germany was 82·5 kg (182 lb) per head, of which 44·6 kg (98 lb) was taken up by pork.

German cookery naturally presents a wide range of methods for preparing meat dishes. They can be fried, braised, roasted or boiled, and pot-roasting is a method much favoured for many dishes. The use of spices in the preparation of sauces and marinades adds breadth to the range of flavours associated with meat dishes and adequately justifies the extra time and planning which is required for their presentation.

Many butchers in Germany now sell meat in a form suitable for immediate cooking, having taken over the role of the housewife in preparing such dishes as beef olives (Rouladen) and Sauerbraten.

This should have the additional advantage of ensuring that the correct cut of meat is used for the chosen dish.

As will be seen later, many succulent dishes are created with the use of offal, with strong regional variations in methods of preparation.

Meat is almost always served in its own gravy. Gravy brownings and powders are regarded as poor substitutes and are generally avoided by a good housewife. If a roast or joint has been prepared, it is the custom to slice the meat in the kitchen before serving and to arrange the slices on a meat dish, garnished with parsley, tomatoes, lettuce or mushrooms.

A meal for which all ingredients are cooked together in one saucepan might not sound tempting to everyone and is usually regarded as the housewife's emergency method to use up left-overs. There are, however, some hot-pots (Eintopfgerichte) which enjoy great popularity. The secret lies in the wise composition of ingredients and the choice of spices and not in the random use of them. Hot-pots are as popular as a Monday meal in Germany as main course soups are for Saturdays. A number are given in this chapter and others in the chapter on Vegetables.

PORK *(Schweinefleisch)*

The pig is the most important source of meat in Germany. It is the oldest German domestic animal and it has also become the symbol of good luck.

The popularity of pork chops and Kasseler has had an influence on the breeding of pigs. A new strain has been custom-bred to correspond with the consumers' eating habits: pigs with eight pairs of ribs instead of six: with 30 per cent less fat, 25 per cent more lean meat. About 60 per cent of the pig is sold as fresh, salted or smoked meat, the remainder being used for the preparation of sausages (see pages 167–70).

Slaughter Plate *(Schlachtplatte—South Germany)*

People in country areas who have a small holding, or perhaps keep only one or two pigs, still celebrate slaughter day once or twice a year. It is an occasion to which friends and relations are invited to help preserve and to eat. During the winter season, village inns usually have one traditional slaughter day a week when Schlachtplatte is the dish of the day. It usually consists of boiled pork belly, pigs' trotters, chops, a selection of different sausages and sauerkraut. To help the digestion of this rather fatty meal it is accompanied by Schnaps and beer or new wine.

A rather unusual Schlachtplatte is traditional in the South German town which carries the German name for pig—Schweinfurt (near Würzburg). A whole pig is cooked for a Schweinfurter Platte which is meant to be for a group of thirty people. No dishes are used. Everything is served straight on the well-scrubbed wooden table top: salt, pepper, diced rye bread and the pork itself. Everybody helps themselves to the different parts of the pig which are carried in, starting with the belly pork, to the head, trunk, offal and eyes. Fat is not eaten at all. The drink is new wine and Schnaps made from plums. Now and then the feast is interrupted by one of the traditional songs.

Roast Sucking Pig *(Gebratenes Spanferkel—South Germany)*

3–6 weeks old piglet
salt, pepper
50 g (2 oz) fat or oil
¼ l (½ pt) beer
4 tablespoons soured cream

Filling (optional)
30 g (1¼ oz) butter
piglet's liver and heart (chopped)
1 medium-sized onion (chopped)
250 g (9 oz) minced pork
2 slices of white bread soaked in warm milk
2 eggs
2–3 tablespoons breadcrumbs
1 teaspoon salt
½ teaspoon pepper
½ teaspoon marjoram
½ teaspoon thyme

Wash and dry the piglet; sprinkle with salt and pepper; place in a roasting pan. Fry the ingredients for the filling in the butter for 10 minutes. Fill the piglet and sew it up. Roast for 2–3 hours (according to size) at 190 °C (375 °F, gas mark 5), in a mixture of the fat and beer. Baste frequently. Add the soured cream to the gravy. Serve on a meat dish garnished with parsley and lemon slices.

Bavarians eat the piglet with potato dumplings and sauerkraut or dressed lettuce.

Westerwald Barbecue

(Westerwälder Spiessbraten—Rhineland)

boned middle piece of a pig's back
½ bottle of red wine
400 g (14 oz) sliced onions
1 teaspoon ground black pepper
2 teaspoons marjoram
6–10 tablespoons vegetable oil

Mix the onions, pepper, marjoram and oil; leave for 30 minutes then pour the mixture over the meat and leave for 3 hours.

Slowly roast the meat in the usual way in the open over a charcoal or wood fire, rotating it all the time. The roasting time depends on the size of the meat. During the last hour of roasting, baste frequently with red wine.

The meat is served with fresh bread rolls and tomato salad and red wine.

Stuffed Pig's Belly

(Gefüllte Schweinebrust—North Germany)

1500 g (3½ lb) belly of pork (boned)
50 g (2 oz) fat
salt, pepper

Filling
175 g (6 oz) white bread soaked in warm milk
1 egg
100 g (4 oz) raisins
1 large apple (peeled and diced)
1 pinch of ground cardamom and clove
1 dessertspoon rum

Mix the ingredients for the filling. Pack into the pig's belly and sew it up. Sprinkle the meat with salt and pepper. Place in a roasting tin with the heated fat. Roast in the oven, frequently basting, at 190 °C (375 °F, gas mark 5), for 70–90 minutes. Serve with boiled potatoes and mixed salad (tomatoes, lettuce, cucumbers).

Pork Pot-roast *(Schweinebraten)*

1000 g (2¼ lb) pork (shoulder or leg)
salt, pepper
½ teaspoon french mustard
40 g (1¾ oz) fat
1 onion
1 carrot
½ bay-leaf
1 clove
1 tomato
1 sprig thyme
1 stem parsley
¼ l (½ pt) hot water
1–2 teaspoons cornflour
2 tablespoons cold water
1 tablespoon dry red wine
1 dessertspoon home-made raspberry juice or cranberry sauce

Wash and dry the meat; rub with salt and pepper and mustard. Heat the fat in a meat roasting pot on the hot plate. Place the joint rind downwards in the hot fat. When the skin is crisp and brown, turn rind upwards; add the onion. Fry until brown. Add the carrot, bay-leaf, clove, tomato, thyme and parsley. Cover with a lid tightly and leave on low to medium heat for another 5–10 minutes. Pour in ⅛ l (¼ pt) hot water. Cover and pot-roast for another 70–90 minutes over low to medium heat.

From time to time check that the meat does not boil dry. Add the remaining ⅛ l (¼ pt) hot water as necessary. When the meat is cooked, remove from the pot, put on to a pre-warmed dish and keep warm. Strain the gravy; bring to the boil, adding the cornflour mixed with cold water. Season to taste with salt, pepper, raspberry juice and wine. Slice the pork and serve with some gravy poured over it.

In Bavaria pot-roasted pork is served with potato dumplings (page 153); in the Rhineland with boiled potatoes.

Smoked Pork Rib (*Kasseler Rippenspeer—Berlin*)

One could easily assume that this well-known dish originates from the Hessian town Kassel. It received its name, however, from the Berlin butcher Cassel who first introduced it to his customers. Kasseler is a salted and smoked boned piece of pork ribs of the typical pink colouring and yellow-brown outside.

It has to be soaked in water for 1 hour before preparing it. It is advisable to cook a slightly larger piece than needed for a particular meal and to serve the cold Kasseler sliced with brown bread for the evening meal. It is rather difficult to obtain fresh Kasseler in England. It is mainly offered in delicatessen shops, cooked and sliced. The following recipe is for fresh Kasseler.

1500–2000 g (3½–4½ lb) fresh Kasseler
¼ teaspoon ground black pepper
1 medium-sized sliced onion
1 dessertspoon honey
juice of 1 orange
⅜ l (¾ pt) hot water
⅛ l (¼ pt) dry red wine
3 tablespoons soured cream

Place the Kasseler and the onion into a roasting pan; sprinkle with pepper and pour the hot water over it. Roast in a pre-heated oven, 210° C (400 °F, gas mark 6), for 70–90 minutes. Add the wine after 45 minutes and baste frequently.

Heat the orange juice with the honey and brush over the Kasseler 20 minutes before cooking time is finished. When cooked, remove on to a pre-heated meat dish. Add the soured cream to the gravy and if necessary thicken with 1 teaspoon cornflour mixed with cold water.

Hot Kasseler is served with sauerkraut and boiled potatoes.

White Cabbage and Pork

(Weisskohl mit Schweinefleisch)

1000 g (2¼ lb) white cabbage
500 g (1 lb 2 oz) potatoes
500 g (1 lb 2 oz) cooking apples
750 g (1¾ lb) belly of pork or other fat pork
30 g (1¼ oz) margarine
1 medium-sized chopped onion
1 teaspoon caraway seeds
25 g (1 oz) sugar
½ teaspoon salt
¼ teaspoon pepper
½ l (1 pt) broth or water and meat cube
¼ l (½ pt) dry white wine
1 tablespoon wine vinegar

In a large saucepan heat the margarine. Add the sugar and brown. Add onion. Halve the cabbage, remove stalk, wash and shred finely. Add to the saucepan with broth, wine, salt and pepper and caraway seeds. Place meat on top. Simmer covered with a lid for about 1 hour. Peel, wash and slice potatoes and apples. Add to the saucepan and simmer for another 30 minutes. Add vinegar and season to taste with salt and pepper. Serve hot.

Pig's Trotters

(Eisbein—Berlin)

For this dish the pig's trotters should be mildly salted and smoked. The name Eisbein (ice-leg) originates from the fact that years ago it was common practice to make ice-skates from the bones in a pig's legs.

1000–2000 g (2¼–4½ lb) pig's trotters (4 trotters of 500 g (1 lb 2 oz) each are ideal for 4 people)
3 peppercorns
1 medium-sized sliced onion
1 bay-leaf
1 carrot
2 l (3¾ pt) cold water

Put the trotters, vegetables and spices into a large saucepan; cover with the water. Bring to the boil and simmer over low heat for 2 hours (longer if 2 big legs are cooked). Serve with plenty of mustard, mashed potatoes and sauerkraut, or the traditional Berlin style with sauerkraut and pea purée.

In Bavaria this dish is called Schweinshaxe and is served on sauerkraut.

Holstein Cutlet

(Holsteiner Schnitzel—North Germany)

4 tender pork cutlets
salt, pepper
1 beaten egg
40–50 g (1¾–2 oz) fine breadcrumbs
100 g (4 oz) butter or margarine
4 fried eggs

Slightly beat the cutlets, rub with salt and pepper. Dip into the beaten egg. Turn in the breadcrumbs. Fry in the hot butter for 20–25 minutes, turning once. Pork chops (Schweinekoteletten) are prepared in the same way. According to the original recipe, the cutlets should be prepared in fresh butter from Holstein in North Germany and served with a fried egg on top.

Neck of Pork in Beer

(Schweinenacken in Bier)

1000–1500 g (2¼–3½ lb) neck of pork
1 leek
1 piece of celery
1 medium-sized sliced onion
2 skinned tomatoes
½ l (1 pt) beer
1–2 teaspoons cornflour

Put the washed meat, vegetables and the beer into a saucepan. Bring to the boil and simmer over a low heat for about 1½ hours. Thicken the gravy by adding cornflour mixed with one tablespoon cold water. Season to taste and serve with mashed potatoes and dressed lettuce.

Sour Pork (*Schweinesauer*)

1000 g (2¼ lb) pork
2 onions
2 leeks
1 piece of celery
2 carrots
⅜ l (¾ pt) cold water
2 tablespoons wine vinegar
1 clove
1 bay-leaf
½ teaspoon sugar
salt and pepper to taste
1–2 teaspoons cornflour

Put the pork and diced vegetables with the spices and vinegar into a saucepan; add the cold water and bring to the boil. Simmer for about 70–90 minutes.

Remove the meat and keep in a warm place. Make the gravy by thickening some of the broth with cornflour mixed with cold water. Add the sugar and seasoning to taste.

Serve with dumplings and sauerkraut.

Pork Goulash (*Schweinegulasch*)

750 g (1¾ lb) lean diced pork
50 g (2 oz) fat
3 medium-sized sliced onions
4 skinned sliced tomatoes
⅛ l (¼ pt) hot water
½ teaspoon wine vinegar
1 teaspoon sweet paprika
salt and pepper
1 tablespoon soured cream
1–2 teaspoons cornflour

Fry the pork in the fat until brown. Add the onions. Cover with a lid and leave over low heat until the onion rings are soft (do not burn the meat). Add the tomatoes, water, vinegar and paprika. Cover and simmer for about 70 minutes. During the cooking process add more water if necessary. Season to taste. Thicken with cornflour mixed with cold water. Add cream and serve with boiled potatoes or noodles.

Shoemaker's Pan

(Schusterpfanne—East Germany)

750 g (1¾ lb) lean pork
salt, pepper
750 g (1¾ lb) raw potatoes
750 g (1¾ lb) small pears (peeled, halved and cored)
2 sliced carrots
¾ l (1½ pt) boiling water

Wash and dry the pork; rub with salt and pepper and put into a deep pan. Arrange potatoes, pears and carrots around the meat. Pour the boiling water over the meat, cover and simmer for 1½–2 hours. This is a typically East German dish where the mixture of sweet and savoury food is very popular.

Tenderloin

(Schweinefilet)

Tenderloin is a very tender, but rather expensive piece of meat. There is, however, no waste, as it is sold without bones and fat.

2 tenderloin
50 g (2 oz) butter or margarine
1 medium-sized onion (halved)
salt, pepper
⅛ l (¼ pt) hot water
1 dessertspoon dry wine
1 tablespoon double or soured cream
1 teaspoon cornflour

Wash and dry the meat; rub with salt and pepper. Brown in the butter adding the onion towards the end of this process. Add the water; cover with a lid and pot-roast for 30–40 minutes. Add more hot water if necessary. Lift meat on to a hot meat dish and keep warm. Thicken gravy with cornflour mixed in cold water. Lastly add wine and cream. Serve with asparagus, red cabbage or cauliflower.

Marinaded Pork *(Schweinepfeffer)*

750–1000 g (1¾–2¼ lb) pork (cut into cubes)
50 g (2 oz) fat
40 g (1¾ oz) plain flour
2 medium-sized onions
¼ l (½ pt) marinade
¼ l (½ pt) boiling water

Marinade
¼ l (½ pt) dry wine
1 tablespoon wine vinegar
1 teaspoon salt
1 sliced onion
3 peppercorns
1 bay-leaf
½ teaspoon mustard seeds
1 dessertspoon finely chopped celery

Prepare the marinade and pour over the meat. Leave overnight. The next day take the meat out of the marinade; dry on kitchen paper and fry in the fat until brown. Add the onion. Dust with flour. Stir in the liquid; cover and simmer for about 60 minutes. Season to taste and serve with potato dumplings (page 153) and any chosen vegetable or dressed lettuce.

Fried or Grilled Pork Sausage *(Bratwurst—South Germany)*

German Bratwurst consists of meat, fat and spices only. Its home is Franken and Bavaria. Sausages for frying and grilling are popular in all parts of Germany, but by no means are they of the same taste or appearance. There are the normal-sized sausages of about 2 cm (¾ in) diameter and 15 cm (6 in) length, prepared to special regional recipes. Well known is the variety from Thüringen in East Germany. A speciality of Nuremberg is the miniature Bratwurst, with a 600-year-old tradition, which only weighs 23 g (¾ oz) and should be grilled over beech wood. Grilled Bratwurst is a popular snack and is sold in bread rolls at market-places and street-stands. Many restaurants offer as one of their cheaper meals, Bratwurst, mashed potatoes and sauerkraut.

The following recipe is suitable for a quick, cheap and tasty lunch:

500 g (1 lb 2 oz) Bratwurst (sausage for frying)
50 g (2 oz) plain flour
50 g (2 oz) fat
1 l (2 pt) water
1 sliced onion
$\frac{1}{8}$ l ($\frac{1}{4}$ pt) beer
1 tablespoon tomato purée

Bring the water to the boil; take off the hot plate. Immerse the sausage and leave for 5–10 minutes. Remove, roll in the flour and fry immediately in hot fat, turning it and pricking a few holes with a fine fork occasionally. When it is crisp and golden brown add the onions. After 5 minutes add beer and tomato purée. Serve with mashed potatoes and dressed lettuce, tomato salad, sauerkraut or red cabbage.

BEEF *(Rindfleisch)*

Recipes for beef include boiling, stewing and roasting. The use of spices, wine and cream plays an important role in the German method of cooking this meat. Pot-roasting, preferably in a cast-iron roasting pot, is commonly used, particularly for cheaper cuts, as it makes them tasty and tender. It is unusual in Germany to serve beef underdone.

Stewed Pickled Beef *(Sauerbraten—Rhineland)*

This dish represents the traditional Sunday lunch for many families in the Rhineland. Its typical sour taste goes particularly well with potato balls and stewed apples. The cheaper cut from the forequarter is very suitable for a sour roast.

1000 g ($2\frac{1}{4}$ lb) piece of beef
50 g (2 oz) fat smoked bacon or 2 tablespoons oil
1 tablespoon tomato purée

Marinade
¼ l (⅛ pt) wine vinegar
¾ l (1½ pt) water
2 medium-sized sliced onions
1 finely diced piece of celery
1 sliced carrot
1 bay-leaf
3 juniper berries
2 cloves
5 peppercorns
¼ teaspoon mustard seeds
1 teaspoon salt
1½ teaspoons sugar

Gravy
1 tablespoon raisins
1 dessertspoon grated almonds
3 tablespoons double or soured cream
salt, pepper, sugar
1 teaspoon cornflour

Wash and dry the meat and put into an earthenware or porcelain dish. Put all the ingredients for the marinade into a saucepan; bring to the boil and leave to cool. Pour marinade over the meat; leave meat in the marinade in a cool place for 2–3 days, turning it daily. Take meat out of marinade and dry. Extract the fat from the bacon by heating, or use cooking oil. Place the meat in the hot fat and brown on all sides. Add the onions, carrot and celery from the marinade and the tomato purée. Pour in ⅛ l (¼ pt) hot water and ⅛ l (¼ pt) strained marinade. Cover and leave to braise over low heat for 1½–2 hours, basting the meat frequently. Add more hot water or marinade (according to taste) as required. During the last 15 minutes, add raisins and almonds. Take out the meat; keep warm. Season the gravy to taste with salt, pepper and sugar. Boil to thicken; if necessary, add 1 teaspoon cornflour mixed in one tablespoon of water. Stir in the cream (do not boil again). Serve meat cut into thick slices.

Lindau Wedding Braised Beef
(Lindauer Hochzeitsbraten—South Germany)

This used to be the traditional meat dish for South German weddings or other family occasions. A piece of hindquarter (topside or silverside) is a suitable cut.

1500–2000 g (3½–4½ lb) beef
150 g (5 oz) lean smoked bacon
20 g (¾ oz) lard
⅛ l (¼ pt) hot water

Marinade
1 l (2 pt) dry white wine
2 sliced onions
1 bay-leaf
2 sprigs thyme
2 cloves
pinch of nutmeg and cinnamon
1 teaspoon salt
2 teaspoons sugar

Gravy
50 g (2 oz) raisins
grated rind from ¼ lemon
1 teaspoon Black Forest cherry water (or other Schnaps)
50 g (2 oz) chopped roasted almonds
1–2 teaspoons cornflour

Wash and dry the meat. Place in an earthenware or porcelain dish. Add the onions, spices and seasoning. Pour over the wine and leave for 2–4 days. Heat the lard and sliced bacon. Dry the meat and fry until brown on both sides. Add the onions from the marinade. Pour in ⅛ l (¼ pt) hot water. Cover and leave to braise for about 2 hours. During this time gradually add ½ l (1 pt) of the strained marinade. Fifteen minutes before the end of the cooking time add the raisins and almonds.

Take out the meat and keep warm. Boil the gravy to thicken; if necessary, add 1–2 teaspoons of cornflour mixed in a little cold water. Add lemon rind and cherry water. Thickly slice the meat, pour over some of the gravy. Serve with noodles.

Beef Pot-roast *(Schmorbraten)*

750–1000 g (1¾–2¼ lb) beef
2 tablespoons vegetable oil
salt, pepper
1 medium-sized sliced onion
1 sliced leek
1 sliced piece of celery
1 carrot
1 skinned tomato
⅛ l (¼ pt) hot water
1 teaspoon tomato purée
1 tablespoon soured cream
2 tablespoons dry red wine
1–2 teaspoons cornflour

Heat the oil in a meat casserole. Add the meat which has been previously washed, dried and rubbed with salt and pepper. Quickly brown the meat on both sides. Add onion and other vegetables. Cover with a lid, turn down to a low heat and add the hot water. Cover and pot-roast for 2–3 hours. Frequently baste and add more hot water as necessary.

Take out the meat and keep warm. Add tomato purée to gravy. Bring to the boil. Add 1–2 teaspoons cornflour mixed in a little cold water if too thin. Strain, add soured cream and wine. Heat, but do not boil again. Thickly slice meat and serve.

Beef Olives *(Rouladen—North Germany)*

4 thinly cut, even slices of topside
50 g (2 oz) fat
salt, pepper, made mustard
2 medium-sized finely chopped onions
50 g (2 oz) lean, smoked diced bacon
1 tablespoon finely chopped parsley
2–3 diced sweet-sour gherkins (page 270)
$\frac{1}{8}$ l ($\frac{1}{4}$ pt) hot water
1–2 skinned tomatoes
1 onion
pinch of paprika powder
1 dessertspoon flour
1–2 teaspoons cornflour mixed in a little cold water
1 tablespoon soured cream

Sprinkle the slices of meat with salt and pepper and thinly spread with mustard. Divide the onion, bacon, parsley, gherkins between the four slices and spread evenly over each slice. Roll up each slice and secure the ends with one or two cocktail sticks, or tie together with cotton thread. Dust the beef olives with the flour and fry in the hot fat until brown all round. Add the sliced tomatoes and onion. Pour in $\frac{1}{8}$ l ($\frac{1}{4}$ pt) hot water; cover and pot-roast for 1$\frac{1}{2}$–2 hours, adding more water if necessary. Take out the beef olives and keep warm. Bring gravy to the boil. Stir in cornflour mixture. Season to taste with salt, pepper and paprika. Add soured cream (do not boil again). Remove cocktail sticks or thread. Serve decorated with lettuce leaves with boiled potatoes and red cabbage, cauliflower or brussels sprouts.

Beef Steaks in Red Wine *(Rindersteaks in Rotwein)*

4 beef steaks
salt, pepper, sweet paprika
2 tablespoons oil
1 sliced onion
1 sliced leek
1 diced piece of celery
3 sliced carrots
¼ l (½ pt) red wine

Sprinkle the steaks with salt, pepper and paprika. Fry in the oil until brown on both sides. Add the onion and other vegetables. Stir in the wine. Cover and leave over low heat for about 30 minutes. If necessary, add some hot water. Remove the steaks, strain the gravy and serve with dumplings or noodles.

Meat Fondue *(Fleischfondue)*

500 g (1 lb 2 oz) beef fillet
fat or oil for frying

Cut the fillet into 2 cm (¾ in) cubes and place into individual dishes. Heat oil in a fondue pan.

Fondue parties are more of a social event than a feast for hungry people! Calculate 125 g (4½ oz) meat per person and not more than 8–10 people per fondue pan. Each person needs two fondue forks. Pierce one piece of meat with the fork and immerse into the hot fat. Whilst eating the cooked meat, fry another piece on the second fork.

Serve white bread and a selection of mixed pickles, herb butter, chutney, mayonnaise and horse-radish with the fondue. Whilst the first frying takes place, serve a brandy or Schnaps. Then offer a white or red wine.

Westphalian Goulash

(Westfälischer Pfefferpotthast)

1000 g (2¼ lb) braising beef
50 g (2 oz) fat
500 g (1 lb 2 oz) sliced onions
1 leek
1 piece of celery
1 carrot
1 skinned tomato
1 l (2 pt) hot meat broth
1 teaspoon salt
½ teaspoon freshly ground black pepper
1 bay-leaf
½ teaspoon caraway seeds
grated rind of ½ lemon
100 g (4 oz) fine breadcrumbs

Cut the meat into cubes and fry in the hot fat, stirring frequently until brown. Add the onions. Fry for another 5–10 minutes. Add the other vegetables, spices and seasoning. Stir in the broth. Cover and simmer for 1½–2 hours. The meat has to be covered with liquid all the time. If necessary, add some hot water from time to time. When the meat is cooked, add the lemon rind and carefully stir in breadcrumbs. Bring to the boil, remove from heat and serve with boiled potatoes and dressed lettuce, tomato or cucumber salad.

Boiled Beef

(Gekochtes Rindfleisch)

This method is a good way of preparing a tasty meal from the cheaper cuts of beef. It is important that the meat is always placed in boiling water, that it is covered with water and cooked over very low heat.

1000 g (2¼ lb) beef for boiling
1 onion
1 teaspoon salt
1 bay-leaf
5 peppercorns
1 leek
1 piece of celery
2 carrots
parsley

Wash the meat and place it with the vegetables, spices and seasoning into a deep saucepan. Add enough boiling water to cover the meat. Cover with a lid. Bring to the boil and simmer over low heat for 2–3 hours.

Take the meat out of the saucepan, slice and serve with roast or fried potatoes and one of the following:

Mustard Sauce (page 179)
Onion Sauce (page 180)
Hot Horse-radish Sauce (page 180)
Frankfurt Green Sauce (page 181)

Savoy Cabbage with Beef
(Wirsing mit Rindfleisch)

1 medium-sized cabbage
50 g (2 oz) margarine or lard
2 medium-sized sliced onions
600 g (1 lb 6 oz) beef (cheap cut for boiling)
700 g (1 lb 10 oz) potatoes
salt, pepper, pinch of paprika
¼ l (½ pt) broth or water with meat cube

Cut the meat into cubes and fry with the onions in the fat. Add the broth, cover with a lid and simmer for 50–60 minutes. Wash and shred the cabbage. Peel, wash and slice the potatoes. Add the cabbage and potatoes to the meat and simmer for 30–40 minutes. Serve hot.

Beef Stewed in Beer
(Gedämpftes Rindfleisch in Bier)

1000 g (2¼ lb) beef (topside)
salt
60 g (2½ oz) smoked sliced bacon
1 large sliced onion
1 carrot
1 diced piece of celery
5 peppercorns
1 teaspoon sugar
½ l (1 pt) beer
¼ l (½ pt) hot water
2 teaspoons cornflour mixed with a little cold water

Fry the bacon and vegetables. Add the washed meat, spices and seasoning. Pour the hot water over the meat. Add the beer and sugar. Bring to the boil and simmer covered for 2–3 hours.

Take out the meat and keep warm. Thicken the gravy with cornflour mixture. Serve the meat in the hot sauce with boiled or roast potatoes.

Wine Goulash *(Weingulasch)*

750 g (1¾ lb) beef, cut into 3 cm (1¼ in) cubes
50 g (2 oz) fat

Marinade
½ l (1 pt) dry red wine
1 sliced onion
1 teaspoon chopped thyme
1 teaspoon chopped marjoram
1 diced carrot
1 sliced leek
1 diced piece of celery
½ teaspoon freshly ground black pepper
1 bay-leaf
2 skinned tomatoes

Put the meat, vegetables and seasoning into an earthenware or porcelain dish. Pour over the wine and leave for 1–2 days. Dry the meat and fry in the heated fat until brown. Add tomatoes and vegetables from the marinade. Add strained marinade and simmer for 1½ hours.

Cured Meat and Fish Hot-pot *(Labskaus—North Germany)*

Labskaus is a typical seaman's dish which originates from the times of long sea journeys when only cured meat and fish were available and left-overs had to be used. It is popular in North Germany where it is said to improve in taste when prepared the day before serving.

600 g (1 lb 6 oz) cured (salted) beef
½ l (1 pt) water
750 g (1¾ lb) cooked potatoes
4 medium-sized chopped onions
4 salted herring fillets
80 g (3¼ oz) lard or pork dripping
1 bay-leaf
pepper and nutmeg
1 teaspoon sugar
200 g (7 oz) cooked beetroot
1 apple
4 sweet-sour pickled gherkins (page 270)
salt to taste
4 eggs
3–4 sprigs of parsley

Wash the meat. Bring the water with bay-leaf to the boil. Add meat and simmer for 60 minutes. Meanwhile, mash potatoes. Soak herring fillets in cold water for 20 minutes. Chop finely. Put cooked meat through the mincer. Dice beetroot and gherkins. Fry the onion in the lard. Add chopped herring fillets and some meat broth. Mix in mashed potatoes and minced meat. Leave until the next day. Heat Labskaus; add diced beetroot and gherkins, chopped apple, and pepper, sugar and nutmeg. If too dry, stir in more meat broth but avoid the Labskaus becoming a soup. Add salt to taste. Fry the eggs. Serve Labskaus sprinkled with parsley with fried eggs on top.

VEAL *(Kalbfleisch)*

Veal, because of its tenderness and juiciness, is a very popular meat in Germany. As lamb is not so common as in England, veal takes its place where a young tender meat is required. Some veal dishes have achieved international recognition as for example Wiener Schnitzel, which, although bearing an Austrian name, appears with equal prominence on the German menu. There is a variety of Schnitzel dishes; they are tasty and require little time for preparation. The meat for Schnitzel comes from the hindquarter of the calf. Ideally they should be about 1 cm (⅜ in) thick and should be slightly beaten before cooking.

Viennese Cutlet (*Wiener Schnitzel*)

4 veal steaks
salt, pepper
1 beaten egg
25 g (1 oz) plain flour
30 g (1¼ oz) fine breadcrumbs
60 g (2½ oz) butter

Wash the steaks; sprinkle with salt and pepper. Turn them in the flour, dip them into the beaten egg and turn in the breadcrumbs. Immediately fry in the hot butter until golden brown on both sides. It may be necessary to add more butter as the breadcrumbs soak up much of the fat. Serve on a hot meat dish garnished with lemon segments. New boiled potatoes, tossed in butter, and dressed lettuce are often eaten with this dish.

Veal Cutlet à la Holstein (*Kalbschnitzel à la Holstein—Berlin*)

This dish should not be confused with Holstein cutlet which is a form of pork cutlet (page 90). The Veal Cutlet à la Holstein was created in Berlin a hundred years ago in response to a request from a certain Councillor Holstein who asked to be provided with a quick meal which could serve as both first and main course.

4 veal cutlets
salt, pepper
50 g (2 oz) butter
4 slices of buttered toast
4 teaspoons caviare
4 slices smoked salmon
4 anchovy fillets
4 fried eggs (Spiegelei)

Sprinkle the cutlets with salt and pepper and fry on both sides in the butter until golden brown. Meanwhile make the toast. With a pastry-cutter cut 3 toasted discs from each slice. Butter and arrange them on a plate. Put a teaspoon of caviare on one disc, a slice of salmon on the next and an anchovy fillet on the third. Prepare 4 fried eggs (the yolk must still be soft when serving). Take the cutlets out of the pan; arrange between the toast discs; place fried eggs on top of each cutlet and serve with fried potatoes.

Hunter's Cutlet (*Jägerschnitzel*)

4 veal cutlets (1½ cm (⅝ in) thick)
salt, pepper
50 g (2 oz) fat
120 g (4½ oz) sliced mushrooms
1 very finely chopped onion
2 tablespoons plain flour
2 tablespoons very finely chopped herbs (parsley, borage)
20 g (¾ oz) butter
1 teaspoon cornflour

Mix the herbs and onion in the melted butter. Wash and dry the cutlets; sprinkle with salt and pepper. Cut 2 or 3 pockets into each cutlet; fill with the herb and onion mixture and press together. Turn each cutlet in the flour and fry in the fat until golden brown on both sides. Add the mushrooms and 4–6 tablespoons of hot water. Cover the pan with a lid and leave simmering over low heat for 15–20 minutes. If necessary thicken with 1 teaspoon cornflour mixed in a tablespoon of cold water.

Cutlet in Cream Sauce (*Rahmschnitzel*)

4 veal cutlets
salt, pepper
40 g (1¾ oz) butter or margarine
1 finely chopped onion
1 tablespoon mixed chopped fresh herbs (parsley, chives)
⅛ l (¼ pt) water or wine
1 teaspoon cornflour mixed in 1 tablespoon cold water
⅛ l (¼ pt) soured cream
1 teaspoon lemon juice

Sprinkle the cutlets with salt and pepper and brown on both sides in the butter. Add the onion, herbs and the water or wine. Cover with a lid and leave to simmer over low heat for 20 minutes. Remove the cutlets and keep warm. Thicken the gravy with cornflour. Season to taste with lemon juice, salt and pepper. Add the cream. Serve with boiled potatoes or noodles.

Paprika Cutlet (*Paprikaschnitzel*)

4 veal cutlets
salt
1 teaspoon paprika
40 g (1¾ oz) butter
1 green pepper cut into strips
1 sliced onion
¼ l (½ pt) meat broth or water
1 teaspoon cornflour mixed in 1 tablespoon cold water
1 tablespoon soured cream

Season the cutlets with salt and some of the paprika. Brown on both sides in the butter. Add the onion and green pepper. Stir in the broth. Cover with a lid and leave over low heat for 15 minutes. Take out the cutlets and keep warm. Thicken with the cornflour. Season the gravy with salt and the rest of the paprika. Add the soured cream and serve pouring the gravy over the cutlets.

Meat Cushions (*Fleischpolster*)

4 thin veal cutlets
4 thin slices smoked or boiled ham
4 thin slices cheese or 4 teaspoons cream cheese
40 g (1¾ oz) butter
⅛ l (¼ pt) wine
salt, pepper
1 teaspoon cornflour mixed in 1 tablespoon cold water

Cover each cutlet with a slice of ham and cheese. On each cutlet fold the four corners towards the centre and secure with a wooden cocktail stick. Brown the meat cushion in the butter on both sides. Add the wine. Cover and simmer for 5–10 minutes. Remove the meat cushions and keep warm. Thicken the gravy with cornflour. Season to taste and serve with boiled potatoes and dressed lettuce.

Birds' Nests

(Vogelnester—Schleswig-Holstein and Baden Württemberg)

4 thin slices of veal
salt, pepper, sweet-sour mustard
4 slices smoked ham
4 hard-boiled eggs, shelled
50 g (2 oz) fat
¼ l (½ pt) hot water
1 tablespoon soured cream
1 teaspoon cornflour mixed with a little cold water

Season the veal slices with salt, pepper and a little mustard. On each piece place one slice of ham and an egg. Roll up and secure the ends with a wooden cocktail stick. Fry in fat until brown all over. Add the hot water. Cover with a lid and simmer for 40–50 minutes. Add more water if necessary. Remove birds' nests and keep warm. Season the gravy to taste, and thicken with cornflour; add the soured cream and serve with noodles and tomato or cucumber salad. The birds' nests are served cut in half across their diameters.

Veal and Kidney Roast

(Kalbsnierenbraten—Westphalia)

This is a very popular Sunday roast. It is usually bought oven-ready. Since this is not possible in this country, the full recipe is given.

1000 g (2¼ lb) boned loin of veal with some of the kidney and breast
salt, pepper
175 g (6 oz) veal kidney
100 g (4 oz) minced pork and 100 g (4 oz) minced veal, mixed with ½ teaspoon salt added
100 g (4 oz) sliced smoked ham
60 g (2½ oz) fat
2 onions (halved)
1 carrot
1 sliced leek
1 teaspoon parsley
1 sliced piece of celery
1 sprig thyme
¼ l (½ pt) hot water
⅛ l (¼ pt) dry red wine
1–2 teaspoons cornflour mixed with 1 tablespoon cold water

Wash, dry and season the veal. Line with some slices of smoked ham. Fill with the minced veal and pork. Press in the kidney. Cover with the rest of the smoked ham. Roll the veal so that the filling is inside and secure several times with string. Place the meat in the hot fat in a roasting pan and baste. Roast in a pre-heated oven, 190 °C (375 °F, gas mark 5), for 1½–2 hours. After 20–30 minutes add onions, herbs and other vegetables and half the water. Baste frequently and add the rest of the water gradually.

Take the roast out of the pan and keep warm. Pour the red wine into the pan. Stir and boil the gravy to loosen all the brown sediments. Strain through a sieve. Stir in cornflour mixture and bring to the boil. Season to taste. Remove string from the meat and cut the roast into thick slices. Pour over a little gravy.

Serve the rest of the gravy separately with boiled new potatoes and young tender vegetables (peas, brussels sprouts, asparagus, salsify).

Braised Knuckle of Veal *(Kalbshaxe)*

1 knuckle of veal
1 l (2 pt) water
1 teaspoon salt
1½ tablespoons vinegar
1 medium-sized sliced onion
1 clove
1 bay-leaf
1 carrot
1 piece of celery
60 g (2½ oz) butter
salt, pepper
1–2 teaspoons cornflour mixed with 1 tablespoon cold water
2 tablespoons double cream

Bring the water, salt, vinegar, clove, bay-leaf and vegetables to the boil. Add the knuckle of veal and simmer over low heat for 25–30 minutes. Take the meat out of the broth and place in a colander to dry. Brush with butter. Heat the rest of the butter in a roasting pan. Place the knuckle of veal into the hot butter and brown in the oven at 190 °C (375 °F, gas mark 5) for 50–60 minutes. Take out the meat and keep warm. Add enough veal broth to the pan to make up ¼ l (½ pt). Bring to the boil. Add the cornflour mixture. Stir in the cream. Season to taste with salt and pepper. Serve with potato balls, potato salad, tomato or cucumber salad.

Stuffed Breast of Veal
(Gefüllte Kalbsbrust—Württemberg/Bavaria)

It is advisable to prepare a generous quantity as this dish tastes excellent when cold sliced. Do *not* attempt to fill the breast of veal too tightly as this might cause the skin to burst during roasting.

1000–1500 g (2¼–3½ lb) boned breast of veal
40 g (1¾ oz) fat
salt, pepper
1–2 teaspoons lemon juice
1 onion
1 carrot
2–3 bread rolls or white bread (120 g (4½ oz))
2 eggs
¼ l (½ pt) hot milk
1 tablespoon finely chopped onions
½ teaspoon salt
¼ teaspoon freshly ground black pepper
pinch of nutmeg
1 tablespoon finely chopped parsley
1 teaspoon chopped marjoram
100 g (4 oz) butter
¼ l (½ pt) hot water
1 teaspoon cornflour in 1 tablespoon cold water

Wash and dry the breast of veal; sprinkle with salt and pepper and rub with a little lemon juice. Pour the milk over the bread rolls and leave 5–10 minutes to soak. Make the stuffing by melting the butter, adding the tablespoon of chopped onion and cooking them for a few minutes over low heat. (Do not brown!) Mix in the soaked bread rolls, eggs, parsley, salt, pepper, marjoram and nutmeg. If the stuffing feels too moist, add a tablespoon of breadcrumbs. Pack the mixture into the breast of veal, roll and sew together with needle and thread.

Melt the fat in a roasting pan. Place the stuffed breast of veal upside down in the pan with the onion and carrot. Roast for 20 minutes, covering with a lid. Then add the hot water. Roast for another 90 minutes, basting frequently.

Remove the meat and keep warm. Prepare the gravy by thickening with the cornflour mixture. Season to taste. Remove thread and thickly slice the meat. Arrange slices on a hot meat dish, garnished with parsley. Serve with boiled potatoes and any vegetable or salad.

Veal Fricassee (*Kalbsfrikassee*)

500 g (1 lb 2 oz) veal cut into cubes
½ l (1 pt) water
1 bay-leaf
½ teaspoon mixed herbs
1 leek
3 peppercorns
50 g (2 oz) butter
50 g (2 oz) plain flour
4–6 tablespoons dry white wine
salt and pepper
2 egg yolks
2–3 tablespoons single cream
1–2 teaspoons lemon juice

Bring the water, leek, herbs and spices to the boil. Add the meat, cover and simmer for 1 hour. Melt the butter, add the flour; gradually stir in enough of the broth to make a smooth sauce. Boil for 15 minutes stirring all the time. Take off the hot plate. Add the wine. Mix the yolks with the cream and carefully whisk into the sauce. Season to taste with salt, pepper and lemon juice. Add the meat. Re-heat but do not boil.

Cooked, sliced asparagus or mushrooms can be added to the fricassee. Serve with rice, noodles or in puff pastry cases.

LAMB (*Lamm*)

In 1974/75 the average consumption of lamb in West Germany was only 0·5 kg (1 lb) per head—this being less than one per cent of the total meat consumption. The following recipe is popular for the preparation of an Easter meal. (It is also suitable for breast of lamb.)

Marinaded Leg of Lamb *(Gebeizte Lammkeule)*

1500 g (3½ lb) leg or breast of lamb
1 medium-sized chopped onion
50 g (2 oz) sliced smoked bacon
salt and pepper, paprika
1 teaspoon cornflour mixed in 1 tablespoon cold water
2 tablespoons soured cream

Marinade
½ l (1 pt) buttermilk
¼ l (½ pt) dry wine (red or white)
1 tablespoon wine vinegar
6 tablespoons water
1 sliced onion
1 carrot
½ piece celery
1 piece of parsley root
1 clove of garlic
2 peppercorns
2 cloves
1 bay-leaf
3 juniper berries
½ teaspoon chopped thyme

Wash and dry the meat; rub with salt and pepper. Place in an earthenware dish. Prepare the marinade and pour over the meat; leave the meat in the marinade for 2 days (in a cool place). Then take out and dry. Put half of the bacon in a roasting pan; place the lamb on top and cover with the rest of the bacon. Cover roasting pan with a lid and roast at 180 °C (350 °F, gas mark 4) for about 1½ hours. Add onion. Take off the lid during the last 20–30 minutes to brown the meat. Take out of the pan and keep warm.

Prepare the gravy by adding enough of either the marinade or wine to make up ¼ l (½ pt). Season to taste with salt, pepper and paprika. Thicken with the cornflour mixture. Add the cream. Serve with stewed cranberries, potatoes or noodles.

MIXED MEAT DISHES *(Fleischspeisen)*

Apart from Goulash and Pichelstein Hot-pot, this category of dishes uses minced meat as a basis. Most German households have at least one meal a week prepared from minced meat since it is easy to prepare and relatively cheap. Before the introduction of the meat mincer, the meat used to be chopped into small pieces and the German name for the raw meat is chopped meat (Hackfleisch) which originates from this time.

German butchers sell three types: minced pork (Schweinehack); minced beef (Rinderhack) and Tatar. Tatar is a German speciality. It is best beef steak (without fat) finely minced and eaten uncooked (page 173).

Fried Meat Balls *(Frikadellen—Rhineland)*

500 g (1 lb 2 oz) minced meat (half beef, half pork)
1 egg
1 level teaspoon salt
½ level teaspoon freshly ground black pepper
1 finely chopped or grated medium-sized onion
1 tablespoon finely chopped parsley
1–2 tablespoons fine natural breadcrumbs
1 tablespoon oil or 20 g (¾ oz) fat

Mix all the ingredients to a meat dough adding the breadcrumbs last. Form 8–10 meat balls and fry over medium heat until brown on both sides, and cooked inside. The whole cooking time is about 30 minutes.

Frikadellen are served with fried potatoes and any dressed salad or vegetable. They also taste delicious cold in a bread roll. The Rhinelanders like them cold with mustard.

Königsberg Meat Balls *(Königsberger Klopse—East Prussia)*

500 g (1 lb 2 oz) minced meat (pork and/or beef)
100 g (4 oz) butter
2 eggs
200 g (7 oz) fine natural breadcrumbs
1 tablespoon finely chopped onions
1 level teaspoon salt
½ level teaspoon freshly ground black pepper
pinch of nutmeg

grated rind of ½ lemon
50 g (2 oz) chopped anchovies
¾ l (1½ pt) water or meat broth
2 sliced onions
1 clove
1 bay-leaf
1 tablespoon lemon juice
60 g (2½ oz) butter
60 g (2½ oz) plain flour
1 tablespoon capers
2 egg yolks
2 tablespoons double or sour cream
2 tablespoons dry white wine

Cook the chopped onions in the 100 g (4 oz) butter and add with the nutmeg, seasoning, lemon rind, anchovies, eggs and breadcrumbs to the minced meat. Bring the water, clove, bay-leaf, lemon juice and sliced onions to the boil. Form small balls (about 12) and poach (covered with a lid) for 30 minutes. Take out of the broth and keep warm.

Prepare the sauce by melting the 60 g (2½ oz) butter and mixing in the flour. Take off the hot plate and stir in some of the broth. Return to the hot plate, bring to the boil, stirring all the time, gradually making up to ½ l (1 pt) of sauce. Season to taste with salt and pepper. Add capers. Beat yolks gradually adding a few tablespoons of the hot sauce. Return the egg/sauce mixture to the saucepan. Add wine and cream. Place meat balls in the sauce. Reheat, but do not boil. Serve meat balls in the sauce with boiled potatoes and any dressed salad.

Stuffed Green Peppers *(Gefüllte Paprikaschoten)*

4 large green peppers
500 g (1 lb 2 oz) minced beef dough (see recipe for Fried Meat Balls, page 111)
30 g (1¼ oz) butter
⅛ l (¼ pt) meat broth
1 tablespoon tomato purée
1 tablespoon soured cream
salt, pepper
½ teaspoon sugar
1 teaspoon lemon juice
1 teaspoon cornflour

Prepare the meat dough. Cut the stem with the bottom off the peppers; scoop out seeds, wash thoroughly. Fill peppers with the meat dough. Melt butter in a deep saucepan. Place the peppers upright in the saucepan and fry them for 3–5 minutes over low heat. Add the broth; cover with a lid and simmer for 30 minutes. Season to taste with salt, pepper, sugar and lemon juice. Add tomato purée. If necessary, thicken by adding 1 teaspoon cornflour mixed in a little cold water to the boiling sauce. Add the cream and serve with rice or boiled new potatoes.

Cabbage Meat Rolls *(Kohlrouladen)*

1 white cabbage
1 l (2 pt) boiling salt water
250 g (9 oz) minced meat dough (see recipe for Fried Meat Balls, page 111)
50 g (2 oz) butter
2 tablespoons tomato purée
salt, pepper, nutmeg
2–3 teaspoons cornflour in a little cold water
1 tablespoon cream

Clean the cabbage and remove the stalk. Simmer in the salt water for 10 minutes. Remove and dry the large outer leaves. Retain ½ l (1 pt) of cabbage broth. Prepare the meat dough. Place a sausage of meat dough on to each leaf. Fold over two opposite corners of the leaf and roll up the other way.

Secure by winding cotton thread around each cabbage roll. Fry the cabbage rolls in the hot butter, turning frequently. Add ½ l (1 pt) of the cabbage broth; cover with a lid and stew over low heat for about 50 minutes. Take out the cabbage rolls and keep warm. Add the tomato purée to the sauce. Season to taste with salt, pepper and nutmeg. Thicken with the cornflour mixture. Add the cream. Serve the cabbage rolls in the hot sauce with boiled or roast potatoes.

Liver Cheese *(Leberkäse—Bavaria)*

The name of this South German speciality does not provide an accurate description of the dish since it contains no cheese and only a small amount of liver. Its name probably derives from the shape of the finished piece and that it is usually eaten sliced. It is best obtained from a Bavarian butcher or from an inn. It should be served fresh and warm, sliced in a bread roll as an in-between snack, or for lunch or evening meal in a thick slice, browned in butter, topped with a fried egg and accompanied by roast potatoes and dressed lettuce or tomato salad.

500 g (1 lb 2 oz) minced beef
500 g (1 lb 2 oz) minced pork
200 g (7 oz) minced liver
100 g (4 oz) minced smoked bacon
1 l (2 pt) milk
100 g (4 oz) plain flour
2 eggs
1 finely chopped medium-sized onion
1–2 teaspoons salt
1 level teaspoon freshly ground black pepper
1 teaspoon finely chopped or dried marjoram
1 teaspoon finely chopped or dried thyme

The meat, liver and bacon must be minced very finely and if necessary, should be passed through the mincer twice. Mix all the ingredients to a dough. Line a bread tin (loaf-shaped) with buttered greaseproof paper. Fill with the meat dough, brush the top with cold water and bake at 190 °C (375 °F, gas mark 5) for 2 hours.

Mixed Goulash *(Gulasch von dreierlei Fleisch)*

250 g (9 oz) veal
250 g (9 oz) beef
250 g (9 oz) pork
60 g (2½ oz) fat
2–3 sliced onions
1 tablespoon plain flour
200 g (7 oz) skinned tomatoes
1 dessertspoon wine vinegar
½ l (1 pt) hot water
½ teaspoon paprika
½ teaspoon caraway seeds
2 tablespoons dry red wine
4 tablespoons soured cream
salt, pepper

Cut the meat into cubes (about 2 cm (¾ in)). Fry the beef in the hot fat for 5 minutes, then add the pork. After a further 5 minutes add the veal. Brown the meat over medium heat. Dust with the flour;

leave to brown. Add the onions, then the tomatoes, stirring well. Add salt, pepper, spices, hot water and vinegar. Cover with a lid and leave to stew over low to medium heat for 1 hour. Add more hot water if necessary. Stir in the wine and cream. Serve with noodles, rice, potatoes and any kind of vegetable or dressed salad.

Pichelstein Hot-pot *(Pichelsteiner Topf—Bavaria)*

This recipe, which originated in the Bavarian Forest, is just as popular in North Germany as in the South.

250 g (9 oz) cubed beef
250 g (9 oz) cubed pork
80 g (3¼ oz) bone marrow or fat
500 g (1 lb 2 oz) peeled, washed and sliced potatoes
100 g (4 oz) sliced onions
250 g (9 oz) scraped, washed and sliced carrots
1 piece of diced celery
1 sliced leek
500–600 g (1 lb 2 oz–1 lb 6 oz) washed and shredded savoy or white cabbage
salt, pepper
1 teaspoon marjoram
1 teaspoon caraway seeds
1 tablespoon chopped parsley
½ l (1 pt) meat broth or water with a meat cube

Melt the marrow in a deep saucepan. Put layers of meat, onions, vegetables and potatoes into the saucepan. Season each layer with a pinch of salt, pepper, marjoram, caraway seed and parsley. Pour over the meat broth. Cover tightly with a lid; bring to the boil and simmer over very low heat for 2 hours. Do *not* open lid and do *not* stir.

LIVER, KIDNEYS, TONGUE *(Leber, Nieren, Zunge)*

Liver—Berlin Style *(Leber auf Berliner Art)*

For this dish calves' liver is preferred as it is very tender and has a mild taste.

500 g (1 lb 2 oz) liver cut into slices
80 g (3¼ oz) butter or margarine
30 g (1¼ oz) plain flour
2 medium-sized sliced onions
2 medium-sized cored, peeled and sliced apples
salt, pepper

Wash and dry the liver; roll in the flour and place into the very hot butter. Lower to medium heat and finish frying until liver is crisp and brown all over This should not take longer than 4–6 minutes on each side. Take out liver, season with pepper and salt and keep warm. Fry the onions and apple slices in the fat for 5 minutes. Use for garnishing the liver slices. Serve with mashed potatoes and dressed lettuce. It is important that the liver is seasoned after it has been fried. It loses some of its tenderness if salt and pepper are added before frying.

Liver in Wine *(Leber in Wein—Rhineland)*

500 g (1 lb 2 oz) liver cut into slices 1 cm (⅜ in) thick
60 g (2½ oz) butter
40 g (1¾ oz) fine breadcrumbs
2 medium-sized sliced onions
salt, pepper
½ teaspoon finely chopped thyme
½ teaspoon finely chopped marjoram
⅛ l (¼ pt) dry white wine
100 g (4 oz) sliced mushrooms

Wash and dry the liver; turn in the breadcrumbs and place in the very hot butter. Fry 2–3 minutes on each side, lowering the heat to medium. Sprinkle with salt and pepper. Add the onions. Fry for 2 minutes. Pour in the wine; add thyme, marjoram and mushrooms. Cover with a lid and continue cooking for 2 minutes. Serve immediately with mashed potatoes and dressed lettuce.

Liver Dumplings (Leberknödel—South Germany)

375 g (13 oz) liver
1 bread roll or 1 slice of white bread cut into cubes and soaked in 3 tablespoons warm milk
1 egg
1 medium-sized onion
2 tablespoons fine breadcrumbs
100 g (4 oz) diced smoked bacon (Speck)
3 tablespoons plain flour
1 level teaspoon salt
¼ teaspoon freshly ground black pepper
½ teaspoon marjoram
½ teaspoon thyme
1½ l (3 pt) water (add 1 teaspoon salt)
1 medium-sized sliced onion
50 g (2 oz) diced smoked bacon

Pass the raw liver, 100 g (4 oz) bacon, 1 onion and soaked bread roll (squeezed out) through the mincer. Add the egg, breadcrumbs, flour, herbs and seasoning to the mixture and stir well. Bring the water and salt to the boil; turn down the heat and keep the water just below boiling. Hold a tablespoon in the water for a few seconds. With the hot spoon, scoop a dumpling into the water. The dumpling sinks to the bottom of the saucepan and should float to the top after a few minutes. If the test dumpling does not stay in one piece, the dough is too thin and more flour should be added. If the mixture has proved to be of the right consistency, continue scooping dumplings into the hot water. The spoon must be heated as described before each scoop. Poach the dumplings for 20–30 minutes according to size. Cut one dumpling to test if they are cooked. During the whole of the cooking time the water should be kept just below boiling point. Take the dumplings out of the water and keep warm.

Fry the 50 g (2 oz) diced bacon until crisp; fry the other onion in the bacon fat. Pour fried onions and bacon over the liver dumplings and serve with mashed potatoes and sauerkraut. Liver dumplings are also popular as a soup garnish. In this case, teaspoon-sized dumplings are prepared from a quarter of the mixture.

Meat on Skewers (Fleischspiesse)

250 g (9 oz) lambs' liver
250 g (9 oz) lambs' kidneys
2 sliced onions
cucumber slices
125 g (4½ oz) lean smoked bacon
oil
salt, pepper

Marinade
2 tablespoons oil
4 tablespoons lemon juice
½ teaspoon sugar
pinch of salt and pepper

Whisk the ingredients for the marinade and place the sliced liver and kidney (½ × 3 cm (¼ × 1¼ in)) into it. Leave for 1 hour. Successively spike pieces of liver, onion, cucumber, bacon and kidney on to metal or wooden skewers. Brush on the oil; sprinkle with a little pepper and salt. Cook under the grill or in the pre-heated oven, 220 °C (425 °F, gas mark 7), for 20 minutes.

Serve with fresh bread rolls and tomato salad.

Sour Kidneys (Saure Nieren)

500 g (1 lb 2 oz) kidneys (pigs', calves' or ox)
¼ l (½ pt) milk and ¼ l (½ pt) water mixed
50 g (2 oz) fat
2 medium-sized sliced onions
20 g (¾ oz) plain flour
salt, pepper
½ teaspoon sugar
¼ l (½ pt) water
1 tablespoon wine vinegar
2 tablespoons dry wine
½ teaspoon marjoram
2 tablespoons soured cream
1 teaspoon brandy

Skin the kidneys; remove the cores; wash and soak for 30 minutes in the milk and water mixture. Dry, slice and fry with the onions in the hot fat, stirring all the time. Dust with the flour and brown. Add the water, vinegar, wine and marjoram. Cover with a lid and simmer for 15–20 minutes. Season to taste with salt, pepper and sugar. Stir in soured cream and brandy. Do not boil again. Serve with noodles, dumplings or potatoes and young vegetables or dressed salad.

Boiled Tongue (*Gekochte Zunge*)

1 ox tongue
3 peppercorns
1 bay-leaf
1 clove
1 sliced onion

Wash and brush the tongue thoroughly and soak for 1 hour in water. Put the tongue into a saucepan covered with cold water. Add the onion and spices. Bring to the boil, cover and simmer until tender (30 minutes per 500 g (1 lb 2 oz) plus 20 minutes). Lift out and remove skin. Slice, keep warm and serve hot with the following sauce:

60 g (2½ oz) butter
40 g (1¾ oz) plain flour
¼ l (½ pt) broth (from cooking the tongue)
¼ l (½ pt) wine (or beer)
salt, pepper
1 teaspoon finely chopped chives (or parsley with beer sauce)

Melt the butter; mix in the flour. Take off the hot plate. Stir in the broth. Return to hot plate. Bring to the boil, stirring continuously for 5 minutes. Add the wine or beer and herbs. Season to taste.

POULTRY (*Geflügel*)

As in other European countries, the popularity of chicken has increased above all other poultry. Roast chicken, although a very common and widespread recipe, is an inseparable part of Munich and its 'October feast'.

In most families the goose is the festive roast for the Christmas season. The young geese are fattened during the weeks before

Christmas. The traditional day for starting this process is Martin's Day (11 November), which is celebrated in Germany in memory of the benevolent St Martin. Children carrying lanterns follow St Martin, riding a horse, to a bonfire. Very often these processions have at the end an open cart bearing a cage full of geese. In some areas it is customary to have a raffle for the geese on Martin's evening.

Smoked goose drumsticks and breast are a particular feature in parts of Germany.

Bremen Chicken Ragout (*Bremer Kükenragout*)

2 very young chickens (500 g (1 lb 2 oz) each)
salt, pepper
50 g (2 oz) butter
$\frac{1}{8}$ l ($\frac{1}{4}$ pt) hot water
100 g (4 oz) mushrooms (sliced)
120 g ($4\frac{1}{2}$ oz) shrimps or prawns (peeled)
4 tablespoons dry white wine
75 g (3 oz) cooked or frozen peas
75 g (3 oz) cooked or tinned asparagus tips
1–2 teaspoons cornflour mixed in a little cold water
2 tablespoons soured or double cream
1 teaspoon brandy
1 teaspoon lemon juice

Wash and dry the chickens; cut into portions. Sprinkle with salt and pepper and brown in the butter. Add the hot water; cover with a lid and simmer until cooked, for 20–30 minutes. Take out the chicken portions and keep warm. Add the wine, the shrimps, peas and mushrooms to the chicken gravy and bring to the boil. Simmer over low heat for 10 minutes. Then add enough of the cornflour mixture to obtain a smooth consistency. Stir in the cream, brandy and lemon juice. Season to taste with salt and pepper. Lastly add the asparagus tips. Reheat but do not boil. Arrange the chicken portions on a meat dish and coat with the hot sauce. Serve with mashed potatoes and dressed lettuce or vegetables.

Roasted Goose (*Gänsebraten*)

1 goose (about 4000–5000 g (9–11¼ lb))
salt, pepper
2 medium-sized onions
½ teaspoon marjoram
2 cloves
1 l (2 pt) hot water
⅛ l (¼ pt) cold salt water
2–3 teaspoons cornflour mixed in a little cold water

Wash and dry the goose. Season with salt and pepper inside and out. Place the goose, breast down, on the grid of a large roasting pan. Pour over ¼ l (½ pt) boiling water and bake in a pre-heated oven, 210 °C (400 °F, gas mark 6), for 40–50 minutes. Then take out the grid, remove the fat from the pan and return the goose, breast up. Pour over another ¼ l (½ pt) boiling water. Add the onions, marjoram and cloves; cover with a lid and roast the goose for another 2 hours at 190–200 °C (375–400 °F, gas mark 5–6). Baste frequently, adding more boiling water. To allow the fat to run out, prick the skin around the neck and the wings a few times. For the last 15 minutes take off the lid, open oven door slightly and brush the goose frequently with cold salt water. This ensures a crisp skin. Take the goose out of the roasting pan and keep warm. Remove the fat from the pan. Add a little more boiling water to the pan, stirring well to loosen the browning. Strain the gravy through a sieve and pour into a small saucepan. Bring to the boil, thicken with the cornflour mixture and season to taste with salt and pepper. Serve the goose decorated with steamed apples or apple sauce, potato dumplings (page 154) or roast potatoes and hot red cabbage (page 140). The gravy is served separately.

If a stuffing is preferred for the goose, one of the following can be used with the above recipe. Do not fill too tightly.

1.

250 g (9 oz) cooking apples
120 g (4½ oz) minced beef
250 g (9 oz) prunes
60 g (2½ oz) breadcrumbs
1 teaspoon icing sugar
salt, pepper to taste

1 small, finely chopped onion
1 egg yolk
1–2 tablespoons milk

Wash the prunes; soak in boiling water and leave overnight. Stone and dice. Peel, core and slice the apples. Mix all the ingredients. Fill goose with the mixture. Sew up and roast as previously described.

2.
goose liver, heart and skinned stomach
2 small finely chopped onions
120 g (4½ oz) white bread or bread roll (soaked in milk)
1 tablespoon chopped parsley
½ teaspoon marjoram and thyme
salt, pepper

Finely chop or mince the liver, heart and stomach. Squeeze out excess liquid from the bread. Mix all the ingredients. Stuff the goose. Sew up and roast.

3.
500 g (1 lb 2 oz) peeled and skinned sweet chestnuts
1 small chopped onion
4 peeled, cored and sliced apples
50 g (2 oz) butter
4–6 tablespoons hot water
salt, sugar

Heat the onion in the hot butter; add the chestnuts, water, salt and sugar. Cover with a lid and simmer for 10–15 minutes. Add the apple slices. Stuff and sew up the goose and roast as described above.

4. Three or four cored apples can be placed inside the goose. Sew up the goose and roast as above.

Goose dripping is popular as a sandwich spread. Heat in a saucepan with two sliced onions and one large peeled, cored and quartered apple. Leave to cool, pour into an earthenware or glass dish and place in the refrigerator to set.

Neuenahr Goose Breast *(Neuenahrer Gänsebrust)*

This recipe is not very widely known. Neuenahr is a spa in the centre of a red wine area. The use of red wine in this preparation is therefore not surprising.

1 boned goose breast
$\frac{1}{4}$ l ($\frac{1}{2}$ pt) red Ahr wine
1 finely chopped onion
$\frac{1}{2}$ teaspoon finely chopped fresh thyme
1 teaspoon finely chopped fresh marjoram
salt, freshly ground black pepper
puff or short-crust pastry (to cover goose breast)
1 egg

Mix the wine, herbs and onion and pour into an earthenware dish. Leave the goose breast in this marinade for 3 hours, turning once. Take out and dry. Season with pepper and salt. Roll out a rectangle of pastry $\frac{1}{4}$ cm ($\frac{1}{8}$ in) thick. Place the meat in the middle of the pastry; fold over the corners to the middle. Wet edges with water and press together. With a skewer or fork prick a few holes in the top of the pastry. Put the pastry coated meat into a greased roasting pan. Brush the pastry top with the beaten egg and bake at 180 °C (350 °F, gas mark 4) for about 60–90 minutes. Heat the marinade and gradually pour half of it (including onions and herbs) into the pan. Serve with roast potatoes and young tender vegetables.

Roast Duck *(Entenbraten)*

For the preparation of roast duck, use the recipe for goose (page 121).

GAME *(Wild)*

Compared with meat from domestic animals, game is darker, firmer and has less fat. This lack of fatty tissues has to be taken into consideration in the preparation of game. More fat is used and frequently the meat is larded. The taste of game is supposed to be enhanced during the cold winter months.

Roast Pheasant (*Fasanbraten*)

The best time for fresh pheasant is from December to the end of February.

1 pheasant
salt, pepper
¼ teaspoon thyme
2 large slices smoked bacon (50 g (2 oz))
80 g (3 oz) butter
1 teaspoon cornflour mixed in a little cold water
3–4 tablespoons soured cream
1 teaspoon brandy

Rub the pheasant with salt and pepper. Secure the legs and wings with string. Place slices of bacon on top. Put into a roasting pan with the heated butter. Roast in a pre-heated oven, 200 °C (400 °F, gas mark 6), basting frequently. If the fat in the pan becomes too dark add a few tablespoons hot water. After about 1 hour remove the bacon. Pour the cream over the pheasant and roast for another 15 minutes. Take out the pheasant and keep warm. Boil the gravy adding a little more hot water. If necessary, thicken with the cornflour mixture. Season to taste with salt, pepper, thyme and brandy. Serve with sauerkraut or peas and potato dumplings.

Saddle of Venison (*Rehrücken*)

Venison should have been hung for 3 weeks before preparation.

1200 g (2¾ lb) saddle of venison
salt, pepper
175 g (6 oz) smoked bacon
60 g (2½ oz) butter
2–4 teaspoons cornflour mixed in a little cold water
4 tablespoons soured cream
1 tablespoon stewed cranberries

Skin the meat, wash and dry. If the meat is from a young animal, wrap it in a cloth wrung out in wine vinegar. Leave in the cloth for 24 hours. Keep the cloth moist all the time. Treat the meat from older animals in one of the following marinades for 2 days, basting it frequently.

Marinade 1:
1 l (2 pt) buttermilk
5 juniper berries
3 lemon slices
8 peppercorns

Mix and pour cold over meat.

Marinade 2:
⅜ l (¾ pt) water (add 1 level teaspoon salt)
⅛ l (¼ pt) wine vinegar
¼ l (½ pt) dry red wine
2 medium-sized sliced onions
1 sliced carrot
1 parsley root
1 piece of celery
5 juniper berries
6 mustard seeds
1 bay-leaf
1 level teaspoon thyme
8 peppercorns
1 level teaspoon marjoram

Bring the water to the boil. Add vegetables. Cover with a lid and simmer over low heat for 20 minutes. Add juniper berries, peppercorns, mustard seeds, bay-leaf, thyme and marjoram. Simmer for another 10 minutes. Stir in vinegar and wine. Bring to the boil. Take off the hot plate; leave to cool and pour over the venison.

Dry the meat. Rub with salt and pepper. Cover with the sliced smoked bacon. Place in a roasting pan. Pour over the very hot butter. Roast in a pre-heated oven, 220 °C (425 °F, gas mark 7), for about 90 minutes, basting frequently. After 20 minutes cover with a lid, and if marinade 2 has been used, add vegetables. For the last 15 minutes remove the bacon and the lid to brown the meat. Take out of the roasting pan and keep warm. Add a few tablespoons of hot water to the gravy. Bring to the boil. Season with salt and pepper. Thicken with the cornflour mixture. Add the cream and cranberries. Serve with potato dumplings (page 154), red cabbage (page 140) and cranberry or redcurrant jelly.

Game Ragout (Wildragout)

750 g (1¾ lb) game
marinade 2 (see Saddle of Venison, page 125)
60 g (2½ oz) smoked diced bacon
2 medium-sized sliced onions
30 g (1¼ oz) plain flour
3 skinned tomatoes
150 g (5 oz) sliced mushrooms
1 bay-leaf
5 peppercorns
4 juniper berries
¼ l (½ pt) hot water
¼ l (½ pt) red wine
⅛ l (¼ pt) soured cream
⅛ l (¼ pt) single cream
salt, pepper
¼ teaspoon powdered paprika

Wash the meat and leave in the marinade overnight. Dry, cut into cubes and fry in the heated bacon. Add the onions. Fry for another 3–5 minutes. Dust with flour. Add the tomatoes and mushrooms. Cover with a lid and keep over low heat for 10 minutes. Stir in the water and wine. Add spices. Cover and simmer for 50 minutes. Add the cream, season to taste with salt and pepper. Serve with potato dumplings (page 154) or noodles and apple sauce or steamed cranberries.

Roast Wild Boar (Wildschweinbraten—Bavaria)

The wild boar lives in the forest areas of the Rhineland, Bavaria and Prussia. The animals can be hunted throughout the year. Particularly tender and easily digestible is the meat from the young wild boar (up to 15 months). Wild boar from the Spessart in North Bavaria is a traditional delicacy.

1500 g (3½ lb) young wild boar (saddle or leg)
salt, pepper
1 tablespoon gin
80 g (3¼ oz) butter or lard
2 medium-sized sliced onions
1 carrot
5 peppercorns
3 juniper berries
1 bay-leaf
grated crust from one slice of brown bread (preferably rye bread)

¼ l (½ pt) dry red wine or dark beer
2–3 teaspoons cornflour in a little cold water
4 tablespoons soured cream
1 tablespoon redcurrant jelly

Remove the skin and wash the meat under running water. Dry the meat; sprinkle with the gin and rub with salt and pepper. Roast in the heated fat, basting frequently. After 10 minutes add the onions, other vegetables and spices. Add the red wine (or beer) and bread crust; cover with a lid and roast in a hot oven, 210 ° C (400 °F, gas mark 6). Baste frequently and if necessary add some hot water. After 80 minutes take off the lid and brown the meat for 30 minutes. Take out the meat and keep warm. Add a little more hot water to the gravy, bring to the boil to loosen the browning and strain. Thicken with enough cornflour mixture to give a smooth consistency (gradually add to the boiling gravy). Stir in redcurrant jelly and soured cream. Serve the roast garnished with lemon slices accompanied by potato dumplings (page 154) or mashed potatoes and brussels sprouts or noodles and mushrooms.

Roast Hare *(Hasenbraten)*

This recipe is also suitable for the preparation of rabbit.

1 hare
salt, pepper
80 g (3¼ oz) sliced smoked bacon
120 g (4½ oz) butter
2 small onions
1 teaspoon chopped parsley
½ teaspoon chopped thyme
⅛ l (¼ pt) hot water
⅛ l (¼ pt) dry red wine or hot water
2–4 teaspoons cornflour mixed in a little cold water
3 tablespoons soured cream
100 g mushrooms (optional)

Skin, wash and dry the animal. Remove any fat. Rub with salt and pepper. Place in a roasting pan. Cover with slices of bacon. Heat the butter and pour over the meat. Roast in a pre-heated oven, 210 °C (400 °F, gas mark 6), for 15 minutes. Add the onions, herbs and $\frac{1}{8}$ l ($\frac{1}{4}$ pt) water; cover with a lid. Roast for 60–90 minutes, basting frequently. Gradually add more water or the red wine and the mushrooms. Take out the hare and keep warm. Thicken the gravy with cornflour mixture. Season to taste with salt and pepper. Mix in the cream. Serve with potato dumplings (page 154) and stewed apple. Hare or rabbit can also be prepared by marinading it first in one of the preparations described in Saddle of Venison (page 125).

Braised Leg of Moorland Lamb
(Heidschnucken Lammkeule—North Germany)

Schnucken are the wild sheep of the heath around Lüneburg in North Germany. The animals with their typically bent horns provide a meat which is more similar to game than to lamb. Roast Moorland Lamb is the speciality of the Lüneburg Heath. People in Lower Saxony enjoy it with potato dumplings or new potatoes tossed in fried onions and brussels sprouts or cooked red cabbage.

1500 g (3½ lb) boned leg of moorland lamb
Marinade 1 (*see Saddle of Venison, page 125*)
80 g (3¼ oz) fat
salt, pepper
2 medium-sized sliced onions
1 teaspoon finely chopped marjoram
1 teaspoon finely chopped thyme
1 teaspoon finely chopped sage
1 leek
1 piece of celery
1 level tablespoon plain flour
$\frac{1}{8}$ l ($\frac{1}{4}$ pt) hot water
$\frac{1}{8}$ l ($\frac{1}{4}$ pt) red wine
3 tablespoons buttermilk
3 tablespoons soured cream
1 tablespoon cranberry jelly
1 tablespoon tomato purée
2 teaspoons cornflour

Wash and dry the meat and leave in the marinade for 24 hours. Take out and dry. Rub with salt and pepper. Heat the fat in a roasting pan on top of the stove. Brown the meat all over in the fat. Add the herbs and vegetables. Dust with the flour. Stir in the water, wine, buttermilk and tomato purée. Cover the saucepan with a lid and braise in a pre-heated oven, 200 °C (400 °F, gas mark 6), for about 90 minutes. Take out the meat and keep warm. Strain the gravy through a sieve. If the gravy is too thin, thicken with 2 teaspoons cornflour mixed in a little water added to the boiling gravy. Add soured cream and cranberry jelly.

Vegetables and Noodles

(*Gemüse und Nudeln*)

Onions in Wine	Zwiebelgemüse
Leeks	Lauchgemüse
Beetroot	Rote Rüben
Salsify	Schwarzwurzelgemüse
Kohlrabi	Kohlrabi
Asparagus	Spargel
Green Beans	Grüne Bohnen
Broad Beans and Bacon	Dicke Bohnen und Speck
Peas in Sauce	Erbsen in Sosse
Pea Purée	Erbspurée
Lentils	Linsen
Lentil Hot-pot	Linseneintopf
Cucumber	Gurkengemüse
Red Cabbage	Rotkohl
Savoy Cabbage	Wirsing
White Cabbage	Weisskohl
Cooked Sauerkraut	Gekochtes Sauerkraut
Sauerkraut Hot-pot	Sauerkrautauflauf
Borecole	Grünkohl
Spinach	Spinat
Mushrooms	Pilze
Hop Shoots	Hopfensprossengemüse

Leipzig Mixed Vegetables	Leipziger Allerlei
Vegetable Hot-pot	Gemüseeintopf
Potato Dishes, Noodles and Dumplings	**Kartoffelgerichte, Nudeln und Knödel**
Potatoes in Sauce	Lackkartoffeln
Apple Potatoes	Apfelkartoffeln
Pot-roasted Potatoes	Rösttopfkartoffeln
Halved Potatoes	Halbierte Kartoffeln
Potatoes in Wine Sauce	Kartoffeln in Weinsosse
Potato Soufflé	Kartoffelauflauf
'Heaven and Earth'	'Himmel und Erde'
Fried Potatoes	Bratkartoffeln
Potato Dumplings:	Kartoffelklösse:
from raw potatoes	Klösse aus Rohen Kartoffeln
from cooked potatoes	Klösse aus Gekochten Kartoffeln
from raw and cooked potatoes	Thüringer Kartoffelklösse
Warm Potato Salad	Warmer Kartoffelsalat
Noodles	Nudeln
Swabian Noodles with Cheese	'Spätzle' mit Käse
Baked Noodles	Nudelauflauf
Bread-roll Dumplings	Semmelknödel

No meal is complete without vegetables! Sauerkraut is probably the best-known German vegetable, but generally German cooking favours variety in serving vegetables which is mainly achieved by individual preparation methods for different vegetables. Vegetables are not just boiled in salted water but mostly served in or with a sauce or stewed with a number of spices and herbs. Almost all vegetables have their own recipe, passed on from generation to generation and often varying from area to area. This chapter deals with the most common German vegetable preparations, including vegetable hot-pots, only mentioning the ones which differ from the English way of cooking. It contains only recipes for cooked vegetables, lettuce being treated in the chapter on Salads.

Onions in Wine *(Zwiebelgemüse—Hessen)*

Hessians have a love for onions which grow well in the mild climate of this area. They enjoy them as soup, with cheese, on a flan and as a vegetable.

750 g ($1\frac{3}{4}$ lb) fresh small onions
50 g (2 oz) butter
$\frac{1}{8}$ l ($\frac{1}{4}$ pt) meat broth or water
$\frac{1}{8}$ l ($\frac{1}{4}$ pt) dry white wine, cider or apple juice
1 teaspoon salt
$\frac{1}{4}$ teaspoon black pepper
1 teaspoon caraway seeds
2 tablespoons raisins
2 tablespoons fine breadcrumbs

Peel, wash and halve the onions. Cook in the melted butter over low heat for a few minutes covered with a lid. Add the broth, wine, seasoning and caraway seeds. Simmer over low heat, covered with a lid, for 30 minutes. Add the raisins and simmer for another 10 minutes. Mix with the breadcrumbs and serve with fried sausages or Schnitzel and boiled potatoes.

Leeks *(Lauchgemüse)*

1000 g ($2\frac{1}{4}$ lb) leeks
60 g ($\frac{1}{2}$ oz) butter
$\frac{1}{8}$ l ($\frac{1}{4}$ pt) water
salt, pepper, ground nutmeg
1 egg yolk
2 tablespoons double cream
1 dessertspoon lemon juice
1–2 teaspoons cornflour mixed in a little cold water

Cut off roots, outer leaves and dark green tops of the leeks. Wash thoroughly. Cut into 4 cm ($1\frac{1}{2}$ in) long pieces. Heat in the melted butter. Add the water, cover with a lid and simmer for about 15–20 minutes. Add seasoning. Thicken by adding the cornflour mixture to the boiling leeks. Take off the hot plate. Mix the egg yolk and cream and add gradually. Stir in the lemon juice and serve.

Beetroot (*Rote Rüben*)

750 g (1¾ lb) beetroot
50 g (2 oz) butter
1 medium-sized finely chopped onion
⅛ l (¼ pt) water
salt, pepper
1 teaspoon sugar
1 teaspoon lemon juice
1 teaspoon fresh or dried dill herb
1 tablespoon soured cream
1–2 teaspoons cornflour

Wash and peel the beetroot. Cut into thin strips. Heat the onion in the melted fat. Add the beetroot, salt, pepper and sugar. Pour in the water. Cover with a lid and simmer for 20–30 minutes. Add the dill herb, lemon juice and cream. If the sauce is too thin, thicken by adding a little cornflour mixed in some cold water to the boiling vegetable.

Salsify (*Schwarzwurzelgemüse*)

Salsify is a root vegetable with a black-brown skin and a similar taste to asparagus. It is harvested from September to March.

1000 g (2¼ lb) salsify
2 l (3¾ pt) water
4 tablespoons vinegar
2 tablespoons plain flour
½ l (1 pt) water
1 level teaspoon salt
1 teaspoon lemon juice
50 g (2 oz) butter
40 g (1¾ oz) plain flour
4 tablespoons double cream
1 egg yolk
salt, pepper, nutmeg and lemon juice

Scrape or thinly peel the salsify. Leave whole or cut into 5–6 cm (2–2½ in) long pieces. Immediately immerse in the 2 l (3¾ pt) water to which the vinegar and 2 tablespoons flour have been added. This is to keep them white. Bring ½ l (1 pt) water, salt and lemon juice to the boil. Drain the salsify and add to the boiling water. Simmer, covered with a lid, for about 20 minutes until cooked. In another saucepan melt the butter. Stir in the 40 g (1¾ oz) flour. Take off the hot plate and gradually add some of the vegetable broth. Return to heat, stirring all the time. Add more broth if necessary until a sauce of a smooth consistency is obtained. Take off the hot plate. Mix the egg yolk with cream and carefully add to the sauce. Season to taste with salt, pepper, nutmeg and lemon juice. Reheat but do not boil. If the salsify have been left whole, arrange them on a hot vegetable dish and pour the sauce over them. If they have been cut into smaller pieces, add them to the sauce and serve.

Kohlrabi *(Kohlrabi)*

1000 g (2¼ lb) kohlrabi
½ l (1 pt) water
1 level teaspoon salt
50 g (2 oz) butter
40 g (1¾ oz) plain flour
salt, pepper, nutmeg
2 tablespoons soured or double cream

Remove the leaves and peel the kohlrabi. Cut into thick slices and then into strips. Bring the water and salt to the boil. Add the kohlrabi. Cover with a lid and simmer for about 20 minutes or until tender.

In another saucepan melt the butter; stir in the flour. Take off the heat; gradually add ¼ l (½ pt) of the broth. Bring to the boil stirring all the time. Add more broth if necessary to obtain a smooth sauce. Season with salt, pepper and nutmeg. Stir in cream. Add the drained kohlrabi strips. Reheat but do not boil.

Asparagus *(Spargel—Rhineland—Hessen—Lower Saxony)*

Asparagus prefers a mild climate. Green asparagus is of relatively minor importance in Germany. The white, yellow-tipped kind is generally preferred being grown in mounds to avoid exposure to daylight. Official asparagus time is from the middle of April to

24 June when the harvest is brought to an end to give the perennial plant a chance to recover.

Asparagus is traditionally served with ham. First grade asparagus is normally served whole. It is permissible to fold or cut with a knife whilst eating it. The correct way to eat, however, is to hold the stem towards the end between thumb and first finger of the right hand and to lead it to the mouth by supporting the tip with a fork held in the left hand. Bowls with warm water are supplied to wash the fingers. Frequently, asparagus sticks are served with paper frills over the end of each stick to make the handling easier.

Asparagus is best freshly cut. If it cannot be prepared straight away, keep in a cool, dark and damp place.

500 g (1 lb 2 oz) asparagus	*1 teaspoon salt*
½ l (1 pt) water	*½ teaspoon sugar*

Wash the asparagus. Peel each stick from tip to end, starting thinly and becoming thicker. Tie bundles of 5 sticks together and immerse them in the boiling water to which the salt and sugar have been added. Simmer for 20–30 minutes, remove and serve with one of the following:

(*a*) *Browned butter* Brown 50 g (2 oz) unsalted butter and pour over the cooked asparagus.

(*b*) *Egg and parsley* Finely chop 2 hard-boiled eggs, mix with chopped parsley and sprinkle over cooked asparagus.

(*c*) *Butter sauce*

60 g (2½ oz) butter	*1 tablespoon double cream*
2 level tablespoons plain flour	*1 egg yolk*
⅜ l (¾ pt) broth (from boiling the asparagus)	*salt, pepper, nutmeg*

In a saucepan mix the flour with the melted butter. Take off the hot plate. Stir in the broth. Bring to the boil stirring all the time. Season with salt, pepper and nutmeg. Mix the egg yolk and cream.

Take the saucepan off the hot plate and gradually stir the sauce into the egg and cream mixture. Reheat but do not boil.

(*d*) *Wine sauce* Prepare sauce (*c*) above replacing ⅛ l (¼ pt) broth by ⅛ l (¼ pt) dry white wine.

Green Beans *(Grüne Bohnen)*

Runner or french beans can be used for this recipe. They are topped and tailed and cut into 2 cm (¾ in) long pieces.

750 g (1¾ lb) beans
2–3 sprigs bean herb
50 g (2 oz) butter
50 g (2 oz) plain flour
1 small finely chopped onion
½ l (1 pt) broth from boiling the beans
salt, pepper, nutmeg

Simmer the beans with the bean herbs in salted water until nearly tender (do not over cook). In another saucepan heat the onion in the butter. Mix in the flour. Take off the hot plate. Add half the liquid. Return to heat. Bring to the boil, stirring all the time. Gradually add the rest of the liquid. Simmer for 5–10 minutes. Season to taste with salt, pepper and nutmeg. Add the drained beans (leave out bean herb). Heat again and serve.

Broad Beans and Bacon *(Dicke Bohnen und Speck—Westphalia)*

Broad beans and bacon is a traditional German dish. The beans are always cooked with bean herb which is grown in most German kitchen gardens.

750 g (1¾ lb) shelled broad beans
300 g (11 oz) smoked lean bacon or ham
¾ l (1½ pt) water
3 sprigs bean herb
2–3 teaspoons cornflour mixed in a little cold water
1–2 tablespoons chopped parsley
pinch of pepper

Bring the water to the boil. Add the bacon or ham and simmer, covered with a lid, for 40 minutes. Add the beans and bean herb and simmer for another 30–40 minutes. Take out the bean herb. Thicken the sauce by adding the cornflour mixture to the boiling beans. Mix in the parsley and season with pepper. Slice the bacon and serve with the beans and mashed potatoes.

Peas in Sauce *(Erbsen in Sosse)*

750 g (1¾ lb) cooked peas
30 g (1¼ oz) unsalted butter
1 finely chopped onion
40 g (1¾ oz) plain flour
¼ l (½ pt) water
¼ l (½ pt) milk
salt, pepper, nutmeg
1 level teaspoon sugar
1 dessertspoon soured or double cream
1 teaspoon lemon juice

Cook the onion for a few minutes in the butter but do not let it brown. Add the flour. Take the saucepan off the hotplate and mix in the liquid. Bring to the boil, stirring all the time. Season with the rest of the ingredients. Add the drained peas. Heat them again in the sauce and serve.

Peas in sauce is an attractive alternative to serving the cooked peas with a knob of butter.

Pea Purée *(Erbspurée—Berlin)*

350 g (12 oz) dried peas
1 l (2 pt) cold water
1 leek
1 piece of celery
1 level teaspoon salt
80 g (3¼ oz) diced smoked lean bacon
2 medium-sized sliced onions

Soak the peas overnight in the water. Bring to the boil in the water with the leek, celery and salt. Simmer for 1½–2 hours or until soft. Pass through a sieve and whisk to a smooth purée. Heat the bacon in a pan, add onion rings and fry until golden and crisp. Heat the pea purée and serve topped with the fried bacon and onion rings.

In Berlin, pea purée is eaten with sauerkraut and pig's trotters (Eisbein) or Kasseler.

Lentils (Linsen)

375 g (13 oz) lentils (brown type)
¾ l (1½ pt) cold water
½ l (1 pt) water
1 leek
1 piece of celery
40 g (1¾ oz) butter
1 medium-sized chopped onion
30 g (1¼ oz) plain flour
salt, pepper
½ teaspoon sugar
1 tablespoon wine vinegar

Soak the lentils overnight in the ¾ l (1½ pt) water. Bring them to the boil and pour away the water. Add the ½ l (1 pt) water; bring to the boil with the leek and celery. Cover and simmer for about 70–90 minutes until soft. In another saucepan fry the onions in the butter. Add the flour. Stir in enough lentil broth to make a smooth sauce. Add seasoning and vinegar. Heat the lentils in the sauce and serve with fried sausages or pork and mashed potatoes.

Lentil Hot-pot (Linseneintopf—Hessen)

500 g (1 lb 2 oz) lentils (brown type)
2 l (3¾ pt) water
300 g (11 oz) diced smoked bacon
100 g (4 oz) carrots
150 g (5 oz) potatoes
2 leeks
1 piece of celery
3 medium-sized chopped onions
30 g (1¼ oz) flour
2 tablespoons wine vinegar
2 teaspoons sugar
salt, pepper
1 teaspoon sweet-sour mustard
2 tablespoons chopped parsley

Soak the lentils in the water for a few hours. Bring to the boil in the water and simmer for 30 minutes. Wash, peel and slice carrots, potatoes, leeks and celery. Add to the lentils. Simmer for 20 minutes. Fry the bacon and the onions in a frying pan. Mix with the flour. Add bacon, onion, flour mixture to the hot-pot and simmer for 15–20 minutes, stirring occasionally. Season with sugar, salt, pepper, mustard, and vinegar. Sprinkle with parsley and serve.

Cucumber *(Gurkengemüse)*

Young marrows can be prepared in the same way.

2 cucumbers
50 g (2 oz) unsalted butter
1 small chopped onion
4 tablespoons dry white wine
salt, pepper
½ teaspoon sugar
1 teaspoon dried or fresh dill herb
1–2 teaspoons cornflour mixed in a little cold water
2 tablespoons soured or double cream
1 teaspoon lemon juice

Peel the cucumbers; cut into cubes or thick slices. Heat the butter. Add the onion and cucumber and cook in the fat for a few minutes. Pour in the wine. Add salt, pepper, sugar and dill. Cover with a lid and simmer for about 15 minutes until the cucumbers are tender. Thicken by adding the cornflour mixture to the simmering liquid. Stir in the cream and lemon juice and serve hot with boiled potatoes and Liver Cheese (page 113) or any other meat dish.

Red Cabbage *(Rotkohl)*

In some areas the name 'blue cabbage' (Blaukraut) is popular. Depending on the use or avoidance of vinegar in the preparation, the vegetable is either red or blue in colour. Red cabbage tastes best if it is cooked a few hours or even a day before being served.

750–1000 g (1¾–2¼ lb) red cabbage
30 g (1¼ oz) lard
30 g (1¼ oz) margarine
1 medium-sized chopped onion
¼ l (½ pt) water
250 g (9 oz) cooking apples (peeled, cored and quartered)

2 tablespoons wine vinegar (optional)
1 bay-leaf
4 cloves
salt, pepper
1 dessertspoon sugar
2 tablespoons dry red wine
1–2 teaspoons cornflour

Remove outer leaves from the cabbage. Cut the cabbage into quarters; wash and remove the stalk. Shred the cabbage. In a large saucepan cook the onion in the fat until transparent. Add the shredded cabbage. Cover and cook in the fat over low heat for a few minutes, stirring frequently. Add the water, vinegar, a little salt, the bay-leaf and cloves. Place the apples on top of the cabbage, cover with a lid and simmer over low heat for 1–1½ hours. Season to taste with salt, pepper, sugar and wine. If necessary, thicken with 1–2 teaspoons cornflour mixed in a little cold water added to the boiling cabbage. Serve with pork, beef, duck, goose or game.

Savoy Cabbage *(Wirsing)*

750–1000 g (1¾–2¼ lb) savoy cabbage
½ l (1 pt) water with 1 teaspoon salt added
60 g (2½ oz) margarine or butter
1 medium-sized chopped onion
40 g (1¾ oz) plain flour
⅛ l (¼ pt) vegetable broth
salt, pepper, nutmeg

Remove outer leaves and stalk from the cabbage. Loosen leaves and cut off any strong veins. Wash the leaves and simmer in the boiling salted water for 10 minutes. Take out of the water and drain. Pass the leaves through the coarse part of a mincer or finely cut with a sharp knife. In another saucepan fry the onion in the heated butter. Mix in the flour. Stir in the vegetable broth and bring to the boil. Add the minced cabbage, salt, pepper and nutmeg. Cook over low heat, covered with a lid, for about 20 minutes. Serve with boiled beef or fried sausage.

White Cabbage *(Weisskohl—Bavaria)*

750–1000 g ($1\frac{3}{4}$–$2\frac{1}{4}$ lb) white cabbage
60 g ($2\frac{1}{2}$ oz) diced lean smoked bacon
30 g ($1\frac{1}{4}$ oz) butter
1 small chopped onion
150 g (5 oz) peeled, cored and quartered cooking apples
$\frac{1}{8}$ l ($\frac{1}{4}$ pt) meat broth or water
2 teaspoons caraway seeds
salt, pepper
1 dessertspoon sugar
1 dessertspoon wine vinegar
1–2 tablespoons dry white wine
1 dessertspoon flour mixed in a little cold water

Remove outer leaves from the cabbage. Quarter the cabbage; cut out the stalk and finely shred each quarter. Meanwhile fry the bacon and onions in the butter until golden. Add the shredded cabbage and cook in the fat for a few minutes, stirring frequently. Pour in the broth. Add salt, pepper, caraway seeds, sugar, vinegar and apples. Cover with a lid and cook for 30 minutes. Add the wine; thicken by adding the flour and water mixture to the boiling cabbage. Serve with pork, fried sausages, sour roast or any other beef dish.

Cooked Sauerkraut *(Gekochtes Sauerkraut)*

750 g ($1\frac{3}{4}$ lb) sauerkraut
50 g (2 oz) lard or margarine
2 slices lean smoked bacon
2 large peeled and cored grated apples
2 finely chopped medium-sized onions
4 tablespoons dry white wine or champagne
$\frac{1}{8}$ l ($\frac{1}{4}$ pt) water or meat broth
50 g (2 oz) sugar
1 grated raw potato
1 teaspoon caraway seeds

It is important to use the sauerkraut as it is and *not* to wash it. Fry the onions in the lard until golden. Add the sauerkraut, bacon, apples, caraway seeds, wine and broth. Cook covered tightly with a lid for 20 minutes. Add the sugar and grated potato and cook for another 10 minutes. Serve with mashed potatoes and pigs' trotters (Eisbein), Kasseler, smoked belly pork or smoked bacon on the bone. The sauerkraut can also be cooked with the meat which gives the dish a delicious taste. To increase the nutritional value of the meal a small quantity of uncooked sauerkraut should be mixed with the cooked sauerkraut.

Sauerkraut Hot-pot

(Sauerkrautauflauf—Rhineland)

1000 g (2¼ lb) potatoes
20 g (¾ oz) butter
¼ l (½ pt) hot milk
salt, pepper, nutmeg
500 g (1 lb 2 oz) sauerkraut
2 peeled, sliced apples
1 teaspoon sugar
250 g (9 oz) diced lean smoked bacon
30 g (1¼ oz) butter
2 tablespoons grated cheese
2 tablespoons breadcrumbs

Peel, wash and boil the potatoes. Mash and mix with the 20 g (¾ oz) butter, hot milk, salt, pepper and nutmeg. Fry the bacon in a little of the remaining butter. Add the sauerkraut, the apple slices and sugar and cook, stirring frequently, for 10 minutes. Grease a casserole dish. Put in alternate layers of mashed potatoes and sauerkraut. Finish with a layer of potatoes. Cover with grated cheese and breadcrumbs. Dot with butter. Bake in a pre-heated oven, 200 °C (400 °F, gas mark 6), for about 30–40 minutes. Serve hot.

Borecole

(Grünkohl—North Germany)

This is a typical winter vegetable. It has a better taste when picked after the first frost.

1000 g (2¼ lb) borecole
80 g (3¼ oz) diced lean smoked bacon
50 g (2 oz) lard, goose dripping or margarine
2 medium-sized chopped onions

⅛ l (¼ pt) meat broth (or water and meat cube)
salt, pepper
1 dessertspoon oatmeal
4 Mettwürste (smoked beef sausages)
or 500 g (1 lb 2 oz) Pinkel (sausages prepared with oatmeal to a special Bremen recipe)

Strip the green off the stalk, wash and simmer for 5–10 minutes in salted water. Shock the green with cold water, drain. Chop with a sharp knife. Fry the bacon and onions in the lard. Add the chopped borecole, meat broth, salt and pepper and cook, covered, for about 45 minutes. Then add the oatmeal and sausages and cook for another 15 minutes. Serve the borecole with the sausages and boiled potatoes. Grünkohl and Pinkel is a well-known Bremen dish. It is served at the traditional Schaffermahl on the second Friday in February and is exclusively for men. It is a celebration by seamen and the shipping trade to mark the resumption of shipping after the winter months.

Spinach *(Spinat)*

1000 g (2¼ lb) spinach
60 g (2½ oz) butter
40 g (1¾ oz) plain flour
1 small chopped onion
salt, pepper, nutmeg
a few tablespoons spinach broth
2 tablespoons single cream

Remove the thick stalks and veins of the spinach leaves. Wash the leaves and add them to boiling water in a large saucepan. Bring to the boil again. Immediately take spinach out of the water and drain. Pass through a mincer or chop finely. In a saucepan fry the onions in the butter until transparent. Mix in the flour. Add the spinach. Heat, stirring all the time. Add enough spinach broth to prevent burning. Season to taste with salt, pepper and nutmeg. Heat for a few minutes—not longer than 15 minutes as spinach can develop an unpleasant sharp taste. Add the cream and serve with boiled beef or fried eggs.

Mushrooms *(Pilze)*

Chanterelles (Pfifferlinge), yellow boletus (Steinpilze) and mushrooms (Champignons) are the most popular edible fungi found in Germany. The following recipe is equally suitable for any of the three types.

500 g (1 lb 2 oz) mushrooms
125 g (4½ oz) diced lean smoked bacon
30 g (1¼ oz) butter
2 small chopped onions
salt, pepper
2 tablespoons dry white wine
1 teaspoon cornflour mixed in a little cold water
1 tablespoon single or soured cream
1 teaspoon lemon juice
1 tablespoon chopped parsley

Wash the mushrooms. Fry the bacon and onions in the butter. Add the mushrooms. Cook covered for 10–15 minutes. Season with salt, pepper, wine and lemon juice. Thicken by adding the cornflour mixture and bringing to the boil stirring all the time. Take off the hot plate. Stir in the cream and parsley. Serve with fried potatoes and dressed lettuce or tomato salad.

Hop Shoots *(Hopfensprossengemüse—Bavaria and Baden Württemberg)*

Hop shoots taste very similar to asparagus.

500 g (1 lb 2 oz) hop shoots
½ l (1 pt) water with 1 level teaspoon salt added

Wash the hop shoots and add to the boiling water. Simmer over low heat for 10–15 minutes. Remove from boiling water and shock with cold water. Prepare a butter sauce (page 136). Add cooked hops to the butter sauce, reheat and serve with roast meat and potatoes.

Leipzig Mixed Vegetables (*Leipziger Allerlei*)

This is a mixture of young vegetables in a sauce to which shrimps are added.

750 g (1¾ lb) vegetables, made up of equal amounts of carrots, peas, asparagus, beans and cauliflower
50 g (2 oz) butter
40 g (1¾ oz) plain flour
⅜ l (¾ pt) vegetable broth
salt, pepper, nutmeg
2 tablespoons single cream
2 tablespoons shrimps

Cook each vegetable separately in as little water as possible until tender. Drain and keep the broth. In a large saucepan melt the butter; mix in the flour. Take off the hot plate and stir in the vegetable broth. Bring to the boil stirring well. Season to taste with salt, pepper and nutmeg. Add shrimps and vegetables and reheat. Pour the cream over and serve with veal, chicken or beef.

Vegetable Hot-pot (*Gemüseeintopf—Rhineland, Hessen*)

Vegetable Hot-pot used to be prepared during the summer months using all the vegetables in season. With the help of the deep freeze, this very tasty dish can now be prepared at any time of the year.

1½ l (3 pt) broth or water and meat cube
100 g (4 oz) diced smoked bacon
50 g (2 oz) butter
3 medium-sized sliced onions
250 g (9 oz) peeled diced potatoes
½ washed, divided cauliflower
1 leek
1 piece of celery
300 g (11 oz) young green beans
200 g (7 oz) carrots
1 kohlrabi
100 g (4 oz) asparagus
100 g (4 oz) peas
2 or 3 tomatoes
salt, pepper, parsley

Put the vegetables, potatoes, half the smoked bacon and one

onion with the broth into a saucepan. Bring to the boil and simmer, covered with a lid, over a low heat for about 45 minutes. Keep warm. Fry the rest of the bacon and onions in the fat until crisp. Pour over the hot-pot, add seasoning and parsley and serve with fresh bread rolls and hot Frankfurters or Fleischwurst.

POTATO DISHES, NOODLES AND DUMPLINGS
(Kartoffelgerichte, Nudeln und Knödel)

The potato was introduced into Germany from Spain, Italy and the Netherlands during the Thirty Years War (1618–48). It was, however, a hundred years before, through a stratagem of Frederick the Great, the Germans made use of the 'earth-apple' (Erdapfel) or 'ground-pear' (Grundbirne) as the potato is called in some areas. Realizing that nobody took an interest in growing potatoes, Frederick gave orders to plant potatoes in the area around Berlin and to guard the fields. His plan to get his subjects interested in potatoes worked well. People stole the 'valuable' roots and started growing them. Today about a hundred different kinds of potatoes are grown in Germany. Regions known for potato growing are lower Saxony and the Palatinate where potatoes are harvested from June to November. Potatoes sold in Germany have to carry an indication of size (classes 1, 2 and extra), cooking type and company of origin.

Cooking types are important for certain preparations: firm cooking potatoes are recommended for boiling, roasting, frying and for potato salad. The types which tend to crumble when boiled are more suitable for mashing, potato dumplings and cakes. Potatoes should never be stored in polythene bags. They keep best in a cool (4 °C (39 °F)), dark, well-aired cellar, where most German households store them in a potato box.

German cooking employs numerous ways of preparing potatoes. For a foreign visitor it is important to know that during a meal Germans do not cut potatoes with a knife but separate each potato into smaller pieces with the side of the fork. Mashing potatoes and mixing them in gravy on the plate is also discouraged.

In South Germany, noodles, strudel or dumplings are a component of the daily lunch and are preferred to potatoes. Even when potatoes are included, they are usually made into dumplings.

Potatoes in Sauce *(Lackkartoffeln)*

750 g (1¾ lb) potatoes (firm boiling type)
40 g (1¾ oz) butter
50 g (2 oz) diced smoked bacon
40 g (1¾ oz) flour
½ l (1 pt) broth or water
1 level teaspoon salt
1 teaspoon caraway seeds
¼ teaspoon black pepper
½ teaspoon sugar
2 bay-leaves
1 teaspoon marjoram
1 clove
1 tablespoon wine vinegar
2 tablespoons soured cream

Wash the potatoes well and, without peeling, place in a saucepan, covered with cold water. Add 1 teaspoon salt and 1 teaspoon caraway seeds. Bring to the boil and simmer for about 30 minutes until cooked. Prepare a sauce by frying the bacon in the butter, mixing in the flour and gradually stirring in the liquid. Add salt, pepper, sugar, bay-leaves, clove, marjoram and vinegar. Simmer for 5–10 minutes. Add the cream. Peel and slice the boiled potatoes. Add them to the sauce. Reheat and leave over low heat for 10 minutes. Serve with fried sausage (Bratwurst) or meat balls (Frikadellen) and pickled gherkins or beetroot.

Apple Potatoes *(Apfelkartoffeln)*

This potato dish is often served with pork.

750–1000 g (1¾–2¼ lb) potatoes (firm boiling type)
½ l (1 pt) water
1 level teaspoon salt
500 g (1 lb 2 oz) apples
1 medium-sized onion
1 teaspoon sugar
1 dessertspoon wine vinegar

Peel and roughly dice the potatoes. Bring to the boil with the water and salt. After 10 minutes add peeled and diced apples and onion. Simmer for another 10–15 minutes until potatoes and apples are cooked. Season with sugar and vinegar.

Pot-roasted Potatoes *(Rösttopfkartoffeln)*

750 g (1¾ lb) potatoes (firm boiling type)
100 g (4 oz) butter
salt, pepper

For this preparation use an earthenware or other fireproof dish with a lid. Peel, wash and thinly slice the potatoes. Put a layer of potato slices at the bottom of the greased dish. Sprinkle with pepper and salt. Dot with butter. Carry on layer by layer until the potatoes are used. Finish with butter dots on top and use more butter if required. Put on the lid and roast in a hot oven, 210 °C (400 °F, gas mark 6), for about 70 minutes. Serve in the earthenware dish or turned out on to a potato dish with dressed lettuce and any kind of roast meat, sausages or fish.

Halved Potatoes *(Halbierte Kartoffeln)*

New potatoes are particularly suitable for this preparation.

750–1000 g (1¾–2¼ lb) potatoes
50–80 g (2–3¼ oz) unsalted butter
salt, pepper
caraway seeds

Brush the potatoes under running water until clean. Dry and halve them lengthways. Put each potato half on to a greased baking tray with the cut surface upwards. Spread the cut surface with butter. Sprinkle with salt, pepper and a few caraway seeds. Bake in a pre-heated oven, 200 °C (400 °F, gas mark 6), for about 45 minutes.

Potatoes in Wine Sauce (*Kartoffeln in Weinsosse*)

750 g (1¾ lb) peeled and diced potatoes (firm boiling type)
¼ l (½ pt) dry white wine
¼ l (½ pt) water
1 level teaspoon salt
30 g (1¼ oz) butter
60 g (2½ oz) diced smoked lean bacon
25 g (1 oz) plain flour
pepper
1 teaspoon caraway seeds
1 tablespoon soured cream

Bring potatoes, wine, water and salt to the boil. Simmer for 10 minutes. Remove potatoes from the liquid. In another saucepan fry the bacon in the butter; mix in the flour. Stir in enough of the liquid in which the potatoes were boiled, to obtain a smooth sauce. Season with pepper and caraway seeds. Stir in cream. Add potatoes; reheat and leave over low heat for 5–10 minutes. Serve hot with cold poultry, game or pork.

Potato Soufflé (*Kartoffelauflauf*)

750 g (1¾ lb) cooked potatoes (crumbly kind)
50 g (2 oz) butter
⅛ l (¼ pt) milk
1 level teaspoon salt
pinch of nutmeg
3 tablespoons double cream
3 egg yolks
3 beaten egg whites
1 chopped medium-sized onion
120 g (4½ oz) diced lean smoked ham
30 g (1¼ oz) butter
100 g (4 oz) grated cheese
2 tablespoons breadcrumbs
20 g (¾ oz) butter

Mash the cooked potatoes and mix while still hot with the 50 g (2 oz) butter, milk, salt, nutmeg and cream. Beat to a very smooth consistency. Fry the ham and onion in the 30 g (1¼ oz) butter until golden and crisp. Mix with the creamed potatoes. Add the yolks and beaten egg whites. Fill a large greased soufflé dish with the mixture. Top with the grated cheese, breadcrumbs and the 20 g (¾ oz) butter and bake in a pre-heated oven at 210 °C (400 °F, gas mark 6) for about 45 minutes. Serve with tomato salad, cucumber salad or dressed lettuce and fried sausage.

'Heaven and Earth'

('Himmel und Erde'—Rhineland)

The name of this dish derives from the main ingredients, with potatoes representing Earth and apples Heaven.

750 g (1¾ lb) potatoes (crumbly kind)
750 g (1¾ lb) cooking apples
½ l (1 pt) water
40 g (1¾ oz) sugar
1 level teaspoon salt
1 dessertspoon wine vinegar
pepper
50 g (2 oz) butter
30 g (1¼ oz) butter
100 g (4 oz) diced smoked bacon
2 small chopped onions

Peel the potatoes and cut into small pieces. Peel, core and quarter the apples. Put potatoes and apples into a saucepan with the water, salt, sugar and vinegar. Bring to the boil and simmer, covered with a lid, until cooked (15–20 minutes). Mash potatoes and apples, add the 50 g (2 oz) butter and the pepper and mix well. Fry the bacon and onions in the 30 g (1¼ oz) butter and pour over the top of the potato/apple mixture. Serve with fried smoked black pudding (Blutwurst), fried liver, kidneys or sausages.

Fried Potatoes

(Bratkartoffeln)

Fried potatoes are a popular addition to the usual cold evening meal. They can be complemented by the use of eggs, ham or cheese and can be prepared from raw or cooked potatoes. Usually fried potatoes are served with dressed lettuce or tomato and cucumber salad.

1. Fried cooked potatoes Boil the potatoes (firm boiling type) in their skins, peel and leave to cool. Melt butter in a frying pan, add some diced smoked bacon and the sliced potatoes. Fry without a lid, turning the potatoes frequently until crisp and golden. During the last 5 minutes add a small finely chopped onion.

Variations: (a) Very small potatoes can be fried whole.

(b) Whisk 2–4 eggs (according to quantity of potatoes). Pour over the ready fried potatoes and leave to set over low heat.

(c) Sprinkle 2–4 tablespoons grated cheese (according to quantity of potatoes) over the ready fried potatoes. Stir until cheese is melted and serve immediately.

2. *Fried raw potatoes* Peel, wash and dry the potatoes. Cut into thin slices and fry in butter with 1–3 tablespoons diced smoked bacon. Cover the frying pan with a lid for the first 10 minutes. Then take off the lid, turn potatoes with a spatula and carry on frying until golden and crisp. Onions, cheese and eggs can be added towards the end of the frying time as with variations (b) and (c) above.

Potato Dumplings *(Kartoffelklösse)*

Dumplings can be prepared from raw potatoes, cooked potatoes or a mixture of raw and cooked potatoes. In South Germany dumplings are called Knödel.

Dumplings are cooked in an open saucepan in water over very low heat. Always add 2 level teaspoons cornflour mixed in a little cold water to the simmering water before inserting the first dumplings. The dough for the dumplings must be neither too wet nor too dry. To cook good potato dumplings is an art in itself and a question of experience. So one should not despair if the dumplings do not turn out well at the first attempt. Dumplings made from raw potatoes seem to be the most difficult. It is advisable to cook a sample dumpling first and then alter or use the mixture according to the result.

Potato dumplings are served with pork, sour roast, game, goose and duck. In the Rhineland and North Germany dumplings are prepared by pouring a mixture of fried onion rings and fried smoked bacon dice over the dumplings. They are served with stewed dried fruit. Any left-overs from dumplings can be sliced and prepared like fried potatoes (page 151).

Potato Dumplings from Raw Potatoes
(Klösse aus Rohen Kartoffeln)

1000 g (2¼ lb) potatoes
2–3 tablespoons potato flour
1–2 tablespoons plain flour
1 egg
1 teaspoon salt
¼ teaspoon pepper
¼ teaspoon nutmeg
2 l (3¾ pt) water for boiling
2 teaspoons cornflour mixed in a little cold water

Peel, wash and grate the potatoes. Place in a cloth and press out excess water. Add flour, egg and seasoning to the potato mixture. Meanwhile, bring the water with 1 teaspoon salt to the boil; add cornflour mixture. Turn heat down just below simmering point. Form dumplings with flour-dusted hands and place in the water. Leave them in the water for 20–30 minutes. Serve with either a meat dish or smoked diced bacon and onion rings fried in butter.

Potato Dumplings from Cooked Potatoes
(Klösse aus Gekochten Kartoffeln)

750 g (1¾ lb) boiled grated potatoes
80 g (3¼ oz) plain flour
60 g (2½ oz) potato flour
1 egg
2 tablespoons milk
1 level teaspoon salt
¼ teaspoon ground black pepper
¼ teaspoon ground nutmeg
½ teaspoon marjoram
3–4 tablespoons fried bread cubes

2 l (3¾ pt) water for boiling
1 teaspoon salt

Mix the ingredients to a dough. Bring the water with the salt to the boil. Reduce heat to just below simmering point. Form round dumplings of about 5 cm (2 in) diameter. Press 1 or 2 fried bread cubes inside each dumpling and poach in the water for about 15–20 minutes.

Variation: Mix 150 g (5 oz) diced fried smoked bacon with the dumpling dough.

Potato Dumplings from Raw and Cooked Potatoes
(Thüringer Kartoffelklösse—East Germany)

750 g (1¾ lb) boiled potatoes
750 g (1¾ lb) raw potatoes
1 egg
3–4 tablespoons plain flour
1 teaspoon salt
¼ teaspoon ground black pepper
¼ teaspoon ground nutmeg
2 l (3¾ pt) water with 1 teaspoon salt added

Peel, wash and grate raw potatoes. Press out excess water. Mix with grated boiled potatoes. Add egg, flour and seasoning. Bring water and salt to the boil. Reduce heat to just below simmering point. Form dumplings and place them in the water. When they have floated to the surface, leave for another 20 minutes. Serve with goulash or other meat dishes.

Warm Potato Salad *(Warmer Kartoffelsalat)*

Warm potato salad is served at lunch-time with liver cheese (page 113), fried sausage, Frankfurters or hot Fleischwurst. For cold potato salad see page 166.

750 g (1¾ lb) potatoes (firm cooking type) boiled in the skin
⅛ l (¼ pt) hot meat broth
3 tablespoons wine vinegar
2 medium-sized chopped onions
30 g (1¼ oz) butter
50 g (2 oz) diced lean smoked bacon
2 tablespoons plain flour
¼ l (½ pt) water
1 teaspoon salt
¼ teaspoon ground black pepper
1 teaspoon sugar
2–3 tablespoons soured cream
2 tablespoons finely chopped parsley and chives

Peel the hot potatoes and slice them. Pour over the hot meat broth. Keep potatoes warm. Mix vinegar and onions. Fry the bacon in the butter. Add flour. Gradually stir in water. Bring to the boil, stirring well. Add salt, pepper, sugar, onion and vinegar, cream and herbs. Pour sauce over warm potatoes; mix well and serve.

Noodles *(Nudeln)*

Noodles are usually bought ready made. Here is a recipe to make them at home.

300 g (11 oz) plain flour
2 eggs
¼ teaspoon salt
2 tablespoons water (more if necessary)

Mix the ingredients and knead until a stiff pliable dough is obtained. Roll out into even, 2-mm ($\frac{1}{10}$-in) thick pieces. Leave for 20 minutes. Roll up each piece and cut each roll into 7-mm (¼-in) strips. Separate the noodles, dry and store them in a glass jar until needed.

To serve, add noodles to boiling salted water and simmer for about 15 minutes. A dessertspoon of oil in the water keeps the noodles from sticking to each other. Quickly rinse with cold water to prevent them from sticking together. Fry some breadcrumbs in plenty of butter and pour over the noodles.

Swabian Noodles with Cheese *('Spätzle' mit Käse—Württemberg and Bavaria)*

250 g (9 oz) plain flour
1 level teaspoon salt
2 eggs
2 tablespoons cold water
2 l (3¾ pt) salted water for boiling
60 g (2½ oz) grated cheese
40 g (1¾ oz) melted butter
30 g (1¼ oz) butter
1 medium-sized sliced onion

Mix the flour, salt, eggs and water and beat well until a firm dough is obtained. Bring the water to the boil. Divide dough into 2 parts. Roll each piece out on a wooden board and with a sharp wet knife, cut small noodle-like strips and place them in the boiling water. When the Spätzle float to the surface (after 3–5 minutes), take out and plunge into cold water. In a hot dish put layers of Spätzle topped with melted butter and grated cheese. Top with onion rings fried in butter. Serve with roast meat and dressed lettuce.

Baked Noodles *(Nudelauflauf)*

250 g (9 oz) cooked noodles
1 level teaspoon salt
1 medium-sized sliced onion fried in 20 g (¾ oz) butter
150 g (5 oz) grated cheese
3 large sliced tomatoes
⅛ l (¼ pt) milk
1 tablespoon soured cream
2 eggs
salt, pepper, nutmeg
2 tablespoons breadcrumbs
20 g (¾ oz) butter

Butter a soufflé dish. Mix the noodles with the salt. Put successive layers of noodles, cheese, onion rings and tomatoes into the dish. Repeat until the noodles are used up. Mix milk, cream, eggs, salt, pepper and nutmeg and pour over the noodle layers. Top with breadcrumbs and dot with butter. Bake in a pre-heated oven, 200 °C (400 °F, gas mark 6), for about 30 minutes. Serve with tomato salad or dressed lettuce.

Variation: Add 50 g (2 oz) diced boiled ham to the noodle mixture.

Bread-roll Dumplings *(Semmelknödel—Bavaria)*

8 stale bread rolls
⅜ l (¾ pt) hot milk
40 g (1¾ oz) butter
1 small chopped onion
1 tablespoon chopped parsley
2–3 eggs
salt, nutmeg
100 g (4 oz) plain flour
2 l (3¾ pt) water, with 1 teaspoon salt added

Finely slice the bread rolls and soak in the hot milk. Fry the onion and parsley in the butter and add to the soaked bread rolls. Mix in eggs, flour, salt and nutmeg. Bring the water and salt to the boil. Form a test dumpling and cook in the slowly simmering water for 10–15 minutes. If dumpling drops apart, add breadcrumbs to the mixture to make it drier. If dumplings turn out to be too firm, add a little more milk to the mixture. Serve with goulash or roast meat.

Salads, Sausages and Open Sandwiches

(*Salate, Wurst und Belegte Brote*)

Salads	**Salate**
Dressed Lettuce	Grüner Salat
Cucumber Salad	Gurkensalat
Tomato Salad	Tomatensalat
White Cabbage Salad	Weisskrautsalat
Celeriac Salad	Selleriesalat
Bean Salad	Bohnensalat
Asparagus Salad	Spargelsalat
Hop Shoot Salad	Hopfensalat
Sauerkraut Salad	Sauerkrautsalat
Beetroot Salad	Rote Rüben Salat
Cauliflower Salad	Blumenkohlsalat
Carrot Salad	Möhrensalat
Cheese Salad	Käsesalat
Meat Salad	Fleischsalat
Fish Salad	Fischsalat
Noodle Salad	Nudelsalat
Potato Salad	Kartoffelsalat

Sausages and Smoked Meat	**Wurst und Aufschnitt**
Sausage Salad	Wurstsalat

Platters and Open Sandwiches	**Kalte Platten und Belegte Brote**
Salmon Sandwiches	Lachsschnitten
'Vicar and Nun'	'Pfäffchen und Nönnchen'
Open Ham Rolls	Schinkenbrötchen
Tatar Sandwich	Tatarbrot
Bremen Sandwich	Bremer Brot
Hamburger	Hamburger Rundstück
Black Pudding Bread Roll	Flönz mit Öllig
Pumpernickel with Cheese	Pumpernickel mit Käse

In the evening, most German families eat open sandwiches with different kinds of sausages, cold meats and cheese, sometimes accompanied by a salad. In Germany the expression 'salad' stands for cold vegetable, meat, fish or cheese served in a dressing whilst a 'cold platter' means a selection of different kinds of meat, sausage or cheese with bread, butter and a dressed vegetable or pickles. Bread is served sliced and unbuttered. It is left to each individual person to butter a slice of bread and top it with a slice of cold meat, sausage or cheese from a selection on the table. This open sandwich is then eaten with knife and fork. To hold a buttered sandwich in one's hand is only permissible when not sitting at a table. This makes side plates rather superfluous for an uncooked meal, although separate salad dishes are used for dressed lettuce, tomato, cucumber and any other dressed vegetable. They are always placed on the left of the main plate.

SALADS *(Salate)*

Dressed Lettuce *(Grüner Salat)*

1 lettuce *salad dressing (page 181)*

Wash and drain the lettuce leaves. Cut out the strong veins and tear the leaves into small pieces. About 5–10 minutes before serving, toss the lettuce in the dressing.

Variation: Decorate with sliced hard-boiled eggs.

Cucumber Salad *(Gurkensalat)*

1 cucumber

Wash, dry and slice the cucumber. Follow recipe and method for dressed lettuce above, adding one teaspoon of fresh or dried dill leaves. Pour the dressing over the sliced cucumber; mix well. Leave for 15 minutes and serve.

Tomato Salad *(Tomatensalat)*

500 g (1 lb 2 oz) firm tomatoes
1 medium-sized finely chopped onion
1 level teaspoon salt
1 teaspoon sugar
pinch of pepper
½ dessertspoon wine vinegar
1–2 tablespoons freshly chopped herbs (parsley, chives, marjoram, thyme, dill leaves)
1 tablespoon vegetable oil
1 tablespoon single or double cream

Wash and dry tomatoes. Cut them into thin slices and place them into a salad bowl. Add the other ingredients; mix well and serve.

White Cabbage Salad *(Weisskrautsalat)*

500 g (1 lb 2 oz) white cabbage
2 coarsely grated medium-sized apples
70 g (3 oz) diced smoked bacon
1 finely chopped or grated onion
1 teaspoon salt
pinch of pepper
1 teaspoon caraway seeds
½ teaspoon icing or castor sugar
2 tablespoons wine vinegar
2 tablespoons vegetable oil
1 tablespoon soured cream
1–2 tablespoons chopped walnuts

Halve the cabbage and remove the stalk. Shred finely; wash and drain well. Put the cabbage into a bowl. Mix with the salt and pepper and beat or stamp with a wooden spoon for 10 minutes. Fry the bacon until crisp; add the onion and vinegar and pour over the cabbage. Mix with the rest of the ingredients. Leave covered for at least 1 hour and serve.

Celeriac Salad *(Selleriesalat)*

Small portions of this salad go well with poultry, game and cold meat.

1 celeriac root
1 tablespoon wine vinegar

1 tablespoon vegetable oil
1 tablespoon wine vinegar
2 peeled, cored and diced apples
¼ teaspoon sugar
½ teaspoon salt
pinch of pepper
1 tablespoon chopped walnuts
1 small grated onion
1 tablespoon whipped cream

Brush the celeriac under running water until clean, then immerse in boiling water and simmer until soft. Remove from water; pour over 1 tablespoon vinegar and leave to cool a little. Then peel and dice. Mix with the rest of the ingredients and leave for 4–5 hours before serving.

Bean Salad *(Bohnensalat)*

500 g (1 lb 2 oz) cooked young, tender, french beans (preferably yellow kind)
1 small finely chopped onion
1½ tablespoons wine vinegar
1 tablespoon vegetable oil
pinch of pepper
¼ teaspoon sugar
½ teaspoon salt

Cut the cooked beans into 3–4-cm (1¼–1½-in) pieces and place into a salad bowl. Mix with the rest of the ingredients. Leave to stand for 30 minutes and serve.

Asparagus Salad *(Spargelsalat)*

500 g (1 lb 2 oz) cooked asparagus
4–6 tablespoons mayonnaise (page 180)
¼ teaspoon sugar
½ teaspoon salt
pinch of pepper
1 dessertspoon chopped parsley
3 teaspoons lemon juice
2 teaspoons orange juice
1 tablespoon whipped cream
1 finely chopped onion
a little grated lemon rind
1 sliced hard-boiled egg

Cut the cooked asparagus into 4–5-cm (1½–2-in) pieces. Mix with the rest of the ingredients. Arrange in a dish; decorate with slices of hard-boiled egg and serve.

Hop Shoot Salad *(Hopfensalat—South Germany)*

Follow recipe for Asparagus Salad.

Sauerkraut Salad *(Sauerkrautsalat)*

500 g (1 lb 2 oz) sauerkraut (uncooked) (page 271)
125 g (4½ oz) pineapple cubes
2 medium-sized coarsely grated apples
1 small finely chopped or grated onion
1 teaspoon parsley
1 teaspoon chopped dill leaves
½ teaspoon salt
pinch of pepper
1 tablespoon sugar
2 teaspoons lemon juice
2–3 tablespoons vegetable oil
2 tablespoons pineapple juice
2 tablespoons dry white wine
1 diced sweet-sour gherkin

With a sharp knife cut the sauerkraut into 4–5-cm (1½–2-in) lengths. Place in a large bowl adding all other ingredients except for the oil. Mix well. Heat the oil; pour over and mix with the sauerkraut salad. The salad is ready to serve after 1 hour.

Beetroot Salad (Rote Rüben Salat)

500 g (1 lb 2 oz) cooked beetroot
3–4 tablespoons wine vinegar
2 tablespoons hot water
1 level teaspoon salt
pinch of pepper
1 teaspoon caraway seeds
½ teaspoon horse-radish
1 teaspoon sugar
2 tablespoons vegetable oil
1 bay-leaf

Peel and slice the beetroot while still hot and pour over the vinegar and water. Mix in the other ingredients. Leave covered for at least 3–4 hours before serving. It is advisable to prepare beetroot salad 1–2 days before serving. This salad is popular with open sandwiches, boiled beef or fried sausages.

Cauliflower Salad (Blumenkohlsalat)

1 medium-sized cooked cauliflower
1 finely chopped small onion
2 teaspoons lemon juice
1 dessertspoon wine vinegar
1 tablespoon vegetable oil
1 tablespoon single cream
1 tablespoon mayonnaise (page 180)
½ teaspoon salt
pinch of pepper
1 teaspoon chopped parsley

Break the cooked cauliflower into small pieces and place in a bowl. Mix with the rest of the ingredients. Leave for 20 minutes and serve.

Carrot Salad (Möhrensalat)

300 g (11 oz) peeled carrots
200 g (7 oz) peeled and cored apples
juice of 1 orange
1–2 tablespoons chopped walnuts

Grate the carrots and apples. Mix with the walnuts; add orange juice and serve immediately.

This salad is refreshing, tasty and healthy as a first course.

Cheese Salad *(Käsesalat)*

300 g (11 oz) Allgäuer Emmentaler cheese
3 medium-sized peeled and cored apples
2 hard-boiled eggs
1 tablespoon chopped nuts
50 g (2 oz) sliced button mushrooms
5 sliced olives
1 tablespoon chopped parsley and chives

salad dressing (page 181) or mayonnaise (page 180)

Cut cheese, apples and eggs into small cubes. Add the mushrooms, nuts, olives and herbs and the dressing. Mix well and leave for 2–3 hours.

Meat Salad *(Fleischsalat)*

300 g (11 oz) cooked, diced meat (pork, beef, poultry; left-overs from a roast)
3 diced hard-boiled eggs
2 diced sweet-sour pickled gherkins
1 tablespoon freshly chopped herbs (chives, parsley, dill leaves)
2 tablespoons diced cooked mushrooms
1 finely chopped medium-sized onion
2 tablespoons cooked peas
2 teaspoons lemon juice
1 teaspoon sweet-sour mustard
1 teaspoon salt
1 teaspoon sugar
pinch of pepper, curry and paprika
$\frac{1}{8}$ l ($\frac{1}{4}$ pt) mayonnaise
2 tablespoons soured cream

Place the meat, eggs and mushrooms into a salad bowl and add the rest of the ingredients. Mix well and leave covered in the refrigerator for 2–3 hours. Serve on a bed of lettuce leaves.

Fish Salad *(Fischsalat)*

300–400 g (11–14 oz) cooked or smoked fish fillet
2 peeled, cored and diced apples
1–2 tablespoons chopped walnuts
4–6 tablespoons mayonnaise (page 180)
1 dessertspoon wine vinegar
1 diced sweet-sour gherkin
1 small chopped onion
1 teaspoon chopped parsley
1 teaspoon sweet-sour mustard

With two forks tear the fish into small pieces. Mix the rest of the ingredients together and then with the fish. Keep covered in the refrigerator for 1 hour. Serve with roast or fried potatoes or rye bread.

Noodle Salad *(Nudelsalat—South Germany)*

300 g (11 oz) cooked noodles or macaroni
50 g (2 oz) hard diced cheese
200 g (7 oz) diced Fleischwurst Lyoner or Mortadella sausage or cooked chicken
2 peeled, cored and diced apples
1–2 sweet-sour diced gherkins
1 tablespoon cooked peas
¼ l (½ pt) mayonnaise (page 180)
½ teaspoon made mustard
salt and pepper to taste
1 dessertspoon chopped parsley

Place the noodles, cheese, sausage and apples in a bowl. Add the rest of the ingredients and mix well. Leave covered 2–3 hours. If the salad appears to be too dry, add a little single cream. Serve with fresh crisp rolls or rye bread and fresh unsalted butter and a plate of cold meat, smoked sausages and cheese.

Potato Salad *(Kartoffelsalat)*

1000 g (2¼ lb) potatoes (firm boiling type)
⅛ l (¼ pt) hot meat broth to which 1 tablespoon vinegar has been added

1 small to medium-sized finely chopped or grated onion
1–2 sweet-sour pickled diced gherkins
1 teaspoon salt
pinch of pepper
$\frac{1}{8}$ l ($\frac{1}{4}$ pt) mayonnaise (page 180)
1 teaspoon sugar
1 teaspoon sweet mustard
2 tablespoons soured cream
1 tablespoon single cream

Garnish
3 hard-boiled eggs
1 teaspoon chopped parsley or chives
1 sliced tomato

Boil the potatoes in their skins; peel and leave to cool a little. Finely slice the potatoes; place in a bowl and pour over the hot meat broth. Leave to cool completely. In another dish mix the rest of the ingredients and add to the sliced potatoes. Mix well and leave covered in a cool place for at least 3 hours. The salad should be moist. If it is too dry, add more mayonnaise and single cream. Arrange in a salad bowl decorated with the halved hard-boiled eggs, tomato slices and herbs. Serve with hot Frankfurter sausages and crisp bread rolls and beer.

SAUSAGES AND SMOKED MEAT
(Wurst und Aufschnitt)

German butchers offer their customers a wide choice of sausages, and smoked and cooked meats. Each district has its own regional variety of specialities in sausages, smoked ham and bacon, roast beef and pork. Altogether in Germany 1500 kinds of sausages are available. They consist mainly of lean meat and according to the German food law additives such as flour, colouring and preservatives are not allowed. In broad terms there are three groups of sausages:

RAW SAUSAGES (*Rohwurst*)

These consist of salted raw meat and bacon and are smoked and dried to preserve them. The following sausages belong to this group:

Salami: A coarse hard sausage which is consumed in slices. It is produced from beef and pork and spiced with garlic and pepper.

Cervelatwurst: A hard sausage, consumed in slices; produced from beef and pork. It is not as coarse as Salami.

Teewurst: A soft, spreadable sausage in which paprika, juniper and rum are used.

BOILED SAUSAGES (*Kochwurst*)

These are made from pre-cooked meat, offal, spices and herbs. The sausage meat is then filled into the skins, boiled again and slightly smoked. They do not keep as long and as well as raw sausages. The most popular sausages of this group are liver sausage (Leberwurst), tongue sausage (Zungenwurst) and black pudding (Blutwurst).

PARBOILED SAUSAGES (*Brühwurst*)

Together with the boiled sausages, these are fresh and consequently do not keep as well as the raw sausages which are smoked and dried for a lengthy period. In their preparation, the sausage meat is filled into the skins, then the sausages are slightly smoked and finally scalded at a temperature of about 70 °C (158 °F).

Meat Sausage (Fleischwurst) The firm, finely textured sausage of 4–5 cm (1½–2 in) diameter is one of the most popular in Germany. Beef and pork are used for its preparation and garlic is often added. Fleischwurst is served sliced on open sandwiches or warmed with potato salad or in pea, lentil, bean or potato soup.

Lyoner or Mortadella A very fine textured sausage made from beef and pork of about 9–10 cm (3½–4 in) diameter. It is bought and served in thin slices.

Beer Sausage (Bierwurst) This is a spherical-shaped sausage mainly produced from pork and ham and contains some garlic.

Knack and Bock Sausages (Knackwurst und Bockwurst) These individual 100-g (4-oz) sausages are of a similar consistency to Fleischwurst. The smoked skin made from the pig's intestine is edible. They are served warmed with potato salad and one-meal soups. They should not be boiled. Bockwurst gained its name from Bockbier with which it was originally served in public houses.

Frankfurter Sausages (Frankfurter Würstchen) The ingredients are lean pork and bacon, very finely minced. Real Frankfurters are always produced in pairs. They are smoked but are usually sold uncooked. They should be heated in water (65 °C, 149 °F) for about 10–15 minutes but should not be boiled. They are served in crisp rolls, with potato salad or with one-course-meal soups.

White Sausage (Weisswurst) A speciality of Munich, served warm with Bavarian sweet mustard and potato salad.

SMOKED MEAT (*Aufschnitt*)

One of the earliest methods of preserving meat was to salt the raw meat and then hang it in smoke for a period of time. This whole process takes about 2–3 months. The salting gives the meat a fresh red colour and the smoking adds a very distinct taste to it. German people seem to have a liking for salted and smoked meat and in spite of all the modern methods of preserving meat, have maintained this form of preparation. All German butchers' shops have this slightly smoky pleasant scent arising from the sausages and smoked meats on display.

Whilst Speck (smoked bacon) is only used as an ingredient for pot-roasting meat, preparing sauces and vegetables, smoked ham (Schinken) is eaten thinly sliced on open sandwiches. Generally, ham (Schinken), with bone (Knochenschinken) or without bone (Rollschinken), is leg of pork. Salmon-Ham (Lachsschinken), however, is the very tender and lean piece from the pork back. For this the centre piece of the cutlet is wrapped in a layer of fat bacon (Speck) and then cured and smoked.

Each region has its special method of preparing smoked ham (Schinken) which results in a definite difference in taste. The methods of smoking and the kind of wood used produce a difference in aroma, so that the dark-rinded Black Forest Schinken tastes quite different from the lighter Hunsrücker, Westphalian or Eifeler Schinken. Well known for its tenderness and delicious taste is the Holsteiner Katenschinken from Schleswig-Holstein in North Germany. Katenschinken are prepared in houses with thatched roofs called Katen, according to a special wood-smoke technique. Most of these regional methods of preparation are well-guarded secret recipes.

Apart from pork, other kinds of meat have been successfully preserved by the smoked method. Smoked goose drumsticks and goose breast are a real delicacy. Smoked venison is a speciality of the Upper Bavarian region. Another special recipe, smoked beef (Rauchfleisch), comes from the Spa of Bad Neuenahr in the Rhineland. Very thin slices of Rauchfleisch are sprinkled with freshly ground pepper and served with fresh melon as a first course or with farmhouse rye bread and unsalted butter for supper. The best accompaniment is a glass of red Ahr-Burgundy wine.

Sausage Salad *(Wurstsalat—South Germany)*

300 g (11 oz) Meat Sausage (Fleischwurst) Lyoner or Knackwurst (pages 168–9)
2 medium-sized chopped onions
1 tablespoon wine vinegar
1 tablespoon vegetable oil
4 tablespoons mayonnaise (page 180)
1 teaspoon sweet mustard
salt and pepper to taste
2 finely chopped sweet-sour pickled gherkins
½ teaspoon sugar
2 tablespoons cooked peas
1 teaspoon chopped herbs (dill, parsley, chives)

Dice the sausage into 1-cm (⅜-in) size pieces and mix with the other ingredients. Leave covered in the refrigerator for 2 hours and serve with dark rye bread, unsalted butter and a glass of beer.

PLATTERS AND OPEN SANDWICHES
(Kalte Platten und Belegte Brote)

Most restaurants and public houses will serve platters or open sandwiches throughout the day and evening hours. Most German people have a platter or open sandwiches at evening meal-time. Beer, or sometimes tea, is the accompanying drink. For informal invitations after 7 o'clock, guests would be offered wine, beer and a choice of open sandwiches with sliced sausage, smoked or cold roast meat and cheese. Pastes or tinned meats are seldom used and are regarded as cheap substitutes. For buttering the sandwiches use fresh unsalted butter only. The slices of meat sausage or cheese should be big enough to cover the whole slice of bread; otherwise, use more than one slice. These platters are always decorated with hard-boiled eggs, gherkins, tomato slices, bretzels, saltsticks and grapes. In some parts of the country the platter selection is served on a round wooden board.

DECORATIONS FOR PLATTERS

1. Egg slices topped with caviare.
2. Tomato slices with a dot of mayonnaise and a sprig of parsley.
3. Cheese cubes (1½–2 cm (½–¾ in)) crowned with a green or red grape fastened with a cocktail stick.
4. Radishes. Peel the top two-thirds of the radish like an orange, leaving the skin fastened to the base third. Insert in a bowl of water for 15–20 minutes to form a rosette.
5. Mustard eggs (page 61).
6. Gherkins, sliced lengthwise and left joined at the base.
7. Egg 'toadstools'. Place a hard-boiled egg upright on a plate. Place the top third of a scooped out tomato on top and fasten with a cocktail stick. Put about ten mayonnaise dots on the tomato lid.
8. Meat and sausage cones. Place 1–4 teaspoons of meat or sausage salad or a mixture of mayonnaise with horse-radish and

whipped cream on to a slice of Salami, Lyoner, Schinken, roast pork or roast beef. Roll each into a cone shape.

9. Egg halves with a dot of mayonnaise and anchovy fillets.
10. Lemon slices, lettuce leaves, cucumber slices, parsley and dill.
11. Notched tomato halves, filled with meat- or any other salad (see Salad recipes).
12. Two asparagus sticks wrapped in a slice of smoked ham or beef.
13. Filled olives fastened to egg slices with a cocktail stick.
14. Scooped out oranges, grapefruit and pineapples filled with a salad (see Salad recipes).
15. Pumpernickel cubes (Pumpernickelwürfel). Butter a slice of pumpernickel; cover with a slice of cheese and top with a slice of buttered pumpernickel and cheese. Put on another layer of pumpernickel, butter, cheese, butter and pumpernickel. Do not butter the top of the last slice. With a very sharp knife, cut into cubes.
16. Pumpernickel discs (Pumpernickelscheiben). These discs have a diameter of about 4 cm (1½ in) and can be purchased ready cut in packets. If not available, use pastry cutters to cut out discs from rectangular slices. Cover with egg slices, cheese, salmon, or sausage.

Salmon Sandwiches *(Lachsschnitten)*

Butter two slices of rye bread. Cover the bread with slices of smoked salmon. Decorate with egg slices, chopped dill leaves and onion rings.

'Vicar and Nun' *('Pfäffchen und Nönnchen'—Rhineland)*

Butter a slice of pumpernickel. Cover with a slice of cheese and top with half a fresh buttered bread roll.

Open Ham Rolls — *(Schinkenbrötchen)*

With a sharp knife, cut fresh bread rolls horizontally in halves. Butter and cover each with a slice of smoked ham. Decorate with two slices of hard-boiled egg.

Tatar Sandwich — *(Tatarbrot—Berlin)*

100 g (4 oz) Tatar (finely minced best lean fillet steak)
salt, pepper, paprika
½ teaspoon made mustard
1 finely chopped small onion
onion rings
1 fried egg
1 chopped anchovy fillet
slice of buttered rye bread

Mix the raw meat with the salt, pepper, mustard, paprika, anchovy and chopped onion. Place on a buttered slice of rye bread. Top with the fried egg and onion rings.

Variation: Instead of the fried egg, serve topped with a raw egg yolk, which is mixed with the meat before eating.

Bremen Sandwich — *(Bremer Brot)*

Butter a slice of dark rye bread. Cover with fresh shrimps, prawns or crab meat. Top with a fried egg. Decorate with fresh dill herb and parsley. Serve with one tablespoon of mayonnaise in a separate container.

Hamburger — *(Hamburger Rundstück)*

This is the original Hamburger which has been modified in recent years by American cooking.

Halve and butter a fresh bread roll. Cover with 4 slices of hot roast pork or veal. Serve on a lettuce bed with hot gravy, mayonnaise, freshly chopped herbs (parsley, dill and chives), salt, pepper and sliced tomato.

Black Pudding Bread Roll

(Flönz mit Öllig—Cologne)

Flönz is the word for black pudding (Blutwurst) in the Cologne dialect. Öllig means a very sharp mustard. This type of mustard is produced and is popular in the area around Cologne and Düsseldorf whilst South German mustard is milder and sweet.

Cut a rye roll in half. Spread with butter; cover with a slice of smoked tongue sausage or Blutwurst. Spread with mustard and top with onion rings.

Pumpernickel with Cheese

(Pumpernickel mit Käse)

Butter a slice of pumpernickel; cover with a thick slice of cheese. Top with a marinade made from

1 teaspoon finely chopped onion
2 teaspoons vegetable oil
1 teaspoon wine vinegar
pinch of salt
freshly ground black pepper

Serve with a glass of cool beer.

For more suggestions, see chapters on Fish and Appetizers and Light Dishes.

Sauces

(*Sossen*)

Savoury Sauces	**Herzhafte Sossen**
Red Wine Sauce	Rotweinsosse
White Wine Sauce	Weissweinsosse
Brandy Sauce	Weinbrandsosse
Vegetable Sauce	Gemüsesosse
Cream Sauce	Rahmsosse
Dill Sauce	Dillsosse
Mustard Sauce	Senfsosse
Bacon Sauce	Specksosse
Saxony Fish Sauce	Sächsische Fischsosse
Onion Sauce	Zwiebelsosse
Hot Horse-radish Sauce	Warme Meerrettichsosse
Mayonnaise	Mayonnaise
Salad Dressing	Salatsosse
Frankfurt Green Sauce	Frankfurter Grüne Sosse
Soured Cream Sauce	Sauerrahmsosse
Cold Horse-radish Sauce	Kalte Meerrettichsosse
Horse-radish Cream	Meerrettichsahne
Remoulade Sauce	Remouladensosse
Cold Brandy Sauce	Kalte Weinbrandsosse

Sweet Sauces	Süsse Sossen
Wine Sauce	Weinsosse
Wine Cream Sauce	Weinschaumsosse
Rum Sauce	Rumsosse
Hot Chocolate Sauce	Heisse Schokoladensosse
Plum Sauce	Pflaumensosse
Strawberry Sauce	Kalte Erdbeersosse
Vanilla Sauce	Vanillesosse
Cherry Sauce	Kirschsosse

Sauces are of course important accompaniments to many dishes. Although nowadays there are a number of ready made sauces available, a home-made sauce can be much better tailored to complement an individual recipe and is also much cheaper.

SAVOURY SAUCES *(Herzhafte Sossen)*

Most of the cooked sauces have a roux as a base: the melted fat and flour are mixed over heat and then taken off the hot plate. The liquid is then added. The mixture is returned to the heat and brought to the boil, stirring continuously.

Red Wine Sauce *(Rotweinsosse)*

30 g (1¼ oz) butter
30 g (1¼ oz) diced smoked bacon
1 chopped onion
30 g (1¼ oz) flour
⅜ l (¾ pt) meat broth or water with meat cube
⅛ l (¼ pt) red wine
pinch of pepper, salt
¼ teaspoon sugar
1 teaspoon redcurrant jelly

Fry the bacon in the butter. Add the onion. Make a roux by adding the flour and liquid. Simmer for 10–15 minutes. Add the rest of the ingredients and serve hot with boiled ham, tongue or game.

White Wine Sauce *(Weissweinsosse)*

100 g (4 oz) butter
1 tablespoon flour
¼ l (½ pt) meat or fish broth
⅛ l (¼ pt) dry white wine
salt, pepper
juice of ½ lemon
1 egg yolk
20 g (¾ oz) butter

Make a roux from the 100 g (4 oz) butter, flour and liquid. Simmer for 10 minutes. Season with salt, pepper and lemon juice. Add 20 g (¾ oz) butter and leave to melt. Take the sauce off the hot plate and whisk in the yolk. Serve with fish.

Brandy Sauce *(Weinbrandsosse)*

30 g (1¼ oz) butter
20 g (¾ oz) plain flour
⅛ l (¼ pt) red wine
1–2 tablespoons brandy
salt, pepper

Stir the flour into the melted butter; remove from heat and stir in some of the wine. Return to heat stirring all the time until the sauce thickens. Stir in the rest of the liquid. Simmer for 2–3 minutes, season and serve with fish.

Vegetable Sauce *(Gemüsesosse)*

It is common in Germany to serve vegetables in a sauce. This sauce is suitable for beans, peas, carrots, beetroot. Add bean herb and nutmeg with beans. Add ½ teaspoon sugar with peas and carrots.

40 g (1¾ oz) butter
1 medium-sized chopped onion
2 tablespoons flour
¼ l (½ pt) vegetable broth
¼ l (½ pt) milk
salt, pepper

Fry the onion in the butter. Make a roux and season. Simmer for 10 minutes. Add the drained cooked vegetables and serve.

Cream Sauce *(Rahmsosse)*

This sauce is suitable to serve with asparagus, cauliflower, salsify, steamed fish or boiled chicken.

2 egg yolks
100 g (4 oz) butter
$\frac{1}{8}$ l ($\frac{1}{4}$ pt) vegetable broth
3 tablespoons single cream
2 tablespoons soured cream
salt, pepper, nutmeg
1 dessertspoon lemon juice

Divide the butter into small pieces. Place a dish in simmering water. Melt 30 g ($1\frac{1}{4}$ oz) butter in the dish. Stir in a little broth and an egg yolk. Beat well. After a while, gradually add more liquid, butter and the other egg yolk, beating all the time until sauce thickens. Add the cream and seasoning.

Dill Sauce *(Dillsosse)*

1 small chopped onion
50 g (2 oz) butter
30 g ($1\frac{1}{4}$ oz) plain flour
1 tablespoon chopped parsley
$\frac{3}{8}$ l ($\frac{3}{4}$ pt) meat or vegetable broth
2 tablespoons chopped dill leaves
3 tablespoons soured cream
2 teaspoons lemon juice
salt, pepper
$\frac{1}{2}$ teaspoon sugar
1 egg yolk

Lightly fry the onion and parsley in the butter. Mix in the flour; gradually stir in the broth. Bring to the boil, stirring all the time. Add dill, lemon juice, sugar, seasoning and cream. Mix 2 tablespoons of the sauce thoroughly with the egg yolk and add to the sauce. Do *not* boil sauce again. Serve with steamed fish or boiled meat.

Mustard Sauce (*Senfsosse*)

2 eggs
60 g (2½ oz) made mustard
20 g (¾ oz) plain flour
½ l (1 pt) broth or water
⅛ l (¼ pt) dry white wine
½ teaspoon sugar
75 g (3 oz) butter

Place all the ingredients, apart from the butter, in a saucepan. Heat and gradually bring to simmering point, whisking the mixture all the time. Add the butter gradually, keeping the sauce just below boiling point. Beat well and remove from the hot plate. Serve with fish, boiled beef or boiled eggs.

Bacon Sauce (*Specksosse*)

100 g (4 oz) diced smoked bacon
1 medium-sized chopped onion
30 g (1¼ oz) plain flour
½ l (1 pt) broth or water
salt, pepper
1 teaspoon lemon juice
1 tablespoon soured cream

Fry the bacon until golden and crisp. Add the onion and fry for a few minutes until transparent. Mix in the flour and stir in the liquid. Bring to the boil and simmer for 5–10 minutes. Add lemon juice, seasoning and cream and serve with potatoes or with fish.

Saxony Fish Sauce (*Sächsische Fischsosse*)

75 g (3 oz) butter
1 tablespoon plain flour
2 small chopped onions
⅛ l (¼ pt) fish stock
¼ l (½ pt) white wine
1 dessertspoon lemon juice
1 dessertspoon made mustard
pinch of pepper and sugar

Melt half the butter. Mix in the flour and brown. Add the onions. Gradually stir in all the liquid. Add the mustard and other seasoning. Simmer for 5–10 minutes. Just before serving add the remaining butter.

Onion Sauce (*Zwiebelsosse*)

250 g (9 oz) finely chopped onion
60 g (2½ oz) butter
35 g (1½ oz) plain flour
⅛ l (¼ pt) dry wine
⅜ l (¾ pt) broth or water
salt, pepper
1 bay-leaf
1 teaspoon sugar
1 teaspoon lemon juice
grated rind of ¼ lemon

Fry the onion in the butter until golden. Mix in the flour and stir in the liquid. Bring to the boil, stirring all the time. Add the bay-leaf and simmer for about 15 minutes. Remove the bay-leaf. Pass the sauce through a sieve or liquidizer. Add sugar, lemon rind, juice and seasoning and serve with boiled beef.

Hot Horse-radish Sauce (*Warme Meerrettichsosse*)

50 g (2 oz) butter
30 g (1¼ oz) plain flour
½ l (1 pt) milk
2 tablespoons horse-radish
salt, pepper
3 teaspoons lemon juice
2 egg yolks
½ teaspoon sugar

Make a roux (page 176) from the butter, flour and milk. Add the horse-radish and other seasoning. Beat the yolks with 3 tablespoons of the sauce. Add to the sauce. Mix in sugar and lemon juice. Do not boil again. Serve with boiled beef.

Mayonnaise (*Mayonnaise*)

2 egg yolks
⅛–¼ l (¼–½ pt) vegetable oil
1 teaspoon lemon juice
2 tablespoons wine vinegar

½ teaspoon salt
pinch of pepper
1 teaspoon made mustard
½ teaspoon sugar
1 tablespoon double cream
1 tablespoon single cream

It is important that all ingredients are at the same temperature. Stir the 2 egg yolks with a whisk and gradually stir in a few drops of the oil. Continue adding very small amounts of oil, stirring well all the time until the mixture begins to thicken. Once the mayonnaise is thickened, larger amounts of oil can be added until all the oil is used up. Stir in the vinegar, lemon juice, salt, pepper, sugar, mustard and cream. Use as a basic sauce for potato salad or as salad cream.

Salad Dressing *(Salatsosse)*

2 tablespoons oil
1 tablespoon wine vinegar
1 level teaspoon salt
¼ teaspoon sugar
pinch of pepper
1 teaspoon lemon juice
1 small finely chopped onion
1 tablespoon cream or soured cream

Mix all the ingredients. Just before serving, toss the washed and divided lettuce leaves in the sauce. For tomato or cucumber salad, slice, mix with the dressing and leave for 20 minutes.

Variation: Add herbs (dill, marjoram, thyme, parsley, chives) to the dressing.

Frankfurt Green Sauce *(Frankfurter Grüne Sosse)*

Green sauce—one of the specialities of Frankfurt—obtains its green colour from the variety of herbs used in the preparation. The sauce goes well with boiled meat, poached or boiled eggs, new potatoes or farinacious food.

yolks of 4 hard-boiled eggs
finely chopped white of 2 hard-boiled eggs
⅛ l (¼ pt) vegetable oil
4–6 tablespoons soured cream
juice of ½ lemon
1 teaspoon made mustard
½ grated garlic clove
1½ tablespoons wine vinegar
salt, nutmeg, pepper
½ teaspoon sugar
1 small finely chopped onion
1 finely chopped sweet-sour pickled gherkin
as many of the following very finely chopped herbs as possible: parsley, chives, sorrel, chervil, cress, dill, borage

Mix the 4 egg yolks with the oil to a smooth paste. Add the cream, lemon juice, vinegar and the remainder of the ingredients. Prepare the sauce 1–2 hours before serving.

Soured Cream Sauce *(Sauerrahmsosse)*

¼ l (½ pt) soured cream
1 finely chopped onion
2 teaspoons made mustard
1 dessertspoon lemon juice
1 dessertspoon vegetable oil
salt, pepper

Mix mustard, oil, onion and lemon juice well. Add soured cream and seasoning. Serve with fish.

Cold Horse-radish Sauce *(Kalte Meerrettichsosse)*

This sauce is excellent with cold roast beef or pork.

1 small finely chopped onion
3 tablespoons vegetable oil
juice of ½ lemon
3–5 tablespoons soured cream
1 tablespoon horse-radish
salt, pepper
½ teaspoon sugar

Mix all the ingredients and serve.

Horse-radish Cream *(Meerrettichsahne)*

100 g (4 oz) whipping cream
2 teaspoons horse-radish or more if desired (from a jar)
pinch of salt and pepper

Whip the cream and mix with the other ingredients. Serve with fish.

Remoulade Sauce *(Remouladensosse)*

This sauce is often served with cold meat or fried fish.

$\frac{1}{8}$ l ($\frac{1}{4}$ pt) mayonnaise (page 180)
1 small finely chopped onion
1 teaspoon finely chopped capers
1 finely chopped anchovy fillet
1 finely chopped sweet-sour pickled gherkin
1 tablespoon finely chopped herbs
1 tablespoon soured cream
pinch of sugar

Mix all the ingredients and serve cold.

Cold Brandy Sauce *(Kalte Weinbrandsosse)*

1 egg yolk
$\frac{1}{8}$ l ($\frac{1}{4}$ pt) vegetable oil
3–5 tablespoons brandy
salt, pepper
1 tablespoon mixed finely chopped herbs (marjoram, parsley, chives)
1 finely chopped sweet-sour pickled gherkin

Add oil to the yolk a few drops at a time, stirring continuously. Once the mixture starts to thicken more oil can be added at once. When all the oil has been used, mix in the brandy and the remainder of the ingredients.

Serve with boiled beef, fish or egg dishes.

SWEET SAUCES *(Süsse Sossen)*

Wine Sauce *(Weinsosse)*

½ l (1 pt) wine or cider
75 g (3 oz) sugar
3 teaspoons vanilla sugar
grated rind of ½ lemon
piece of cinnamon bar
1 clove
20 g (¾ oz) cornflour

Mix a few tablespoons of cold wine with the cornflour. Bring the rest of the wine with the sugar, vanilla sugar, lemon, clove and cinnamon to the boil. Take off the hot plate and stir in the cornflour mixture. Return to heat and bring to the boil again, stirring all the time. Serve hot or cold with Bavarian Steamed Noodles (page 204), Bread Pudding (page 210), baked apples or Karthäuser Dumplings (page 203).

Wine Cream Sauce *(Weinschaumsosse)*

¼ l (½ pt) dry white wine
100 g (4 oz) sugar
juice and grated rind of ½ lemon
2–3 eggs (according to size)
1 teaspoon cornflour

Put all the ingredients in a large bowl. Stand the bowl in simmering water. Beat the mixture with a hand or electric mixer until light, frothy and rising. Take off the heat and carry on beating. Avoid boiling of the cream. Serve as for Wine Sauce (above).

Rum Sauce *(Rumsosse)*

½ l (1 pt) cold milk
1 tablespoon custard powder
2 eggs
40 g (1¾ oz) sugar
2–3 tablespoons rum

Stir eggs, milk, sugar and custard powder together in a saucepan. Beat with a whisk whilst bringing to the boil. Take immediately off the hot plate when mixture starts to thicken. Add rum and serve with sweet dumplings.

Hot Chocolate Sauce (*Heisse Schokoladensosse*)

½ l (1 pt) milk
60 g (2½ oz) bitter chocolate
40 g (1¾ oz) sugar
1 egg
1 teaspoon cornflour

Break the chocolate and melt in a saucepan with a few tablespoons milk over low heat. Stir frequently. Mix the rest of the milk with the sugar, egg and cornflour and add to the chocolate. Increase heat slightly and beat mixture whilst bringing it to boiling point. Take off the hot plate immediately.

Serve with ice cream or other desserts.

Plum Sauce (*Pflaumensosse*)

500 g (1 lb 2 oz) fresh plums
2–4 tablespoons sugar
2 teaspoons vanilla sugar
1 tablespoon cornflour mixed in a little cold water
pinch of cinnamon

Stone the plums and heat without water for 20 minutes, stirring occasionally. Add sugar, vanilla sugar and cinnamon. Stir in cornflour mixture. Serve with dumplings or puddings.

Strawberry Sauce (*Kalte Erdbeersosse*)

½ l (1 pt) mushed strawberries (cheap, third-rate fruit can be used)
75 g (3 oz) icing sugar
4–5 tablespoons dry wine

Pass the strawberries through a sieve or a liquidizer. Add the sugar and wine.

This sauce can be served either cold or hot. If served hot, bring to the boil and add 1 teaspoon cornflour mixed with a little cold water. Serve with dumplings, ice cream or other desserts.

Vanilla Sauce *(Vanillesosse)*

½ l (1 pt) milk
50 g (2 oz) sugar
½ vanilla pod
2 egg yolks
3 teaspoons cornflour

Mix the cornflour and yolks with a few tablespoons cold milk. Heat the milk and vanilla pod and leave for 5–10 minutes. Take out the vanilla pod. Add the sugar and egg yolk mixture to the milk. Bring to the boil, whisking all the time. Take the mixture from the heat as soon as it thickens. Serve with Bavarian Steamed Noodles (page 204) or stewed fruit.

Cherry Sauce *(Kirschsosse)*

250 g (9 oz) stoned cherries
50 g (2 oz) sugar
1 dessertspoon lemon juice
1 level tablespoon cornflour

Mix the sugar and cornflour; add to the cherries and slowly heat in a saucepan until the sugar is dissolved and the mixture begins to thicken. Add the lemon juice and serve, hot or cold, with ice cream.

Desserts

(*Nachspeisen*)

Fruit Blancmange	Rote Grütze
Wine Apples	Weinäpfel
Stewed Apples	Apfelkompott
Apple Purée	Apfelmus
Redcurrant Cup	Johannisbeerbecher
Plum Dessert	Pflaumenspeise
Grapefruit Dessert	Pampelmusenspeise
Orange Dessert	Apfelsinenspeise
Chocolate Flummery	Schokoladenflammeri
Lemon Dessert	Zitronenspeise
Chocolate Dessert	Schokoladenspeise
Hazel-nut Dessert	Haselnusspeise
Coffee Dessert	Kaffeesüsspeise
Caramel Dessert	Karamelspeise
Grape Dessert	Traubenspeise
Wine Dessert	Weinspeise
Hazel-nut Ice Cream	Haselnusseis
Chocolate Ice Cream	Schokoladeneis
Strawberry Ice Cream	Erdbeereis
Fruit-Rum Ice Cream	Frucht-Rum Eis
Prince Pückler Ice Bomb	Fürst-Pückler Eisbombe
Black Forest Cup	Schwarzwälder Becher

Ice Cream Fruit Cup	Frucht-Eisbecher
Chocolate Curd Cheese	Schokoladenquark
Fruit Curd Cheese	Fruchtquark
Orange Curd Cheese Cream	Orangenquarkkrem
Wine Curd Cheese Cream	Weinquarkkrem
Curd Cheese Cup	Quarkbecher
Beer Pancakes	Biereierkuchen
Cream Cheese Pancakes	Eierkuchen mit Sahnequark
Apple Pancakes	Apfelpfannkuchen
Filled Dumplings	Gefüllte Knödel
Apples in Dressing-gowns	Apfel im Schlafrock
Karthäuser Dumplings	Karthäuser Klösse
Steamed Noodles	Dampfnudeln
Baked Bavarian Noodles	Rohrnudeln
Cherry Michael	Kirschenmichel
Emperor's Pancake	Kaiserschmarren
Nockerln	Nockerln
Apple Strudel	Apfelstrudel
Cherry Strudel	Kirschstrudel
Plum Strudel	Zwetschgenstrudel
Curd Cheese Strudel	Quarkstrudel
Potato Strudel	Kartoffelstrudel
Pumpernickel Pudding	Pumpernickel Pudding
Dark Bread Pudding	Schwarzbrot Pudding
Frankfurt Bread Pudding	Frankfurter Brot Pudding

Fruit Blancmange *(Rote Grütze—North Germany)*

This dish is frequently prepared in North Germany during the time when red currants, raspberries and cherries are harvested.

250 g (9 oz) red currants
250 g (9 oz) raspberries
250 g (9 oz) cherries
boiled water
100–150 g (4–5 oz) sugar (according to taste)
150 g (5 oz) sago or semolina

Either pass the washed fruit through a juice extractor or obtain the juice by heating the fruit for a short time with a little water and passing it through a sieve. Add enough boiled water to the juice to make 1 l (2 pt). Bring the liquid to the boil with the sugar. Stir in the sago or semolina and leave over low heat for 10–15 minutes. Rinse a glass dish with cold water; fill with the mixture and keep in a cool place to set. Serve with vanilla sauce (page 186), ice-cold milk or cream.

Variation: It is possible to use the whole fruit in the preparation of this dish rather than just the fruit juice. For this alternative, add the fruit to ¼ l (½ pt) boiling water and simmer, covered with a lid, until the fruit starts to fall to pieces. Add enough water to make 1 l (2 pt) and add the sugar. Bring to the boil, add sago or semolina and continue the preparation as described above.

Wine Apples *(Weinäpfel—Rhineland)*

4 apples
1 tablespoon chopped nuts or almonds
1 tablespoon sultanas
sugar
cinnamon
unsalted butter
⅛ l (¼ pt) Rhine wine

Wash and core the apples and place into a well-buttered fireproof dish. Pour boiling water over the sultanas, drain and mix the sultanas with the chopped nuts, sugar and cinnamon. Fill the apples with the sultana mixture and dot with butter. Pour the wine over the apples and bake in the oven at 160 °C (325 °F, gas mark 3) for 20–30 minutes. Serve hot with vanilla sauce (page 186) or whipped cream.

Stewed Apples *(Apfelkompott)*

1000 g (2¼ lb) apples
100–120 g (4–4½ oz) sugar
2 teaspoons vanilla sugar
⅜ l (¾ pt) water
¼ l (½ pt) white wine
grated rind of ¼ lemon
2–3 teaspoons cornflour mixed with a little cold water

Wash, peel, core and quarter the apples. Bring to the boil with the water, sugar and lemon rind. Simmer until soft, but do not allow to become a pulp. Add the wine. Take out the apples and put into a serving dish. Bring the liquid to the boil and thicken by adding the cornflour mixture. Pour the sauce over the apples and serve hot or cold.

Pears can be prepared in the same way.

Apple Purée *(Apfelmus)*

1000 g (2¼ lb) cooking apples
75 g (3 oz) sugar
¼–⅜ l (½–¾ pt) water
grated rind of ½ lemon
2 tablespoons sultanas
3–4 tablespoons white wine or cider
3 tablespoons chopped, roasted almonds

Wash, peel, core and cut up the apples. Bring them to the boil with the water and simmer them until they become pulp, stirring occasionally. Add the sugar, lemon rind, sultanas and wine. Bring to the boil once again and pour into a serving dish. Cover with roasted almonds and sprinkle with a little sugar. Serve hot or cold as dessert or with potato pancakes (page 258).

Redcurrant Cup *(Johannisbeerbecher)*

500 g (1 lb 2 oz) red currants
200 g (7 oz) sugar
2 packets gelatine
¼ l (½ pt) whipped cream

Pass the red currants through a liquidizer. Add the sugar and slightly heat the fruit pulp to dissolve the sugar. Add the dissolved gelatine to the pulp and leave until starting to set. Stir in the whipped cream, pour into individual glasses and put into the refrigerator to set. Garnish with fresh red currants and whipped cream just before serving.

Variation: Instead of red currants, raspberries or strawberries may be used.

Plum Dessert (*Pflaumenspeise*)

500 g (1 lb 2 oz) ripe dark-blue plums
200 g (7 oz) sugar
½ l (1 pt) water
juice and grated rind of 2 lemons
2 envelopes dissolved gelatine
2 tablespoons brandy or rum
¼ teaspoon cinnamon
1 dessertspoon vanilla sugar
50 g (2 oz) chopped almonds
⅛ l (¼ pt) whipped cream

Halve and stone the plums and heat with the water for 15–20 minutes. Pass through a liquidizer; return to heat and gradually stir in the sugar and juice and rind of the lemons. Take off the heat when the sugar is dissolved. Leave to cool for a short while and then add the dissolved gelatine, brandy or rum, cinnamon and vanilla sugar. Rinse a mould with cold water and fill with the plum dessert. Leave to cool and keep in the refrigerator for 2–3 hours. Immerse mould in hot water for a few seconds before turning out dessert. Sprinkle with chopped almonds and decorate around the base with whipped cream.

Grapefruit Dessert (*Pampelmusenspeise*)

½ l (1 pt) grapefruit juice
100 g (4 oz) sugar
3 teaspoons vanilla sugar
2 tablespoons custard powder
1 egg yolk
1 beaten egg white
⅛ l (¼ pt) whipped cream
grapefruit segments

Mix the custard powder with 3–4 tablespoons juice and the egg yolk. Bring the rest of the juice and the sugar to the boil. Remove from the hot plate; stir in custard powder mixture. Return to the heat and bring to the boil, stirring all the time. Mix the beaten egg white with the dessert. Leave to cool and mix with most of the whipped cream. Pour into individual glasses and keep cool. Just before serving, decorate with whipped cream and grapefruit segments.

Orange Dessert *(Apfelsinenspeise)*

juice from 4 oranges
grated rind of 1 orange
$\frac{1}{8}$ l ($\frac{1}{4}$ pt) white wine
6 egg yolks
6 beaten egg whites
150 g (5 oz) sugar
3 envelopes gelatine
$\frac{1}{8}$ l ($\frac{1}{4}$ pt) whipped cream
orange segments

Beat the egg yolks and sugar with an electric mixer until creamy. Add the orange rind and juice and the wine. Pour into a saucepan and heat until boiling, beating the mixture all the time. Take off the hot plate. Dissolve the gelatine in water, add to the boiled mixture, and leave to cool. When the mixture is cool and starts to set, mix in the beaten egg whites and pour into a large glass bowl or individual dishes. When set decorate with orange segments and whipped cream.

Chocolate Flummery *(Schokoladenflammeri)*

$\frac{1}{2}$ l (1 pt) milk
120 g (4$\frac{1}{2}$ oz) sugar
200 g (7 oz) chocolate
80 g (3$\frac{1}{4}$ oz) cornflour
$\frac{1}{4}$ l ($\frac{1}{2}$ pt) milk
2 tablespoons sliced almonds
$\frac{1}{8}$ l ($\frac{1}{4}$ pt) whipped cream

Mix the cornflour with the $\frac{1}{4}$ l ($\frac{1}{2}$ pt) milk. Warm the $\frac{1}{2}$ l (1 pt) milk and dissolve the chocolate in it, then bring to the boil with the sugar. Add the cornflour and milk mixture and boil, stirring continously, until the flummery comes away from the sides of the saucepan. Pour into a mould, rinsed with cold water, and leave until cold and set. Turn out of the mould and decorate with sliced almonds and whipped cream.

Lemon Dessert *(Zitronenspeise)*

juice from 2 lemons
grated rind of 1 lemon
1 envelope gelatine powder
4 egg yolks
4 egg whites
1 tablespoon brandy
120 g (4½ oz) icing sugar
¼ l (½ pt) whipped cream

Dissolve the gelatine powder in water and keep ready. Beat the egg yolks and sugar until creamy. Add the lemon rind, juice and brandy and lastly the dissolved gelatine. Mix with the beaten egg white and half the whipped cream. Pour into a glass bowl or individual dishes and place in the refrigerator to set. Decorate with whipped cream and serve.

Chocolate Dessert *(Schokoladenspeise)*

50 g (2 oz) unsalted butter
4 egg yolks
4 egg whites
80 g (3¼ oz) sugar
grated rind of ½ lemon
150 g (5 oz) ground almonds
100 g (4 oz) grated chocolate
¼ l (½ pt) whipped cream
3 teaspoons vanilla sugar
½ tablespoon icing sugar

Cream the butter and gradually add the egg yolks, lemon rind and two-thirds of the sugar. Whisk well with an electric mixer until creamy. Beat the rest of the sugar into the beaten egg white. Pour the egg white on to the egg yolk cream; top with the almonds and chocolate and mix lightly. Pour the mixture into a greased, sugar-dusted pudding basin and steam for about 60 minutes. Turn out the chocolate dessert, leave to cool and serve with cream, whipped with the icing and vanilla sugar. Decorate with a little grated chocolate.

Hazel-nut Dessert (Haselnussspeise)

½ l (1 pt) milk
8 egg yolks
220 g (8 oz) sugar
1 tablespoon vanilla sugar
2 envelopes gelatine
100 g (4 oz) ground hazel-nuts
100 g (4 oz) chopped roasted nuts
½ l (1 pt) whipped cream
hazel-nuts for decoration

With an electric mixer whisk the egg yolks and sugar. Then heat and gradually add the milk, beating all the time. When the mixture starts to rise, take off the hot plate. Add the dissolved gelatine. Leave to cool. Just before setting point, mix in the nuts and whipped cream. Pour into individual glasses and decorate with hazel-nuts.

Coffee Dessert (Kaffeesüsspeise)

125 g (4½ oz) sugar
5 egg yolks
1 teaspoon cornflour
3 teaspoons vanilla sugar
¼ l (½ pt) strong filter coffee
¼ l (½ pt) milk
2½ envelopes gelatine
¼ l (½ pt) whipped cream
grated chocolate or chocolate mocha beans

In a saucepan stir together the sugar, vanilla sugar, egg yolks, cornflour and milk. Add the coffee and bring to the boil whilst whisking with an electric mixer. Take off the hot plate and add the dissolved gelatine. Leave to cool. Just before setting, mix with the whipped cream and pour into a glass bowl. When set, decorate with grated chocolate or chocolate mocha beans.

Caramel Dessert (Karamelspeise)

60 g (2½ oz) sugar
4 egg yolks
40 g (1¾ oz) sugar
¼ l (½ pt) milk
1 envelope gelatine
3 beaten egg whites

In a pan heat the 40 g (1¾ oz) sugar until golden brown. Whisk the egg yolks with the 60 g (2½ oz) sugar and milk and add to the roasted sugar. Bring to the boil. Remove from heat and add dissolved gelatine. Beat mixture for a while until it has cooled down a little. Just before the mixture reaches setting point, mix in the beaten egg whites. Pour into a glass bowl and place in the refrigerator to set.

Grape Dessert *(Traubenspeise—Rhineland)*

250 g (9 oz) small seedless grapes
50 g (2 oz) sugar
15 g (½ oz) cornflour
grated rind of ½ lemon
3 teaspoons lemon juice
¼ l (½ pt) white wine
4 eggs

Wash the grapes and distribute between 6 individual dishes. Place a heatproof dish in a saucepan with simmering water. Put the sugar, cornflour, wine, rind and juice of the lemon into the dish and stir until the mixture becomes hot. In another container beat the eggs and add half of the heated liquid to them. Return the egg mixture to the dish in the simmering water and heat, stirring all the time until it thickens. Do not boil! Pour over the grapes in the dishes and leave to set.

Wine Dessert *(Weinspeise—Rhineland)*

¼ l (½ pt) white wine
3 egg yolks
3 egg whites
1 egg
80 g (3¼ oz) sugar
grated rind and juice of ½ lemon
1 envelope gelatine
grapes for decoration

Mix the egg yolks, the whole egg, rind and juice of lemon, sugar and wine over a low heat; whisk until the mixture reaches boiling point. Remove from heat, beat in the dissolved gelatine, and continue whisking for a while. Leave to cool until the mixture starts to set. Mix in the beaten egg whites and pour into glass dishes. Decorate with grapes before serving.

Hazel-nut Ice Cream *(Haselnusseis)*

3 egg yolks
1 whole egg
1 tablespoon vanilla sugar
½ l (1 pt) single cream
50 g (2 oz) sugar
¼ l (½ pt) whipped cream
60 g (2½ oz) ground hazel-nuts

In a saucepan mix the egg yolks, the whole egg, the sugar, vanilla sugar and the cream. Heat slowly whilst whisking with an electric mixer until a thick cream is obtained. Then leave to cool. Add ground hazel-nuts and whipped cream; pour into a foil container and freeze for an hour; whisk and return to freezer.

Chocolate Ice Cream *(Schokoladeneis)*

120 g (4½ oz) grated chocolate
½ l (1 pt) single cream
75 g (3 oz) sugar
2 teaspoons vanilla sugar
3 egg yolks
1 whole egg
¼ l (½ pt) whipped cream

Melt the chocolate with 2–3 tablespoons single cream over low heat. Stir in the sugar, egg yolks, egg and the remainder of the single cream; heat and whisk until a thick cream is obtained. Leave to cool, then mix well with the whipped cream and freeze for about an hour. Then remove and whisk the mixture well. Return to the freezer.

Strawberry Ice Cream *(Erdbeereis)*

For raspberry ice cream use the same recipe, substituting raspberries for the strawberries.

250 g (9 oz) strawberries
100 g (4 oz) sugar (icing or castor)
juice of ½ lemon
¼ l (½ pt) whipped cream

Pass strawberries through a liquidizer and stir in the sugar and lemon juice. Leave in the refrigerator for 1 hour. Mix in the whipped cream and freeze for 1 hour. Stir mixture with a whisk and freeze for another 2 hours.

Fruit-Rum Ice Cream *(Frucht-Rum Eis)*

250 g (9 oz) steamed and drained fruit (apricots, peaches, cherries)
1 tablespoon candied mixed peel
60 g (2½ oz) macaroons
2–4 tablespoons rum
½ l (1 pt) whipping cream
50 g (2 oz) sugar
2 teaspoons vanilla sugar

Cut fruit, peel and macaroons into small cubes and soak with the rum. Leave covered for 30 minutes. Whip the cream, gradually adding the sugar and vanilla sugar. Mix cream with the fruit mixture and freeze for about 1 hour. Then remove and whisk the mixture well. Return to the freezer.

Prince Pückler Ice Bomb *(Fürst–Pückler Eisbombe)*

This ice cream preparation is very popular in Germany and is usually served on festive occasions. During the nineteenth century the recipe was especially created for Prince Pückler by a confectioner from Lausitz in East Germany. The shape of this ice cream dish reminds one of a bomb as it is prepared in a special ice bomb mould. A pudding mould, however, will serve the same purpose. The mould is filled with one part of chocolate ice cream, one part of vanilla ice cream and one part of raspberry ice cream.

Part One

4 egg yolks

⅛ l (¼ pt) milk

100 g (4 oz) grated chocolate

50 g (2 oz) sugar

¼ l (½ pt) whipped cream

Melt the chocolate with 2–3 tablespoons milk over low heat. Add egg yolks, sugar and the remainder of the milk. Whisk the mixture to a thick consistency until boiling point is reached. Leave to cool, then add whipped cream.

Part Two

¼ l (½ pt) whipping cream

20 g (¾ oz) sugar

1 tablespoon vanilla sugar

Whip the cream, gradually adding the sugar until a stiff consistency is reached.

Part Three

⅛ l (¼ pt) thick fresh raspberry purée

¼ l (½ pt) whipping cream

30 g (1¼ oz) sugar

Whip cream, adding sugar. Mix with raspberry purée.

80–100 g (3–4 oz) macaroons

3–5 tablespoons maraschino, arrac or cherry-water (Kirschwasser)

Either one large mould or 2–3 small moulds may be used. Fill the mould one-third full with the Part One mixture and freeze. Meanwhile, chop up the macaroons and soak with the maraschino. When Part One has become firm top with one-third of the soaked macaroons and fill mould two-thirds full with Part Two. Freeze again. Then top with half of the remaining macaroons. Add the rest of the macaroons to the Part Three mixture and with this fill the mould. Freeze and turn out of the mould by partial immersion in hot water for a few seconds.

Black Forest Cup (*Schwarzwälder Becher*)

Place a tablespoonful of pitted cherries in the bottom of a glass or beaker. Pour over a dessertspoonful of Black Forest cherry water (Schwarzwälder Kirschwasser). Leave for a few minutes for the aroma to penetrate the cherries. Top with a scoop each of vanilla and chocolate ice cream. Pour over a little cherry juice or cherry sauce (page 186). Cover with whipped cream and decorate with a few cherries.

Ice Cream Fruit Cup (*Frucht-Eisbecher*)

Crystal or silver goblets are usually used for this preparation. Fill each goblet with layers of fresh or tinned fruit (cherries, strawberries, peaches, raspberries, apricots) and ice cream. Sprinkle each fruit layer with brandy or rum. Top with whipped cream and decorate with fruit and two ice wafers.

Chocolate Curd Cheese (*Schokoladenquark*)

250 g (9 oz) curd cheese
100 g (4 oz) grated chocolate
50 g (2 oz) chopped nuts
2 tablespoons sugar
3 teaspoons vanilla sugar
1 tablespoon rum
3 tablespoons candied peel
¼ l (½ pt) whipped cream with 2 teaspoons sugar added
4–6 chocolate biscuits

Mix the curd cheese with the sugar, rum, peel, chocolate and nuts. If the mixture is very dry, add some top of the milk but do not allow the mixture to become too soft. Add whipped cream and spoon into 4–6 individual dishes. Each dish should be decorated with a chocolate biscuit.

Fruit Curd Cheese *(Fruchtquark)*

250 g (9 oz) curd cheese
50 g (2 oz) sugar
2 teaspoons vanilla sugar
⅛ l (¼ pt) whipped cream
⅛ l (¼ pt) milk
1 egg yolk (optional)
500 g (1 lb 2 oz) fresh fruit (cherries, strawberries, currants, raspberries or blackberries)

Wash and, if necessary, cut and sugar the fruit. Put into a dish. Mix the curd cheese with the milk, sugar, yolk and cream. Pour over the fruit. Chill and serve.

For a variation of this dish, the fruit may be passed through a liquidizer and then mixed with the curd cheese. Chill and serve.

Orange Curd Cheese Cream *(Orangenquarkkrem)*

250 g (9 oz) curd cheese
60 g (2½ oz) sugar
2 egg yolks
⅛ l (¼ pt) orange juice
4 teaspoons gelatine
2 beaten egg whites

Stir the orange juice into the curd cheese. With an electric mixer beat until the mixture is light and creamy, adding the yolks and the sugar. Dissolve the gelatine in a little water (according to instructions) and add to the curd cheese. When the mixture starts to thicken, mix in the beaten egg whites. Pour into individual dishes or a glass bowl immediately and leave in the refrigerator to set.

Wine Curd Cheese Cream *(Weinquarkkrem)*

Use the recipe for Orange Curd Cheese Cream, with white wine instead of orange juice.

Curd Cheese Cup *(Quarkbecher)*

350 g (12 oz) curd cheese
¼ l (½ pt) milk
60 g (2½ oz) sugar
2 teaspoons vanilla sugar
70 g (2¾ oz) grated pumpernickel
3 tablespoons rum
90 g (3¾ oz) grated chocolate
300 g (11 oz) cherries

Beat the curd cheese with an electric mixer, adding the milk and sugar. If the cheese is still fairly dry, add a little more milk. Into glass dishes put a layer of cherries, pumpernickel and chocolate. Sprinkle with rum and cover with a layer of the curd cheese mixture. Continue with alternate layers in the dishes until all the ingredients have been used. Finish with a layer of curd cheese and decorate with cherries and chocolate.

Beer Pancakes *(Biereierkuchen)*

6 eggs
1 tablespoon vegetable oil
125 g (4½ oz) plain flour
¼ l (½ pt) milk
30 g (1¼ oz) butter
4 sugar cubes
pinch of salt
a few tablespoons beer

Mix the flour with the eggs and the oil. Melt the butter in a saucepan, add the milk, salt and sugar cubes. Bring to the boil and leave to cool. Mix with the egg mixture. Add enough beer to give the dough a creamy consistency. The amount of beer depends on the size of the eggs. Make thin pancakes. Serve with fresh fruit sprinkled with brandy and whipped cream.

Cream Cheese Pancakes *(Eierkuchen mit Sahnequark)*

250 g (9 oz) plain flour
½ l (1 pt) water
1 teaspoon vanilla sugar
3 eggs

Filling
250 g (9 oz) cream cheese
grated rind of ½ lemon
enough milk to achieve a thick creamy consistency
3–5 tablespoons cranberry sauce
1 teaspoon sugar

Mix flour, water, eggs and sugar to a smooth consistency. Make fairly thin pancakes. Prepare the filling; spread on each pancake and roll up. Serve cut into 2. Taste delicious with hot filter coffee.

Apple Pancakes *(Apfelpfannkuchen)*

250 g (9 oz) plain flour
½ l (1 pt) milk
3 eggs
pinch of salt
½ teaspoon brandy

Filling
500 g (1 lb 2 oz) sweet-sour apples (peeled and sliced)
2 tablespoons sugar
1 tablespoon raisins
grated rind of ¼ lemon
pinch of cinnamon
4–5 tablespoons water
2–4 tablespoons icing sugar

Mix the flour, milk, eggs, salt and brandy to a smooth consistency. Make not too thin pancakes and keep warm.

For the filling, steam the apple slices with the sugar, raisins, cinnamon and lemon rind in the water until just soft. Pour off the liquid. Spread the apple filling on to half of each pancake; fold over. Sieve with icing sugar and serve at once.

Filled Dumplings *(Gefüllte Knödel)*

250 g (9 oz) plain flour
1 egg
some water
fruit (plums, apricot halves, pieces of apple)

Mix and knead the flour, egg and water to a firm dough which can be rolled out on a board. The amount of water depends on the size of the egg and the consistency of the flour. It should be just as much as the dough will take without becoming too wet. Cut out 10-cm (4-in) squares, wrap around the fruit, press on well and simmer in water for about 10 minutes. Arrange on a hot plate with cream or melted butter and a little sugar and cinnamon. Serve with hot coffee and cream.

Apples in Dressing-gowns *(Äpfel im Schlafrock)*

250 g (9 oz) plain flour
1 level teaspoon baking powder
120 g (4½ oz) butter
60 g (2½ oz) sugar
grated rind of ½ lemon
1 small egg
2 teaspoons vanilla sugar
pinch of salt
4 peeled and cored apples
milk or egg yolk

Mix flour and baking powder. Rub in butter until mixture looks like fine breadcrumbs. Add sugar, vanilla sugar, salt, lemon and egg. Quickly work to a dough and leave for 30 minutes. Roll out to 5 mm (¼ in) thickness. Cut out squares according to size of apples.

Fold around apples. Wet edges with milk and press together. Brush with milk or egg yolk and bake on a baking tray for 20–30 minutes at 200 °C (400 °F, gas mark 6). Serve warm dusted with icing sugar and topped with whipped cream.

Apples in Dressing-gowns are particularly popular during the winter months.

Karthäuser Dumplings
(Kärthauser Klösse—South Germany and Rhineland)

Karthäuser used to be served frequently during Lent in convents and monasteries, Karthäuser being the name of one of the orders.

In the Rhineland Karthäuser dumplings are also called 'poor knights' (arme Ritter).

6–8 stale bread rolls
½ l (1 pt) milk
2 eggs
30 g (1¼ oz) sugar
2 teaspoons vanilla sugar
grated rind of ½ lemon
100 g (4 oz) butter
5–7 tablespoons breadcrumbs
50 g (2 oz) sugar mixed with 1 teaspoon cinnamon

Rub down the outside of the rolls on a grater. Cut rolls into quarters. Mix milk, eggs, sugar and vanilla sugar. Soak bread rolls in this liquid for 10–15 minutes, turning them once or twice. Drain, roll in breadcrumbs and fry in the butter. Roll in the sugar/cinnamon mixture and serve with wine sauce (page 184).

Steamed Noodles *(Dampfnudeln—Bavaria)*

These noodles have more the appearance of dumplings. Also popular in Württemberg, the Palatinate and the Saarland, they are often served as a Friday lunch with potato soup (page 38) as a first course.

500 g (1 lb 2 oz) plain flour
25 g (1 oz) fresh yeast
2 teaspoons sugar
¼ l (½ pt) lukewarm milk
1 egg
pinch of salt
50 g (2 oz) butter
40 g (1¾ oz) sugar
grated rind of ½ lemon
60 g (2½ oz) butter
¼ l (½ pt) milk or water
1 teaspoon salt

Sieve the flour into a bowl; make a well in the middle. Dissolve the yeast and 2 teaspoons sugar in the lukewarm milk. Pour into the well, mix with a little flour and leave to rise covered with a cloth for about 30 minutes. Add sugar, egg, lemon rind, salt and softened butter and work to a dough. Beat well until dough starts to show blisters and comes away easily from the side of bowl. Form dumplings of about 5–6 cm (2–2¼ in) diameter and leave them in a warm place on a floured board until they have risen. In a wide saucepan, bring the milk, butter and salt to the boil. Place the risen noodles in the liquid, which should be no more than halfway up the noodles. Cover tightly with a lid. Reduce heat to prevent burning, the use of an asbestos plate being advisable. Do *not* open lid as the noodles would collapse. The noodles are ready when all the liquid is taken up and a crust forms at the bottom. This is noticeable by a crackling noise after about 25–30 minutes. Carefully lift the lid. Serve noodles, crusty side upwards, with wine sauce (page 184).

Baked Bavarian Noodles *(Rohrnudeln—Bavaria)*

Prepare noodles as in the previous recipe. Instead of steaming them in a saucepan in milk and butter, bake them in the oven. Melt 20 g (¾ oz) butter in a meat tin or casserole. Place the risen noodles in the tin and brush them with some melted butter. Put the tin and a dish with water in the oven and bake for about 30 minutes at 200 °C (400 °F, gas mark 6). Serve in the same way as Steamed Noodles (above).

Variation: Place a stoned plum or cherry inside each noodle and serve with hot coffee.

Cherry Michael *(Kirschenmichel—Palatinate and Württemberg)*

South and West Germany have areas with extensive cherry orchards. The following recipe is a popular evening meal during the cherry harvest and well worth trying.

400 g (14 oz) white bread without the crust
½ l (1 pt) warm milk
3 eggs
75 g (3 oz) sugar
3 teaspoons vanilla sugar
80 g (3¼ oz) chopped almonds
½ teaspoon cinnamon
100 g (4 oz) butter
grated rind of ½ lemon
750 g (1¾ lb) cherries (stoned)
1–2 tablespoons breadcrumbs
20 g (¾ oz) butter
pinch of salt

Soak the bread in the milk. Cream 100 g (4 oz) butter, egg yolks and sugar. Add bread, salt, vanilla sugar, cinnamon, cherries and almonds. Beat the egg whites and carefully stir into the mixture (do not use an electric mixer). Pour mixture into a buttered ovenproof dish. Sprinkle with breadcrumbs and dot with butter. Bake in a pre-heated oven, 200 °C (400 °F, gas mark 6), for 50–60 minutes.

Emperor's Pancake *(Kaiserschmarren—Bavaria)*

Bavarian Schmarren are usually served as a quick lunch or simple evening meal. They can be prepared with bread, semolina or flour.

125 g (4½ oz) plain flour
pinch of salt
3 eggs
¼ l (½ pt) milk
30 g (1¼ oz) sugar
grated rind of ½ lemon
unsalted butter for frying

Cream egg yolks and sugar. Add flour, milk, salt and lemon rind. Beat egg white and carefully stir into the mixture. Pour some of the mixture into hot butter in a frying pan. When baked on one side turn over, add more butter and with two forks tear into small pieces. Finish frying; sprinkle with sugar and serve with stewed or tinned fruit.

Nockerln *(Nockerln—Bavaria)*

This Austrian dish which originated in Salzburg, is very popular in Bavaria.

50 g (2 oz) unsalted butter
5 eggs
30 g (1¼ oz) plain flour
50 g (2 oz) icing sugar
50 g (2 oz) unsalted butter
4 tablespoons single cream
icing sugar

Cream butter. Add egg yolks and sugar gradually, beating all the time until the mixture is light and frothy. Mix in flour. Beat the egg whites and carefully stir into the mixture. Heat butter and cream in a wide shallow oven-proof dish. Place tablespoons of the creamy mixture into the dish and bake in the oven at 220 °C (425 °F, gas mark 7) for about 20 minutes. Dust with icing sugar and serve.

Apple Strudel *(Apfelstrudel—Bavaria)*

The art of strudel making is passed on from mother to daughter in Bavaria. It takes some practice to reach the Bavarian housewife's perfection in 'pulling' the strudel dough to a paper thin consistency. The name strudel means whirl and describes accurately the shape of this dish.

Dough
250 g (9 oz) plain flour
1 egg
1 tablespoon vegetable oil
pinch of salt
4–7 tablespoons lukewarm water

Filling
1000 g (2¼ lb) apples, peeled, cored, quartered and finely sliced
60 g (2½ oz) chopped almonds or nuts
50 g (2 oz) sugar mixed with 1 teaspoon cinnamon
60 g (2½ oz) raisins
grated rind of ½ lemon
1 dessertspoon rum
50 g (2 oz) fine breadcrumbs
3–4 tablespoons soured cream

Sieve the flour into a cake bowl or on to a wooden board. Make a well in the middle. Put in egg, oil and salt. From the middle, work the ingredients into a dough. Add enough water to obtain a firm but elastic dough. The amount of water needed depends on the size of the egg and the dryness of the flour. Knead the dough well until it forms blisters. Leave dough to rest at least for 1 hour, covered with a warm bowl.

For the beginner, strudel making might be made easier by dividing the dough into two or four pieces and preparing several small strudels instead of one large one. Put the dough on to a floured cloth or large tea-towel on the table. Dust with flour and roll out with a rolling pin. To pull out the dough thinly, hold the dough and cloth with one hand and pull the dough with the other hand. Work evenly and carefully without ripping the strudel dough.

Brush with soured cream and sprinkle with breadcrumbs. Spread apple slices, raisins, lemon rind, almonds and sugar over the dough. Sprinkle with rum. By lifting the cloth, roll the dough and filling into a strudel. Push it off the cloth on to a well-buttered baking tin. Brush with melted butter and bake in a pre-heated oven, 190 °C (375 °F, gas mark 5), for about 40–60 minutes (according to size).

Bavarian housewives use a strudel casserole (Strudelreine) for baking. 25 g (1 oz) butter (unsalted) and enough milk to come up 1 cm (½ in) high in the dish are heated in the casserole and the strudel is placed into this mixture. After baking, the strudel is dusted with icing sugar and served (warm or cold) with whipped cream.

Cherry Strudel *(Kirschstrudel)*

For dough ingredients and preparation, see recipe for Apple Strudel (above).

Filling

750–1000 g (1¾–2¼ lb) pitted cherries
30 g (1¼ oz) sugar mixed with 1 teaspoon cinnamon
60 g (2½ oz) chopped almonds or nuts
125 g (4½ oz) fine breadcrumbs

Plum Strudel *(Zwetschgenstrudel)*

For dough ingredients and preparation see recipe for Apple Strudel (above).

Filling

750–1000 g (1¾–2¼ lb) stoned and quartered purple plums

60 g (2½ oz) chopped almonds

50 g (2 oz) sugar mixed with 1 teaspoon cinnamon

125 g (4½ oz) fine breadcrumbs

Curd Cheese Strudel *(Quarkstrudel)*

For dough ingredients and preparation see recipe for Apple Strudel (above).

Filling

400 g (14 oz) curd cheese

1 egg yolk

50 g (2 oz) sugar

2 teaspoons vanilla sugar

2 tablespoons raisins

30 g (1¼ oz) melted butter

grated rind of ½ lemon

Mix the ingredients to a smooth paste. If too dry add a little cream.

Potato Strudel *(Kartoffelstrudel)*

Dough

500 g (1 lb 2 oz) cold, boiled potatoes

80 g (3¼ oz) plain flour

1 egg

pinch of salt

½ l (1 pt) milk

Filling

500 g (1 lb 2 oz) peeled, cored, quartered and finely sliced apples

50 g (2 oz) butter

50 g (2 oz) raisins

50 g (2 oz) sugar with 1 teaspoon cinnamon

Work the ingredients to a dough. Roll out evenly, but not too thinly, with a rolling pin into 20-cm (8-in) diameter discs. Brush with melted butter. Spread with apples, raisins and sugar and roll up to strudel shapes. Place in a buttered casserole and bake in the oven at 190 °C (375 °F, gas mark 5) for 30 minutes. Bring the milk to the boil and pour over the strudel. Continue baking until milk is almost boiled away.

Pumpernickel Pudding
(Pumpernickel Pudding—Westphalia and East Germany)

500 g (1 lb 2 oz) pumpernickel or very dark whole grain rye bread (Vollkornbrot)
750 g (1¾ lb) stewed or tinned cranberries or blackcurrants (sweetened)
2 tablespoons sugar
3 teaspoons vanilla sugar
½ l (1 pt) whipped cream
½ teaspoon cinnamon

Mix cranberries with cinnamon. Whip the cream with 2 tablespoons sugar and the vanilla sugar. Break the pumpernickel slices into small pieces and rub between hands into small crumbs. Into a glass dish put a layer of breadcrumbs, a layer of cranberries, a layer of cream. Continue with layers until all ingredients are used up. Finish with a layer of cream. Put into the refrigerator for 3–4 hours and serve as a dessert or snack.

Dark Bread Pudding
(Schwarzbrot Pudding—Westphalia)

5 eggs
100 g (4 oz) sugar
2 teaspoons vanilla sugar
grated rind of ½ lemon
1 tablespoon rum
1 tablespoon plain flour
60 g (2½ oz) stale, grated or crumbled very dark bread or pumpernickel
60 g (2 oz) grated bitter chocolate

Pour rum over crumbled bread and leave to soak. Beat egg whites; gradually add sugar and egg yolks. Mix in lemon rind, flour, chocolate and crumbled bread. Pour mixture into a buttered pudding basin and steam for about 60 minutes. Serve with wine sauce (page 184).

Frankfurt Bread Pudding

(Frankfurter Brot Pudding—Hessen)

250 g (9 oz) cubed white bread
100 g (4 oz) unsalted butter
1000 g (2¼ lb) peeled and sliced apples
50 g (2 oz) sugar
¼ teaspoon cinnamon
pinch of ground cloves
⅛ l (¼ pt) wine or cider
grated rind of ½ lemon
50 g (2 oz) chopped almonds
50 g (2 oz) sultanas
30 g (1¼ oz) unsalted butter
icing sugar

Lightly fry the bread cubes and almonds in the 100 g (4 oz) butter. Steam the apple slices in the wine with the sultanas, cinnamon, cloves, lemon rind and sugar. Fill a buttered fireproof dish with alternate layers of the bread cubes and the apple mixture. Start and finish with bread cubes. Dot with butter and bake in a pre-heated oven, 160 °C (325 °F, gas mark 3), for about 30 minutes. Dust with icing sugar and serve with whipped cream as a dessert after a main course soup or for an evening meal followed by open sandwiches.

Cakes, Gateaux and Bread

(*Kuchen, Torten und Brot*)

Pastry Recipes	Teigrezepte
Chocolate Nut Cake	Schokoladen-Nuss Kuchen
Gugelhupf	Gugelhupf
Marble Cake	Marmorkuchen
Egg-Balance Cake	Eischwerkuchen
Frankfurt Ring Cake	Frankfurter Kranz
Tree Cake	Baumkuchen
Spice Cake	Gewürzkuchen
Cold Splendour	Kalte Pracht
Rum-Nut Cake	Rum-Nuss Kuchen
Gooseberry Cake	Stachelbeerkuchen
Grape Gateau	Weintraubentorte
Cherry Flan	Kirschboden
Cherry Crumble Cake	Kirsch-Streusel Kuchen
Strawberry Cake	Erdbeertorte
Redcurrant Cake	Johannisbeerkuchen
Apple Cake	Apfelkuchen
Fruit Cake with Yeast Dough	Obstkuchen mit Hefeteig
'Bee-Sting' Cake	Bienenstich
Covered Apple Cake	Gedeckter Apfelkuchen
Crumble Cake	Streuselkuchen
Black Forest Cherry Gateau	Schwarzwälder Kirschtorte

Nut-Cream Gateau	Nuss-Sahne Torte
Rum Gateau	Rumtorte
Basic Gateau	Tortengrundrezept
Buttercream Fillings	Butterkremrezepte
Sugar Glaze	Zuckerglasur
Chocolate Glaze	Schokoladenglasur
Christmas Bread	Weihnachtsstollen
Cologne Muzen	Kölner Muzemandeln
Cream Puffs	Windbeutel
Waffles	Waffeln
Aachen Printen Biscuits	Aachener Printen
Spekulatius	Spekulatius
Cinnamon Stars	Zimtsterne
Peppernuts	Pfeffernüsse
Nuremberg Honey Cake	Nürnberger Lebkuchen
Heather Sand	Heidesand
Vanilla Biscuits	Vanilleplätzchen
Macaroons	Makronen
Marble Biscuits	Marmorplätzchen
Königsberg Marzipan	Königsberger Marzipan
Rum Balls	Rumkugeln
Salt Sticks and Bretzels	Salzstangen und Bretzel
Cheese Biscuits	Käseplätzchen

Baking with Curd Cheese	**Backen mit Quark**
Curd Cheese Pastry	Quarkteig
Traditional Cheese Cake	Traditioneller Käsekuchen
Small Curd Cheese Cakes	Käseküchlein
Curd Cheese Pasties	Quarkmaultaschen
Curd Cheese Gateau	Quarktorte
Curd Cheese and Nut Gateau	Quark-Nuss Torte
Fluted Ring-Mould Cheese Cake	Quarknapfkuchen
Curd Cheese Cherry Cake	Quark-Kirschkuchen
Apple Cheese Cake	Apfel-Quarkkuchen
Curd Cheese Gateau with Raisins	Käsekuchen mit Rosinen

Curd Cheese Cream Gateau	Käse Sahne Torte
Baking with Potatoes	**Gebackenes aus Kartoffeln**
Potato Pasties	Kartoffeltaschen
Potato Gateau	Kartoffeltorte
Sweet Potato Pancakes	'Pickert'
Potato Bread	Kartoffelkuchen
Savoury Potato Pancakes	Kartoffelpfannkuchen
Savoury Potato Pot Cake	Topfkuchen
Bread	**Brot**
Sour Dough	Sauerteig
Rye Bread	Roggenbrot
Mixed Bread	Mischbrot
Wheat Bread Rolls	Weizenbrötchen
Rye Bread Rolls	Roggenbrötchen
Whole Grain Bread—Pumpernickel	Vollkornbrot—Pumpernickel
Nuremberg 'Hutzelbread'	Nürnberger Hutzelbrot

Black Forest Gateaux and Cheese Cake dominate the views of outsiders as typical German cakes. There is, however, a large selection of other cakes and gateaux in the baking tradition of the country which is well worthwhile considering. Germans are enthusiastic cake eaters. This might explain why they do not just regard cake as a third course of a meal but have devoted an entire meal-time to its consumption. From 4 to 5 o'clock in the afternoon is coffee and cake time, when most of the coffee houses have their busiest time and housewives—particularly on Saturday and Sunday—present their families with home-made cakes. The highlight of a birthday is the celebration coffee-time in the afternoon when friends and relations gather around a table with at least three or four different cakes or gateaux. This tradition is also maintained for adult birthdays.

The size of German cakes is thus a true indication of their role. Cakes of the smaller size normally found in England are unknown in Germany. The average round cake is about 24 cm (10 in) diameter. Heavy fruit cakes are also not very common. Most cakes are of a lighter texture and fruit cakes are usually prepared with fresh fruit in season. The latter usually employ a yeast pastry in their preparation and are baked on a shallow baking tin (Kuchenblech) which is the size of the oven, or a round tin with corrugated sides and a diameter of about 28 cm (11 in).

Unless otherwise stated, the following recipes are for rectangular tins similar to bread tins (24 × 12 cm (10 × 5 in)) or for round cake tins (24 cm (10 in) diameter). These round cake tins usually have a loose bottom and sides which can be loosened or tightened to help the turning out of the cake (spring-wire form). For baking, the tins are placed on a shelf in the lower half of the oven, whilst biscuits, small or low cakes are baked on the middle shelf.

A number of recipes in this chapter are based on four types of pastry which are described below and referred to where necessary. Cakes are always eaten with a cake fork.

Short Pastry *(Mürbteig)*

Mix flour and baking powder (or use self-raising flour)—quantities according to recipe—and sieve into a large bowl. Add sugar, salt, spices and fat and work, first with a knife, then with the hands, into a mixture resembling breadcrumbs. Add eggs and liquid if required and quickly work to a firm dough. Place in the refrigerator for about 30 minutes. Then use as described in the recipe.

Stirred Pastry *(Rührteig)*

Detailed instructions are given in each individual recipe. The following advice might, however, be useful. All ingredients should be at room temperature and the fat should be of a soft consistency. But do *not* melt the fat. Sugar and eggs must be beaten well to a creamy mixture. The required amount of milk depends on the size of the eggs. The pastry must never be too runny but should fall away thickly from the wooden spoon. This type of pastry is particularly sensitive during baking. Vibration and shock should be avoided.

Sponge Pastry *(Biskuitteig)*

The lightness of this pastry is due to the whisking of the eggs. Only castor sugar should be used in its preparation. Always line the bottom of the cake tin with greaseproof paper, but do not line or grease the sides of the tin.

Most gateaux are made with sponge pastry.

Yeast Dough *(Hefeteig)*

All ingredients should be at room temperature. The list of ingredients and the quantities are given in the individual recipes. To develop the raising power, the yeast is first mixed with a teaspoon of sugar and dissolved in a few tablespoons of lukewarm milk. Half a tablespoon of flour is added. The mixture is left covered in a warm place until risen and frothy (about 20–30 minutes). Meanwhile, sieve the flour into a warmed bowl and make a well in the middle. When the yeast has risen, pour into the well, add the rest of the lukewarm milk, the sugar, eggs, spices, other flavourings and soft fat. Work to a dough and beat well with a wooden spoon until the dough shows blisters and comes away from the sides of the bowl. Sprinkle some flour in the bottom of the bowl; place the dough on top, cover and leave to rise in a warm place until twice its size. This can take up to 2 hours, depending on the temperature of the room. Do not expose yeast dough to extreme heat as this would kill the yeast. The most suitable temperature is 35 °C (95 °F). After rising, knead the yeast dough again, form into the required shape or place in a cake tin. Leave to rise again and bake.

Chocolate Nut Cake (*Schokoladen-Nuss Kuchen*)

This is a moist but crunchy cake.

5 eggs
250 g (9 oz) unsalted butter
200 g (7 oz) ground hazel-nuts
100 g (4 oz) mixed chopped nuts
200 g (7 oz) icing sugar
2 teaspoons vanilla sugar
150 g (5 oz) plain flour
1½ level teaspoons baking powder
75 g (3 oz) breadcrumbs
1 teaspoon cinnamon
1 tablespoon rum
grated rind of ½ lemon
150 g (5 oz) grated chocolate
50 g (2 oz) chopped chocolate or chocolate drops
*chocolate glaze (**page 238**)*

Cream the butter and add the egg yolks, sugar and vanilla sugar, beating the mixture well using an electric mixer. Stir in the nuts, rum, cinnamon and lemon rind. Sieve in the flour mixed with the baking powder. Add the breadcrumbs and finally the chocolate and beaten egg whites. Spoon the mixture into a ring mould or rectangular cake or bread tin and bake for about 50 minutes at 180 °C (350 °F, gas mark 4). Cool and cover with chocolate glazing.

Gugelhupf (*Gugelhupf—Bavaria*)

This recipe is traditionally Austrian, having been a favourite of Emperor Franz Joseph I. The Gugelhupf or Kugelhopf is popular throughout the whole of South Germany and must have derived its name from the shape, which resembles that of a ball (Kugel). The yeast-based cake is baked in a special Gugelhupf cake tin which is a fluted timbale mould with a core in the centre. These are available in different sizes. The following recipe is for a medium-size cake.

500 g (1 lb 2 oz) plain flour
40 g (1¾ oz) yeast
125 g (4½ oz) sugar
⅛ l (¼ pt) milk
3 eggs
grated rind of ½ lemon
150 g (5 oz) unsalted butter
¼ teaspoon salt

2 teaspoons vanilla sugar
1 tablespoon Black Forest cherry water or rum
100 g (4 oz) raisins
60 g (2½ oz) currants
70 g (2¾ oz) candied peel
75 g (3 oz) chopped almonds
icing sugar for dusting

Prepare the yeast mix as described on page 217. Pour boiling water over the dried fruit, drain, dust with flour, and with the candied peel and almonds add to the dough. Leave to rise for 1–2 hours. Knead again and place in the greased Gugelhupf tin. Leave to rise again for 20–30 minutes and bake in a pre-heated oven at 190–200 °C (375–400 °F, gas mark 5–6) for about 1 hour. Take out of the oven. Leave to cool for 5–10 minutes. Turn out and dust with icing sugar. Serve with whipped cream and hot coffee.

Marble Cake *(Marmorkuchen)*

250 g (9 oz) unsalted butter
250 g (9 oz) sugar
3 teaspoons vanilla sugar
4–5 eggs
grated rind of ½ lemon
500 g (1 lb 2 oz) self-raising flour
⅛ l (¼ pt) milk
40 g (1¾ oz) cocoa
2–3 tablespoons rum or brandy
icing sugar for dusting

Whisk the butter with an electric mixer until soft and creamy. Gradually add the eggs, sugar, vanilla sugar and lemon rind, beating the mixture all the time. Alternately stir in the sieved flour and milk in small quantities. Fill a well-greased Gugelhupf cake tin (fluted timbale mould) with one-third of the mixture. Of the remaining mixture keep back one half and to the other half mix in the cocoa and rum. Spoon the dark mixture on top of the light mixture already in the cake tin and then top with the remaining light mixture. Pull a knife, spoon or fork through the dough in the tin to roughly mix the dark and light parts. Bake at 180 °C (350 °F, gas mark 4) for about 60–70 minutes. Turn out and cool. Dust with icing sugar and serve with whipped cream.

Egg-Balance Cake (*Eischwerkuchen*)

For the dough the weight of the eggs serves as a unit for the other ingredients.

4 eggs
sugar, plain flour and unsalted butter, each equivalent to the weight of the eggs
½ teaspoon baking powder
3 teaspoons vanilla sugar
50 g (2 oz) sultanas
30 g (1¼ oz) chopped almonds
juice and grated rind of ½ lemon

Whisk the eggs and sugar in a warmed bowl until light and frothy. Add the melted butter, lemon, sultanas and almonds. Mix the flour with the baking powder and sieve into the mixture. Bake in a Gugelhupf cake tin (fluted timbale mould) at 180 °C (350 °F, gas mark 4) for about 45 minutes.

Frankfurt Ring Cake (*Frankfurter Kranz—Hessen*)

This cake is baked in a ring mould, filled with buttercream and covered with buttercream and roasted almonds.

125 g (4½ oz) unsalted butter
125 g (4½ oz) sugar
3 teaspoons vanilla sugar
pinch of salt
2 eggs
3 egg yolks
3 egg whites
150 g (5 oz) self-raising flour
75 g (3 oz) potato flour or cornflour
1 tablespoon rum
grated rind of ½ lemon

Cream the fat and sugar; beat in the two whole eggs and three egg yolks, one at a time. Add the lemon rind and rum. Fold in the sieved flour, salt and cornflour. Whisk the egg whites and carefully stir in. Bake in a ring mould at 180 °C (350 °F, gas mark 4) for about 40–50 minutes. Allow to stand for 5–10 minutes before turning out. When the cake is cold (for best results, the following day), cut into two or three layers and prepare the following filling:

250 g (9 oz) unsalted butter
200 g (7 oz) icing sugar
2–3 egg yolks
3 teaspoons vanilla sugar
2 tablespoons rum
apricot jam
80 g (3¼ oz) sugar
60 g (2½ oz) chopped almonds

Cream together the butter and sugar. Add the egg yolks one at a time.

Sprinkle each cake layer with rum and spread with apricot jam and buttercream. Put the layers together and spread buttercream over the whole cake. Keep back some of the buttercream for decoration.

Brown the sugar in a pan and add the chopped almonds. Leave to cool on a buttered plate. Chop finely and sprinkle over the buttercream all round the cake. To finish the cake put some buttercream rosettes along the top of the ring.

Tree Cake *(Baumkuchen—Berlin)*

The traditional Tree Cake has a height of 1–2 metres (3–6½ feet). It is baked over an open fire. Very thin layers of dough are spread on a continuously turning plate with a pole in the centre. When one layer is browned, the next one is poured on, so that the cake gradually grows to its full height. The finished cake is covered with sugar glaze. The traditional Tree Cake requires professional equipment. For domestic preparation, the following recipe can be used with a 24 × 13-cm (10 × 5-in) rectangular cake tin.

250 g (9 oz) unsalted butter
250 g (9 oz) sugar
3 teaspoons vanilla sugar
grated rind of 1 lemon
6 egg yolks
6 egg whites
75 g (3 oz) ground almonds
125 g (4½ oz) plain flour
125 g (4½ oz) cornflour or potato flour
1 tablespoon rum
2 tablespoons apricot jam

Cream the butter with the egg yolks and half the sugar and vanilla sugar. Add the lemon rind, almonds and rum. Whisk the egg whites with the rest of the sugar to a stiff consistency and fold with the flour and cornflour into the egg cream. Grease the cake tin and put 1 or 2 tablespoons of the mixture on to the bottom of the tin. Bake at 190 °C (375 °F, gas mark 5) for 4–5 minutes until golden. Pour on another layer and bake again until golden on top. Continue this baking process for about 14 further layers. Heat the apricot jam with ½ tablespoon water. Brush the cake with this hot apricot sauce and cover with sugar glazing (page 237).

Spice Cake *(Gewürzkuchen)*

This type of cake is usually eaten during the winter months.

200 g (7 oz) unsalted butter
200 g (7 oz) sugar
3 teaspoons vanilla sugar
4 eggs
pinch of salt
1 teaspoon cinnamon
pinch of cardamom
½ teaspoon ground nutmeg
1 teaspoon ground cloves
grated rind of 1 lemon
3 drops bitter almond oil (flavour)
1 tablespoon rum
500 g (1 lb 2 oz) self-raising flour
⅛ l (¼ pt) milk
125 g (4½ oz) grated bitter chocolate or 50 g (2 oz) cocoa
50 g (2 oz) chopped nuts
2 tablespoons mixed peel

Cream the butter and sugar; gradually beat in the eggs. Add the lemon, salt, spices and rum. Stir in the sieved flour and milk. Add the chocolate, nuts and mixed peel. Bake in a well-greased tin at 185 °C (360 °F, gas mark 4–5) for about 70–80 minutes.

Cold Splendour *(Kalte Pracht)*

2–3 packets plain rectangular biscuits
250 g (9 oz) coconut fat
2 eggs
250 g (9 oz) castor sugar
3 teaspoons vanilla sugar
80 g (3¼ oz) cocoa
1 teaspoon instant coffee powder
1 tablespoon rum
pinch of salt

Melt the coconut fat over low heat. Whisk the eggs with an electric mixer gradually adding the sugar and vanilla sugar. Stir in the cocoa, coffee, rum and salt and add the melted coconut fat. Line a bread tin or a 24 × 12-cm (10 × 5-in) cake tin with greaseproof paper. Cover the bottom of the tin with a layer of the chocolate mixture followed by a layer of biscuits. Continue with alternate layers of the chocolate mixture and biscuits. Leave to cool and set. Turn out of the tin. Take off paper and decorate with coarse sugar, almonds and glacé cherries.

Rum-Nut Cake *(Rum-Nuss Kuchen)*

275 g (10 oz) unsalted butter
175 g (6 oz) sugar
grated rind of ½ lemon
3 teaspoons vanilla sugar
4 eggs
200 g (7 oz) plain flour
1 teaspoon baking powder
150 g (5 oz) ground hazel-nuts
100 g (4 oz) finely chopped hazel-nuts
2 tablespoons rum
2 tablespoons apricot jam
1 tablespoon water
100 g (4 oz) chocolate and a knob of coconut fat

Cream the butter and gradually beat in the sugar, lemon rind, vanilla sugar and eggs. Stir in the sieved flour, mixed with the baking powder, and the hazel-nuts. Spoon into a rectangular greased cake tin (24 × 12 cm (10 × 5 in)) lined with greaseproof paper. Bake at 175 °C (350 °F, gas mark 4) for about 70 minutes. After baking turn out of the tin, prick the surface of the hot cake several times with a skewer and brush with rum. Bring the apricot jam and the water to the boil; pass through a sieve and brush the cake with the sauce. Leave to cool. Break the chocolate into a basin. Stand the basin in a saucepan of hot water. When the chocolate is melted, stir in the coconut fat. Cover the cake with chocolate.

Gooseberry Cake *(Stachelbeerkuchen)*

750 g ($1\frac{3}{4}$ lb) gooseberries
300 g (11 oz) sugar
2 teaspoons vanilla sugar
250 g (9 oz) plain flour
pinch of salt
grated rind of $\frac{1}{2}$ lemon
2 egg yolks
3 egg whites
125 g ($4\frac{1}{2}$ oz) unsalted butter
30 g ($1\frac{1}{4}$ oz) breadcrumbs

Top and tail and wash the gooseberries. Place in a saucepan with 50 g (2 oz) sugar and 6 tablespoons water and heat gradually for 5 minutes covered with a lid. The gooseberries must not fall apart or become too soft. Turn the gooseberries on to a sieve to drain.

For the pastry, sieve the flour into a bowl and add the salt, 100 g (4 oz) sugar, vanilla sugar and lemon rind. Cut the butter into small pieces. First with a knife and then with the hands, work the ingredients until they resemble breadcrumbs. Add the egg yolks and quickly work to a dough. Place in the refrigerator for 20–30 minutes. Line a 24-cm (10-in) round cake tin with the pastry and bake for 15 minutes at 210 °C (400 °F, gas mark 6). Leave to cool in the tin. Cover the baked pastry case first with breadcrumbs and then with the gooseberries. Beat the egg white and gradually add 150 g (5 oz) sugar. Cover the gooseberries with the egg white mixture and bake at 150 °C (300 °F, gas mark 2) for 25 minutes.

Grape Gateau *(Weintraubentorte—Rhineland)*

Pastry
250 g (9 oz) plain flour
150 g (5 oz) unsalted butter
80 g ($3\frac{1}{4}$ oz) sugar
1 egg
pinch of salt

Prepare the pastry according to the instructions for Short Pastry (page 216). Line the bottom of a 24-cm (10-in) spring-wire tin and bake in the centre of the oven at 210 °C (400 °F, gas mark 6) for 15–20 minutes. Leave in the tin to cool.

Filling
1000 g ($2\frac{1}{4}$ lb) seedless grapes
5 egg whites
50 g (2 oz) sugar
3 teaspoons vanilla sugar
100 g (4 oz) finely ground nuts
2 egg whites
100 g (4 oz) sugar

Wash the grapes and put 120 g ($4\frac{1}{2}$ oz) aside. Cut the other grapes into halves. Beat the 5 egg whites, then gradually add 50 g (2 oz) sugar and the vanilla sugar. Stir in the nuts. Spread half of this mixture on to the cooled pastry case in the tin. Top with the halved grapes and cover with the remainder of the egg white and nut mixture. Bake at 150 °C (300 °F, gas mark 2) for about 45–50 minutes. Meanwhile, beat the 2 egg whites and gradually add 100 g (4 oz) sugar. Top the baked gateau with the whole grapes which were set aside and the egg white mixture. Bake again at 150 °C (300 °F, gas mark 2) for 20 minutes.

CHERRY CAKES (*Kirschkuchen*)

Cherries are grown abundantly in Germany, particularly in the south-west part of the country. In this region cherry orchards are seen with as much frequency as are the small groups of cherry trees in domestic gardens. The cherry harvest begins in June with the yellow or light to dark red sweet cherries. The sweet-sour morello cherries ripen later. They are particularly suitable for use in cakes and the preparation of juice and jam. The simplest and quickest methods of cherry cake preparation are given here and they can also be used with other fruits.

Cherry Flan ***(Kirschboden)***

Two alternative recipes are given for the preparation of the pastry.

Pastry

1.

180 g (6½ oz) plain flour
75 g (3 oz) sugar
¼ teaspoon baking powder
120 g (4½ oz) unsalted butter
1 small egg
pinch of salt

Prepare the pastry according to the instructions for Short Pastry (page 216). Line a greased 28-cm (11-in) flan tin with the pastry and bake at 200 °C (400 °F, gas mark 6) for about 20 minutes. Turn out of the tin and leave to cool.

or 2.

75 g (3 oz) unsalted butter
75 g (3 oz) sugar
2 teaspoons vanilla sugar
2 eggs
pinch of salt
150 g (5 oz) plain flour
1 level teaspoon baking powder
1–2 tablespoons milk

Cream the butter, gradually adding the sugar, vanilla sugar, salt and eggs. Mix the flour with the baking powder and sieve into the mixture. Add the milk. Spoon into a greased 28-cm (11-in) flan tin and bake at 180 °C (350 °F, gas mark 4) for 25–30 minutes. Turn out of the tin and leave to cool.

Filling

500–750 g (1 lb 2 oz–1¾ lb) pitted cherries
¼ l (½ pt) water
4 tablespoons sugar
¼ l (½ pt) cherry juice
25 g (1 oz) sugar
25 g (1 oz) cornflour or 1 envelope dissolved gelatine
flaked almonds
whipped cream

In a saucepan bring the cherries to the boil together with the water and 4 tablespoons sugar. Remove from heat and drain. Fill the flan case with the cherries. Cover cherries with a jelly prepared from cherry juice, 25 g (1 oz) sugar and cornflour (or gelatine). Spread flaked almonds along the edge of the cake; decorate with whipped cream and serve with extra cream.

Cherry Crumble Cake (*Kirsch-Streusel Kuchen*)

This cake would usually be prepared on a flat baking tin of approximately the same size as the base of the oven. The following quantities are, however, for a continental-size round cake tin.

250 g (9 oz) plain flour
15 g (½ oz) yeast
⅛ l (¼ pt) milk
40 g (1¾ oz) sugar
50 g (2 oz) butter
1 small egg
pinch of salt

Prepare a yeast dough from the above ingredients as described under Yeast Dough (page 217) and line the bottom of the cake tin with it.

500–750 g (1 lb 2 oz–1¾ lb) pitted cherries
150 g (5 oz) plain flour
100 g (4 oz) unsalted butter
60 g (2½ oz) sugar
2 teaspoons vanilla sugar
¼ teaspoon cinnamon

Fill the cake tin with the cherries and top with crumble made from the rest of the ingredients. Bake for about 50 minutes at 200 °C (400 °F, gas mark 6). Sprinkle with sugar just before serving. Eat whilst fresh.

Variation: For the cake base use curd cheese pastry (page 249) instead of yeast dough.

Strawberry Cake (*Erdbeertorte*)

This cake is prepared in the same way as Cherry Flan (page 225) using strawberries instead of cherries, but instead of heating the fruit, fresh strawberries should be used.

Redcurrant Cake *(Johannisbeerkuchen)*

Prepare either in the same way as Cherry Flan (page 225) or use the following recipe:

Pastry

180 g (6¼ oz) plain flour
75 g (3 oz) sugar
½ level teaspoon baking powder
80 g (3¼ oz) unsalted butter
1 egg
pinch of salt

Prepare as described under Short Pastry (page 216).

Filling

750–1000 g (1¾–2¼ lb) red currants
40–60 g (1¾–2½ oz) sugar
5 egg whites
250 g (9 oz) sugar
125 g (4½ oz) ground almonds

Wash the red currants; remove the stalks and mix with the 40–60 g (1¾–2½ oz) sugar. Beat the egg whites until stiff, then gradually beat in the rest of the sugar and the almonds. Line a cake tin (24-cm (10-in) diameter) with the pastry. Stir the red currants into half the almond meringue mixture and spread on to the pastry. Top with the remainder of the meringue and bake at 180 °C (350 °F, gas mark 4) for about 50 minutes.

Apple Cake *(Apfelkuchen)*

125 g (4½ oz) unsalted butter
125 g (4½ oz) sugar
3 teaspoons vanilla sugar
3 eggs
grated rind of ½ lemon
200 g (7 oz) plain flour
2 level teaspoons baking powder
1–3 tablespoons milk
500 g (1 lb 2 oz) peeled, cored and quartered apples
2 tablespoons apricot jam
1 tablespoon water
icing sugar

Cream the butter and gradually add the sugar, vanilla sugar and eggs, beating well. Add the lemon rind, the sieved flour (to which the baking powder has been added) and the milk.

Spoon into a round spring-wire tin (24 cm (10 in) diameter) and top with the apple quarters, which should be slightly pressed into the pastry. Bake at 190 °C (375 °F, gas mark 5) for 55–60 minutes. Leave to cool in the tin for 10 minutes. Then remove the ring. Heat the apricot jam with the water; pass through a sieve and brush the top of the cake whilst hot. When the cake is cooled, dust with a little icing sugar. Serve with whipped cream.

Fruit Cake with Yeast Dough
(Obstkuchen mit Hefeteig)

This type of cake (Blechkuchen) is almost always baked on a shallow tin of the size of the oven base as large amounts of fresh cake are eaten, particularly in rural areas. In the Palatinate, for example, a very popular midday meal is potato soup with yeast plum cake. The following recipe, however, is for a 28-cm (11-in) fruit flan tin with low sides.

Yeast dough

250 g (9 oz) plain flour
15 g (½ oz) yeast
⅛ l (¼ pt) milk
40 g (1¾ oz) sugar
50 g (2 oz) butter
1 small egg
pinch of salt
grated rind of ¼ lemon

Prepare dough as described under Yeast Dough (page 217), and line the tin with it. Cover with the fruit and bake for about 30–35 minutes at 210 °C (400 °F, gas mark 6). Use the following fresh fruit in season:

Plums The area around Bühl near Baden-Baden in Baden-Württemberg is well known for its plum harvest. The blue-violet plums with a juicy yellow flesh are favoured for plum cakes and are also used for the preparation of plum brandy. Wash and stone 500–750 g (1 lb 2 oz–1¾ lb) dark-blue plums. Sprinkle 2 tablespoons breadcrumbs on the cake base. Make quarter incisions in the plums and place them on the base, tightly packed, starting from the outer rim. Each circle of plums should overlap the previous one by about one-third of a plum. Sprinkle with a little sugar after baking and some more just before serving. Plum cake should be eaten fresh and tastes delicious with sweet whipped cream.

Apples Peel, core and slice the apples. Place the slices tightly together along the outside of the tin, gradually moving towards the centre. Sprinkle 1–2 tablespoons of raisins over the apples. Cover the cake with some greaseproof paper before baking. After baking, sprinkle with sugar mixed with a little cinnamon and when cool serve with whipped cream.

Variation: For the cake base use curd cheese pastry (page 249) instead of yeast dough.

'Bee-Sting' Cake *(Bienenstich)*

Prepare a yeast dough as for Fruit Cake with Yeast Dough (page 229) and line the bottom of a 24–28-cm (10–11-in) greased cake tin with it. Leave to rise whilst preparing the following topping:

100 g (4 oz) unsalted butter
100 g (4 oz) flaked almonds
100 g (4 oz) sugar
2 teaspoons vanilla sugar
2–4 tablespoons milk

Heat the butter and stir in the sugar, vanilla sugar, almonds and finally the milk. Do not brown the almonds. Spread on to the dough in the cake tin. Bake at 190 °C (375 °F, gas mark 5) for about 40 minutes. When the cake is cooled, cut into 8 equal portions. Slice each portion horizontally and fill with the following mixture:

60 g (2½ oz) sugar
2 eggs
1 tablespoon plain flour
1 teaspoon vanilla sugar
¼ l (½ pt) milk
60 g (2½ oz) unsalted butter

Stir all the ingredients, apart from the butter, together in a saucepan. Then whisk whilst heating the mixture until it becomes a thick cream. Remove from the heat and stir until cooled down a little and mix in the creamed butter.

Variation: For the cake base use curd cheese pastry (page 249) instead of yeast dough.

Covered Apple Cake *(Gedeckter Apfelkuchen)*

Pastry
400 g (14 oz) plain flour
250 g (9 oz) unsalted butter
1 egg
50 g (2 oz) sugar
4 teaspoons vanilla sugar
1 teaspoon baking powder
3–6 tablespoons wine or milk (adding gradually as required)

Filling
1000 g (2¼ lb) apples
75 g (3 oz) sugar
¼ teaspoon cinnamon
75 g (3 oz) sultanas
50 g (2 oz) chopped almonds
1½ tablespoons rum
grated rind of ¼ lemon
milk
rum-sugar glaze (page 237)

Prepare the pastry as described under Short Pastry (page 216). Use a little more than half the pastry to line the bottom of a spring-wire cake tin (about 24 cm (10 in) diameter) forming a 3-cm (1¼-in) high rim. Prick the bottom of the pastry several times with a fork. Peel, core and slice the apples and sprinkle with the rum. Mix with the sugar, cinnamon, lemon, sultanas and almonds. Cover the pastry with the apples. Roll out the remainder of the pastry; cut to the size of the cake tin and place on top of the apple filling. Brush the top with a little milk and bake at 190 °C (375 °F, gas mark 5) for about 45 minutes. Cover top with a rum-sugar glaze and when cool serve with whipped cream.

Crumble Cake *(Streuselkuchen)*

Prepare a yeast dough as for Fruit Cake with Yeast Dough (page 229) and use to line the bottom of a 24–28-cm (10–11-in) diameter greased cake tin. Leave to rise whilst preparing the following topping:

30 g (1¼ oz) melted unsalted butter
150 g (5 oz) plain flour
100 g (4 oz) unsalted butter
60 g (2½ oz) sugar
2 teaspoons vanilla sugar
¼ teaspoon cinnamon
grated rind of ¼ lemon
30 g (1¼ oz) chopped almonds

Brush the top of the risen dough with the melted butter. Mix the rest of the ingredients until resembling fine breadcrumbs. Spread on top of the dough and bake at 200 °C (400 °F, gas mark 6) for about 30 minutes.

Variation: For the cake base use curd cheese pastry (page 249) instead of yeast dough.

Black Forest Cherry Gateau *(Schwarzwälder Kirschtorte—Baden Württemberg)*

Black Forest Gateau is popular in all areas of Germany and is reputed to taste its best when made with Black Forest morello cherries. In appearance it reminds one of the Black Forest costume hat with red pom-poms. Wherever it is made, the use of the original Black Forest cherry water (Schwarzwälder Kirschwasser) is essential. This is a clear brandy made from the Black Forest cherries.

It is advisable to bake the cake on one day and to fill it the following day.

Prepare a pastry from the following ingredients:

180 g (6¼ oz) plain flour
½ level teaspoon baking powder
100 g (4 oz) unsalted butter
80 g (3¼ oz) sugar
1 egg
pinch of salt
grated rind of ¼ lemon

For preparation, see Short Pastry (page 216). Line the bottom of a 24-cm (10-in) tin; prick with a fork a few times and bake at 200 °C (400 °F, gas mark 6) for about 20–25 minutes. Remove from tin. This serves as the base of the gateau.

To obtain the two chocolate layers, prepare the following:

200 g (7 oz) sugar
2 teaspoons vanilla sugar
6 egg yolks
100 g (4 oz) ground almonds
50 g (2 oz) cocoa
6 egg whites

Beat the egg yolks, gradually adding the sugar and vanilla sugar until creamy. Stir in the almonds, sieved cocoa and finally the beaten egg whites. Pour into a greased and floured 24-cm (10-in) cake tin and bake at 180 °C (350 °F, gas mark 4) for about 30 minutes. Turn out of the tin. When cool, cut into two layers.

Filling

120 g (4½ oz) redcurrant jelly
500–600 g (1 lb 2 oz–1 lb 6 oz) Morello cherries
50 g (2 oz) sugar
½ l (1 pt) whipping cream
1 envelope gelatine
2 tablespoons icing sugar
2 teaspoons vanilla sugar
3–5 tablespoons Black Forest cherry water (Schwarzwälder Kirschwasser)
50 g (2 oz) grated chocolate

Stone and sugar the cherries and bring to the boil with 2 tablespoons water. Remove from the saucepan and drain. Dissolve the gelatine and leave to cool a little. Whip the cream until just starting to stiffen, then add the sugar, vanilla sugar and gelatine. Continue beating until stiff.

Spread the pastry base with the redcurrant jelly and then a layer of cream. Place one layer of the chocolate base on top and sprinkle with the cherry water. Then spread on a thick layer of whipped cream. Top with the cherries and cover with more cream. Place on the second chocolate cake layer. Cover the top and sides of the gateau with cream. Sprinkle with grated chocolate. Decorate with cherries and cream rosettes.

Nut-Cream Gateau *(Nuss-Sahne Torte)*

5 eggs
150 g (5 oz) sugar
3 teaspoons vanilla sugar
90 g (3½ oz) plain flour
70 g (2¾ oz) cornflour
50 g (2 oz) finely ground hazel-nuts
60 g (2½ oz) unsalted butter
3 level teaspoons baking powder

Beat the eggs, sugar and vanilla sugar until light and frothy. Mix the baking powder with the flour and sieve into the egg and sugar mixture. Add the cornflour and the nuts. Stir in the melted butter. Turn the mixture into a well-greased 24-cm (10-in) spring-wire tin and bake for about 40 minutes at 180 °C (350 °F, gas mark 4). Leave to cool. Cut into three layers and fill with the following mixture:

¾ l (1½ pt) whipping cream
50 g (2 oz) finely ground hazel-nuts
4 teaspoons vanilla sugar

Whip the cream and mix half of it with the vanilla sugar and nuts. Spread the mixture between the layers of the cake. Cover the top and sides of the cake with cream. Decorate the cake using a cream syringe. Decorate with whole hazel-nuts.

Rum Gateau (*Rumtorte*)

100 g (4 oz) unsalted butter
100 g (4 oz) sugar
3 teaspoons vanilla sugar
3 egg yolks
1 tablespoon rum
pinch of salt
100 g (4 oz) ground almonds
50 g (2 oz) breadcrumbs
½ level teaspoon baking powder
4 egg whites

Cream the butter and beat in the egg yolks, sugar, vanilla sugar, rum and salt. Mix the almonds and breadcrumbs with the baking powder and add to the creamed mixture. Stir in the beaten egg whites. Turn the mixture into a well-greased 24-cm (10-in) spring-wire tin and bake at 180 °C (350 °F, gas mark 4) for 40 minutes.

Leave to cool.

Filling
200 g (7 oz) unsalted butter
100 g (4 oz) icing sugar
1 egg yolk
2 tablespoons rum
1 teaspoon lemon juice
3–4 tablespoons raspberry or strawberry jam

Cream the butter. Add the sugar, egg yolk, 1 tablespoon rum and lemon juice. Cut the cake into three layers. Sprinkle each layer with rum, spread with jam and then a layer of the prepared buttercream filling. Cover the top and sides of the gateau with the buttercream. Use the rest of the buttercream for decorating, using a cream syringe.

Basic Gateau (*Tortengrundrezept*)

Gateaux are usually prepared for festive occasions in Germany (birthdays, New Year, Easter, weddings, anniversaries) and are decorated appropriately. Heavy fruit cakes with icing such as for English Christmas, birthday or wedding celebrations are not common in Germany.

The following recipe can be used for a buttercream or whipped cream gateau. If using whipped cream, add 2 tablespoons icing sugar and 1 envelope dissolved cooled gelatine whilst whipping the cream when it is just beginning to stiffen.

4 egg yolks
1–2 tablespoons warm water
150 g (5 oz) sugar
3 teaspoons vanilla sugar
pinch of salt
grated rind of 1 lemon
4 egg whites
100 g (4 oz) plain flour
100 g (4 oz) cornflour
2 level teaspoons baking powder
jam and whipped cream or buttercream (see below)

Beat the egg yolks and water until frothy, gradually adding the sugar, vanilla sugar, salt and lemon rind and beating the mixture until creamy. Beat the egg whites and place on top of the egg cream mixture. Mix the flour, cornflour and baking powder and sieve on to the egg whites. Fold in carefully and quickly and fill into a 24-cm (10-in) spring-wire tin lined with greaseproof paper. Bake immediately for about 30 minutes at about 180 °C (350 °F, gas mark 4). Turn out of the tin. Remove the paper and leave to cool. Cut twice horizontally to form three layers. Spread each layer with jam and buttercream or whipped cream. Assemble the layers. Cover the gateau with buttercream or whipped cream and decorate with the help of a cream syringe. In decorating the cake and marking individual portions accurately, it is useful to use a cake and pie divider, with the help of which it is possible to mark the cake top into 14 or 16 pieces.

Buttercream Fillings *(Butterkremrezepte)*

The following recipes may be used to prepare buttercream.

Method 1
250 g (9 oz) unsalted butter
200 g (7 oz) icing sugar
2 egg yolks
3 teaspoons vanilla sugar

Cream the butter, gradually add the icing sugar, yolks and vanilla sugar, beating well all the time.

Variations:

Nut buttercream Add 75 g (3 oz) finely ground nuts.

Chocolate buttercream Add 100 g (4 oz) melted grated chocolate.

Mocha buttercream Add 2 teaspoons instant coffee powder.

Method 2

250 g (9 oz) unsalted butter

custard prepared from ½ l (1 pt) milk, 2 tablespoons custard powder and 100 g (4 oz) sugar

Leave the custard to cool. Cream the butter. Spoon by spoon, stir the custard into the creamy butter. The butter and custard must be at the same temperature, otherwise they do not mix well. If the mixture curdles, put the dish with the buttercream into a bowl with warm water and beat until it becomes smooth. Then leave to cool.

Variations:

Mocha buttercream Add 3 teaspoons instant coffee powder.

Rum buttercream Add 2 tablespoons rum to the custard.

Strawberry buttercream Add 125 g (4½ oz) mashed strawberries to the hot custard.

Chocolate buttercream Melt 100 g (4 oz) grated chocolate in the hot milk.

Sugar Glaze *(Zuckerglasur)*

250 g (9 oz) icing sugar

2–3 tablespoons water, rum, lemon juice or rose water

Stir sugar and liquid together and heat slightly.

Chocolate Glaze (*Schokoladenglasur*)

1.

150 g (5 oz) chocolate
15 g (½ oz) butter

Break the chocolate into small pieces and place with the butter in a dish standing in hot water. Leave to melt and use immediately.

or 2.

250 g (9 oz) icing sugar
30 g (1¼ oz) cocoa
30 g (1¼ oz) coconut fat
3 tablespoons hot milk

Mix the cocoa, icing sugar and hot milk together in a dish standing in hot water. Add the melted coconut fat and use immediately.

Christmas Bread (*Weihnachtsstollen*)

Stollen is the traditional German Christmas cake. It is shaped as a loaf and is best prepared several weeks before Christmas to allow its delicious taste to develop. Stollen in various forms is popular in all parts of Germany. The recipe from Dresden in East Germany is, however, regarded as particularly tasty.

1000 g (2¼ lb) plain flour
100 g (4 oz) yeast
⅜–½ l (¾–1 pt) milk
200 g (7 oz) sugar
3 teaspoons vanilla sugar
400 g (14 oz) unsalted butter
grated rind of 1 lemon
1 level teaspoon salt
½ level teaspoon ground cardamom
½ level teaspoon ground nutmeg
6 drops rum flavouring
6 drops bitter almond flavouring
200 g (7 oz) chopped almonds
300 g (11 oz) raisins
200 g (7 oz) currants
150 g (5 oz) mixed peel

150 g (5 oz) melted butter
50 g (2 oz) icing sugar

Prepare a yeast dough (page 217). Add the spices, flavouring, almonds and dried fruit. Leave the dough in a warm place to rise. Roll out to a rectangle, making it the length of the finished Stollen. Brush with some of the melted butter, then fold the dough over along the longitudinal axis, leaving an uncovered edge of about 5 cm (2 in). Place on a greased flat baking tin and leave to rise. Then bake at 200 °C (400 °F, gas mark 6) for 70–90 minutes. Cover with buttered greaseproof paper if the surface becomes too dark. Remove from the oven and brush with the remainder of the melted butter. Dust with icing sugar. When cold, cut in half, wrap in foil and keep in an airtight tin for at least a fortnight before serving. This makes one large or two to three smaller Stollen.

Variation: Just before folding into a loaf shape, fill with 300 g (11 oz) marzipan.

Cologne Muzen *(Kölner Muzemandeln)*

These small cakes are baked and eaten during the period of carnival and especially on the Monday (Rosenmontag) throughout the Rhineland. Most bakeries and confectioneries sell them, but they are quite simple and quick to prepare at home.

500 g (1 lb 2 oz) plain flour
2 level teaspoons baking powder
200 g (7 oz) unsalted butter
2 eggs
1 tablespoon rum
1 dessertspoon rose water
150 g (5 oz) sugar
3 teaspoons vanilla sugar
grated rind of ½ lemon
50 g (2 oz) finely chopped almonds
castor sugar

Work the ingredients together according to the instructions for Short Pastry (page 216). Roll out to 1 cm (½ in) thickness and cut into rhombus shapes with diagonal lengths 3 and 5 cm (1¼ and 2 in). Fry them in deep fat until golden brown. Place on kitchen paper to drain and roll in castor sugar. Serve with hot coffee or drinking chocolate.

Cream Puffs *(Windbeutel)*

60 g (2½ oz) unsalted butter
¼ l (½ pt) water
200 g (7 oz) plain flour
4–6 eggs
pinch of salt
1 teaspoon baking powder
sweetened whipped cream
icing sugar

Bring the water, butter and salt to the boil. Remove from heat and add all the flour at once. Return to heat beating well until pastry forms a dumpling and leaves the sides of the pan clean. Remove from heat and turn the dumpling into a bowl. Add the eggs, one at a time, beating thoroughly. When the pastry becomes shiny and drops heavily from the spoon, do not add any more eggs. Finally, stir in the baking powder. Place teaspoonfuls of the pastry on to a greased flour-dusted baking tray leaving about 8 cm (3 in) between each. Bake at 210 °C (400 °F, gas mark 6) for about 30 minutes. The baked pastry should be well risen and be hollow inside. Cut open a lid and when cool fill with sweetened whipped cream, and dust with icing sugar.

Variation: Cover lids with chocolate glaze (page 238).

Waffles *(Waffeln)*

Freshly baked waffles are a welcome surprise at coffee and cake time and require very little preparation. In the Bergische Land in North Rhine-Westphalia, they represent—together with bread, cheese, curd cheese, raisin bread and rice—the standard ingredients of the 4 o'clock coffee table. Most German households possess an automatic electric waffle-iron, which prepares waffles of about 18–24 cm (7–10 in) diameter.

125 g (4½ oz) unsalted butter
50 g (2 oz) sugar
3 teaspoons vanilla sugar
3 eggs
250 g (9 oz) plain flour
2 teaspoons baking powder
⅛ l (¼ pt) lukewarm water
1 teaspoon cinnamon

Cream the butter, sugar and vanilla sugar. Add the eggs, one at a time. Mix the flour with the baking powder and sieve into the mixture, gradually stirring in the water as well. Add the cinnamon. Heat and grease a waffle-iron, fill with some of the mixture; close the iron and bake waffles for about 4 minutes. Serve with sugar and cinnamon, jam, fresh or stewed fruit and whipped cream.

Variation: Add 50 g (2 oz) finely ground hazel-nuts and a table-spoon rum to the pastry.

Aachen Printen Biscuits *(Aachener Printen)*

These are rectangular shaped (3 × 8 cm (1¼ × 3¼ in)) spicy biscuits which are particularly popular at Christmas time.

250 g (9 oz) golden syrup
100 g (4 oz) coarse sugar
pinch of salt
50 g (2 oz) orangeade
2 teaspoons aniseed
2 teaspoons cinnamon
1 teaspoon coriander
pinch each of ground cloves, cardamom and nutmeg
500 g (1 lb 2 oz) self-raising flour
sugar or chocolate glaze (pages 237–8)

Mix the syrup and sugar; heat and leave to cool. Add the spices, salt and orangeade. Knead in the flour. If the pastry is very dry, add a little milk to make it kneadable. Leave the pastry for 12–24 hours in a cool place. Roll out the pastry to about 3 mm (⅛ in) thickness and cut out 3 × 8-cm (1¼ × 3¼-in) rectangles. Place on to a greased and floured baking tray and bake at 200 °C (400 °F, gas mark 6) for about 15 minutes. When cool cover with sugar or chocolate glaze.

Spekulatius *(Spekulatius)*

These are the main Christmas biscuits in the Rhineland. South Germans call them Springerle. They are prepared by pressing the spicy butter pastry into carved wooden moulds to produce particular shapes or pictures. The pastry is then turned out and baked. The tradition dates from the old Germanic customs. Nowadays, Spekulatius moulds are mostly mass produced. Centuries ago they were regarded as works of art which were passed on within the family. There are animal motifs as well as religious themes and traditional Christmas scenes.

500 g (1 lb 2 oz) plain flour
2 level teaspoons baking powder
250 g (9 oz) unsalted butter
200 g (7 oz) sugar
3 teaspoons vanilla sugar
2 eggs
1 level teaspoon cinnamon
½ level teaspoon ground cloves
½ level teaspoon ground cardamom

Mix and knead the ingredients according to guidelines for Short Pastry (page 216). Roll out and cut according to the size of the moulds. Press into the floured moulds; turn out and bake on a well-greased baking tray at 180–190 °C (350–375 °F, gas mark 4–5) for about ten minutes. When cool, keep in a tin. If moulds are not available, the dough can be rolled out and cut with different shaped pastry cutters (hearts, stars, animals, Christmas trees, etc.).

Cinnamon Stars *(Zimtsterne)*

Cinnamon stars also belong to the group of Christmas biscuits.

500 g (1 lb 2 oz) icing sugar
7 egg whites
10 g (⅓ oz) cinnamon
500 g (1 lb 2 oz) unblanched ground almonds
175 g (6 oz) very finely chopped candied peel
grated rind of ½ lemon
1 tablespoon rum

Beat the egg whites and gradually add the icing sugar and the cinnamon. Keep back 4–5 tablespoons of the mixture for covering the stars later. Add all the other ingredients to the remainder. Dust a board with icing sugar and roll out the dough to about 6 mm

($\frac{1}{4}$ in) thickness. With a pastry cutter cut out stars and place them on a baking tray lined with buttered greaseproof paper. Add a little rum to the 4–5 tablespoons sugar and egg white mixture and cover the stars with this glaze. Bake at 150 °C (300 °F, gas mark 2) for about 30 minutes.

Peppernuts *(Pfeffernüsse)*

Peppernuts are part of the Christmas biscuit range.

2–3 eggs (depending on size)
250 g (9 oz) icing sugar
grated rind of ½ lemon
1 dessertspoon rum
1 level teaspoon cinnamon
pinch of each of the following ground spices: nutmeg, pepper, cardamom, cloves
60 g (2½ oz) finely chopped candied peel
250 g (9 oz) plain flour
50 g (2 oz) cornflour
1 teaspoon baking powder
sugar glaze (page 237)

Whisk the eggs, gradually adding the sugar, for about 15 minutes until creamy. Stir in the lemon rind, candied peel, spices and rum. Sieve together the flour, cornflour and baking powder and add to the egg cream. Knead well. Roll out to ½–1 cm (¼–½ in) thickness and cut out biscuits of about 3 cm (1¼ in) diameter. Leave for at least 1 hour. Then bake on a greased baking tray at 190 °C (375 °F, gas mark 5) for about 10–15 minutes. Cover with sugar glaze whilst still hot.

Nuremberg Honey Cake *(Nürnberger Lebkuchen)*

The city of Nuremberg is not only known for its toy-making industry but can also look back on a 600-year-long tradition of honey-cake making. Spicy Nuremberg Honey Cakes are particularly popular during Christmas time. They are sold on the Nuremberg Christmas Market and sent to all parts of Germany and even abroad. The art of honey-cake baking flourished in Nuremberg for two reasons: the forests around Nuremberg provided a ready supply of honey and the business men from this city, through their world-wide trade connections, provided the spices from other countries.

2 eggs
200 g (7 oz) icing sugar
3 tablespoons honey
3 teaspoons vanilla sugar
grated rind of ½ lemon
1 level teaspoon cinnamon
pinch of ground cardamom, nutmeg and cloves
½ teaspoon aniseed
75 g (3 oz) finely chopped candied peel
175 g (6 oz) blanched ground almonds
250 g (9 oz) plain flour
1 tablespoon cornflour
1 teaspoon baking powder
rice paper (6–8 cm (2½–3 in) diameter)
sugar or chocolate glaze (pages 237–8)

Whisk the eggs, honey and sugar until thick and creamy. Stir in the spices, peel and almonds. Mix the flour, cornflour and baking powder and sieve into the mixture. Spread the mixture about 1½ cm (½ in) thick on to the paper and bake at 180 °C (350 °F, gas mark 4) for about 15 minutes. Cover with sugar or chocolate glaze. Keep in a tin until the biscuits become soft.

If rice paper is not available, put teaspoonfuls of the mixture on to a buttered biscuit tray and bake at 160 °C (325 °F, gas mark 3) for 15 minutes. Then proceed as above.

Heather Sand *(Heidesand)*

275 g (10 oz) unsalted butter
250 g (9 oz) sugar
3 teaspoons vanilla sugar
2 tablespoons milk
375 g (13 oz) plain flour
1 level teaspoon baking powder

Melt and brown the butter in a saucepan and leave to cool. Later, cream the butter and gradually add the sugar, vanilla sugar and milk. Carry on beating the mixture until it becomes light and frothy. Mix the flour with the baking powder and sieve into the sugar and butter mixture. Knead well and form cylinders or rolls of about 4 cm (1½ in) diameter. Place in the refrigerator for several hours to harden. Cut each roll into ½ cm (¼ in) thick slices and bake on a greased baking tray at 180 °C (350 °F, gas mark 4) for about 20 minutes.

Vanilla Biscuits *(Vanilleplätzchen)*

300 g (11 oz) plain flour
½ teaspoon baking powder
200 g (7 oz) icing sugar
250 g (9 oz) unsalted butter
3 egg yolks
100 g (4 oz) ground almonds
1 teaspoon vanilla flavouring
1 lightly beaten egg white
chopped almonds

Stir the vanilla flavouring into the beaten egg yolks. Then prepare the pastry according to the procedure given for Short Pastry (page 216). Place the pastry in the refrigerator for 1 hour. Then roll out to about 3–4 mm (⅛–¼ in) thickness. Cut out discs or figures with pastry cutters or a small glass. Brush with the egg white. Sprinkle with almonds and bake at 195 °C (375 °F, gas mark 5) for about 10 minutes.

Macaroons *(Makronen)*

3–4 egg whites
250 g (9 oz) finely ground almonds or nuts
250 g (9 oz) icing or castor sugar
3 teaspoons vanilla sugar
1 teaspoon lemon juice
grated rind of ½ lemon
pinch of salt
melted chocolate

Beat the egg whites until stiff. Then gradually add the sugar, vanilla sugar and salt. Stir for 10–15 minutes. Mix in the ground almonds, lemon juice and rind. Line a baking tray with greaseproof paper. Place teaspoonfuls of the mixture on to the paper and bake in the lower part of the oven at 160 °C (325 °F, gas mark 3) for about 20 minutes. When cool, dip the top of each macaroon into melted chocolate and leave to set.

Marble Biscuits *(Marmorplätzchen)*

125 g (4½ oz) unsalted butter
250 g (9 oz) plain flour
100 g (4 oz) sugar
¼ teaspoon baking powder
1 egg
3–4 drops vanilla flavour
2–3 teaspoons cocoa

Work the ingredients, except the cocoa, to a pastry as described for Short Pastry (page 216). Mix half the pastry with the cocoa. Roll out each pastry to 4–5 mm (¼ in) thickness. Put the dark pastry sheet on top of the light one and roll together to form cylinders of about 4 cm (1½ in) diameter. Place in the refrigerator for about 1 hour then cut into slices of about ½ cm (¼ in) thickness and bake at 180 °C (350 °F, gas mark 4) for about 10–15 minutes.

Königsberg Marzipan *(Königsberger Marzipan)*

250 g (9 oz) ground blanched almonds
250 g (9 oz) icing sugar
3 tablespoons rose water
juice from ½ lemon
60 g (2½ oz) icing sugar mixed with enough orange juice to make a smooth glaze
candied fruit for decorating

Pass the almonds through a grinder twice. Mix them with the sugar, rose water and lemon juice. Knead well and place in the refrigerator for 2–3 hours. Knead again and on a surface dusted with icing sugar roll out to about 4 mm (¼ in) thickness. Cut out heart shapes with a pastry cutter. Place them on a buttered baking tray. Mark patterns on the heart surfaces with a pin. The marzipan hearts are then dried rather than baked in the oven at 130 °C (260 °F, gas mark ½–1) for about 10 minutes (leaving the oven door open). Then place them under the grill and slightly brown the tops. Originally, this was achieved by placing them under glowing charcoal. Cover with the glaze and decorate with candied fruit.

Rum Balls *(Rumkugeln)*

60 g (2½ oz) unsalted butter
200 g (7 oz) grated chocolate
2 tablespoons rum
1 tablespoon ground almonds
1 tablespoon finely cut raisins
3–5 tablespoons chocolate grains

Cream the butter and knead with the chocolate and enough rum to obtain a manageable mixture. Add the almonds and raisins. Form small balls of about 2 cm (¾ in) diameter and roll in the chocolate grains.

Salt Sticks and Bretzels *(Salzstangen und Bretzel)*

Salt sticks and bretzels are popular for cocktail parties as they go well with beer or wine. In South Germany, however, salt sticks and bretzels are also a popular daytime snack. Fresh salt sticks and bretzels of 15–20-cm (6–8-in) lengths are sold in the streets.

250 g (9 oz) plain flour
½ teaspoon salt
15 g (½ oz) yeast
approx. 3 tablespoons lukewarm water
1 egg
coarse salt
caraway seeds

Sieve the flour and salt into a warmed bowl. Cream the yeast with the water and add to the flour. Knead to a firm dough adding more water. Leave to rise in a warm place for about 1 hour. Then form sticks and bretzels. For the bretzels, form a 30-cm (12-in) long, 4-mm (⅛–¼-in) diameter cylinder shape first and then fold into the bretzel shape. Place sticks and bretzels on a greased baking tray and leave 30–40 minutes. Brush with beaten egg and sprinkle with salt and caraway seeds. Bake at 220 °C (425 °F, gas mark 7) for 10–12 minutes or until golden brown.

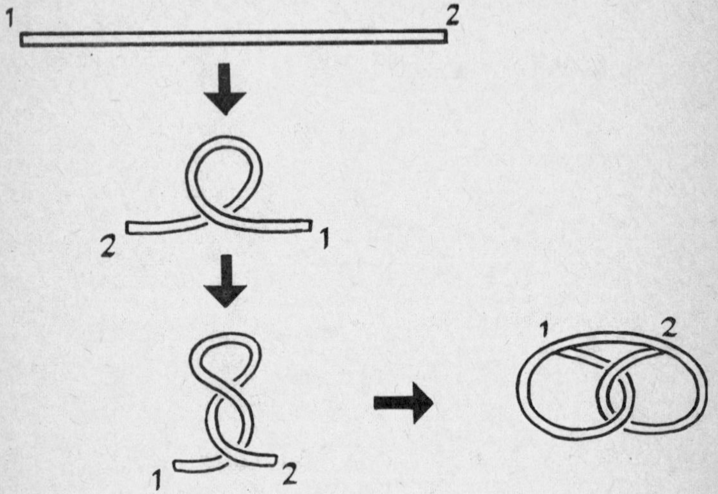

Cheese Biscuits (Käseplätzchen)

100 g (4 oz) plain flour
75 g (3 oz) potato flour or cornflour
¼ teaspoon baking powder
150 g (5 oz) grated cheese
1 small egg
½–1 tablespoon soured cream
100 g (4 oz) butter
1 beaten egg yolk
1 teaspoon caraway seeds
1 teaspoon poppy seeds

Sieve the flour and potato flour into a bowl and mix with the baking powder and cheese. Cut the butter into small pieces and add. Work the ingredients to a breadcrumb-like consistency. Add egg and cream and quickly knead to a dough. Leave in the refrigerator for 30–40 minutes. Then roll out on a floured board to 5 mm (¼ in) thickness. With a glass or pastry cutter, cut out the biscuits. Brush each biscuit with beaten egg yolk and sprinkle with caraway or poppy seeds. Bake at 200 °C (400 °F, gas mark 6), for about 10 minutes or until golden. Serve as accompaniment to wine or beer.

BAKING WITH CURD CHEESE *(Backen mit Quark)*

Curd cheese is notably the basic ingredient for the well-known German cheese cake, but it can also be used for the preparation of pastries. Unless otherwise mentioned, continental-size cake tins (25 cm (10 in) diameter with a 7 cm (2¾ in) rim) should be used.

Curd Cheese Pastry *(Quarkteig)*

150 g (5 oz) curd cheese
6 tablespoons milk
6 tablespoons vegetable oil
80 g (3¼ oz) sugar
pinch of salt
3 teaspoons vanilla sugar
300 g (11 oz) self-raising flour

Mix the curd cheese with the milk, oil, sugar, vanilla sugar and salt. Gradually stir in half the flour. Knead in the rest of the flour.

This pastry serves as a base for fruit cakes and crumble cake.

For Fruit Cake Roll out on a floured board and line 2 continental-size cake tins (28 cm (11 in) diameter). Cover tightly with apple slices, stoned cherries or stoned sectioned plums. Bake at 200 °C (400 °F, gas mark 6) for about 20–30 minutes. Serve with whipped cream.

For Crumble Cake Line the cake tins as for fruit cake. Prepare the crumble from 300 g (11 oz) plain flour, 150 g (5 oz) sugar, 3 teaspoons vanilla sugar, ½ teaspoon cinnamon, 150 g (5 oz) unsalted butter. Spread the crumble on the pastry and bake at 180 °C (350 °F, gas mark 4) for 20–30 minutes.

Traditional Cheese Cake

(Traditioneller Käsekuchen)

There are countless recipes for cheese cakes in Germany and almost every family seems to have its own way of preparing the cake. The traditional German cheese cake is made by using curd cheese as a basic ingredient and baking it in the oven for a certain length of time. The unbaked variations have been introduced recently and are generally regarded as a somewhat inadequate substitute for the real thing.

Some experience is required to produce a good cheese cake. One should not despair if success is not achieved at the first attempt. The following recipe is suitable for a continental type of cake.

Pastry

250 g (9 oz) plain flour
125 g (4½ oz) unsalted butter
80 g (3¼ oz) sugar
1 egg
grated rind of ½ lemon

Filling

750 g (1¾ lb) curd cheese
¼ l (½ pt) single cream
8 egg yolks
8 beaten egg whites
2 tablespoons plain flour
300 g (11 oz) sugar

Prepare the pastry according to the instructions for Short Pastry (page 216). Line the bottom of the cake tin with the pastry, forming a 3 cm (1¼ in) high rim. For the filling, beat the egg yolks and sugar with an electric mixer until creamy. Gradually add curd cheese, cream and flour. Carefully stir in beaten egg white and pour on to the pastry. Bake at 190 °C (375 °F, gas mark 5) for 80–90 minutes. If the cake becomes too dark at the top, cover with greaseproof paper during the last 30 minutes. Take out of the oven; leave in the tin for about 5 minutes. Then turn upside down, still in the tin, on to a grid for 15–20 minutes. This prevents sagging in the centre. Turn out of the tin and leave to cool. Arrange on a cake plate and serve with whipped cream.

Small Curd Cheese Cakes (*Käseküchlein*)

375 g (13 oz) curd cheese
250 g (9 oz) grated boiled potatoes
2 eggs
80 g (3¼ oz) plain flour
pinch of salt
70 g (2¾ oz) raisins
50 g (2 oz) sugar
2 teaspoons vanilla sugar
100 g (4 oz) butter or margarine

If the cheese is very dry, mix in a few tablespoons milk. Add the potatoes and the other ingredients apart from the butter and mix to a manageable dough. With a spoon, place small cakes into the heated butter in a frying pan. Fry on both sides until golden. Serve with stewed fruit and coffee or tea.

Curd Cheese Pasties (*Quarkmaultaschen*)

500 g (1 lb 2 oz) curd cheese
250 g (9 oz) plain flour
75 g (3 oz) butter
1 egg
jam
icing sugar

Mix the curd cheese, flour, butter and egg with a knife. Knead to a dough and roll out on a floured board. Cut into 8–10 cm (3–4 in) squares. Place a teaspoonful jam in the middle of each square. Fold to a triangle, pressing the edges well together and bake at 190 °C (375 °F, gas mark 5) for about 20 minutes until golden. Dust with icing sugar and serve with hot coffee and cream.

Curd Cheese Gateau (*Quarktorte*)

150 g (5 oz) french toast (Zwieback)
50 g (2 oz) sugar
50 g (2 oz) melted unsalted butter
¼ teaspoon cinnamon

Topping
750 g (1¾ lb) curd cheese
¼ l (½ pt) whipped cream
175 g (6 oz) sugar
3 teaspoons vanilla sugar

5 eggs
2 egg yolks
grated rind of 1 lemon
30 g (1¼ oz) plain flour
pinch of salt
2 tablespoons double cream
2 tablespoons single cream

Break the french toast into small pieces; put into a strong polythene bag and crush to crumbs. Keep back 2 tablespoons of crumbs and mix the remainder with the sugar, cinnamon and melted butter. Press on to the bottom of a continental cake tin, making a 2 cm (¾ in) high rim. For the filling mix the curd cheese, flour and whipped cream. Then add lemon rind, sugar, salt, eggs, egg yolks, single and double cream. Pour into the pastry lined tin, sprinkle with rusk crumbs and bake in a pre-heated oven at 225 °C (425 °F, gas mark 7) for 10 minutes. Then turn down heat to 130 °C (260 °F, gas mark ½–1) and finish baking for about 90 minutes until cheese is firm. Leave to cool in the tin.

Curd Cheese and Nut Gateau *(Quark-Nuss Torte)*

100 g (4 oz) unsalted butter
125 g (4½ oz) sugar
4 egg yolks
grated rind of ½ lemon
100 g (4 oz) curd cheese
100 g (4 oz) finely ground nuts
4 beaten egg whites

Filling
200 g (7 oz) apricot jam
50 g (2 oz) grated bitter chocolate

Cream the butter; gradually add sugar, egg yolks and lemon rind. Beat well with an electric mixer. Add curd cheese and ground nuts and finally stir in beaten egg whites.

Fill the mixture into a well-greased and flour-dusted continental cake tin and bake at 175 °C (350 °F, gas mark 4) for 45–50 minutes. When the gateau has cooled, heat the jam and brush over the top. Sprinkle with grated chocolate.

Fluted Ring-Mould Cheese Cake

(Quarknapfkuchen)

This cake is similar to a Gugelhupf (page 218) and the same tin can be used.

125 g (4½ oz) softened unsalted butter
200 g (7 oz) sugar
5 teaspoons vanilla sugar
2 eggs
200 g (7 oz) curd cheese
300 g (11 oz) self-raising flour mixed with 1½ teaspoons baking powder
⅛ l (¼ pt) milk
70 g (2¾ oz) ground hazel-nuts
70 g (2¾ oz) raisins
icing sugar

Beat the butter, sugar and eggs until creamy. Gradually add the curd cheese, flour and milk. Mix in the nuts and raisins. Fill the dough into a well-greased flour-dusted fluted ring mould (Napfkuchenform) and bake at 190 °C (375 °F, gas mark 5) for 1 hour. Turn out of the tin and dust with icing sugar. Serve with whipped cream.

Curd Cheese Cherry Cake ***(Quark-Kirschkuchen)***

Pastry
250 g (9 oz) plain flour
125 g (4½ oz) unsalted butter
80 g (3¼ oz) sugar
1 egg

Filling
750 g (1¾ lb) stoned cherries (preferably sweet-sour type)

Topping
½ l (1 pt) milk
80 g (3¼ oz) semolina
pinch of salt
80 g (3¼ oz) sugar
grated rind of 1 lemon
375 g (13 oz) curd cheese
3 egg yolks
3 beaten egg whites
3 tablespoons sliced almonds

Prepare the pastry as for Traditional Cheese Cake (page 250). Spread the cherries on top. For the topping, bring the milk to the boil and stir in the semolina and salt. Take off the hot plate and leave for 10–15 minutes to cool. Add the beaten egg yolks, lemon rind, sugar and curd cheese. Carefully stir in the beaten egg white. Pour the mixture over the cherries, top with almonds and bake at 190 °C (375 °F, gas mark 5) for 50–60 minutes taking care that the top of the cake does not become too dark.

Apple Cheese Cake *(Apfel-Quarkkuchen)*

125 g (4½ oz) softened unsalted butter
3 egg yolks
250 g (9 oz) sugar
1 tablespoon custard powder
pinch of salt
1000 g (2¼ lb) curd cheese
75 g (3 oz) semolina
1 teaspoon baking powder
3–4 medium-sized peeled and finely sliced apples
3 beaten egg whites

Beat the butter, sugar and egg yolks until creamy. Gradually add the curd cheese, salt, semolina and custard powder mixed with the baking powder. Mix in the apple slices and finally the beaten egg whites. Pour into a well-greased flour-dusted cake tin and bake at 200 °C (400 °F, gas mark 6) for 60 minutes. Turn off the heat but leave in the oven for another 5–10 minutes. When cool serve with whipped cream.

Curd Cheese Gateau with Raisins *(Käsekuchen mit Rosinen)*

Pastry
as for Traditional Cheese Cake (page 250)

Topping
600 g (1 lb 6 oz) curd cheese
100 g (4 oz) softened unsalted butter
100 g (4 oz) sugar
3 teaspoons vanilla sugar
4 egg yolks
4 beaten egg whites
grated rind of 1 lemon
⅛ l (¼ pt) soured cream
50 g (2 oz) plain flour
100 g (4 oz) raisins
1 teaspoon baking powder

Line the cake tin with the pastry, forming a 3 cm (1¼ in) rim. Beat the butter; add the egg yolks, sugar and vanilla sugar and beat until creamy. Stir in the cheese and the rest of the ingredients, adding the beaten egg whites last. Bake at 175 °C (350 °F, gas mark 4) for about 60 minutes, cool and serve with whipped cream.

Curd Cheese Cream Gateau *(Käse-Sahne Torte)*

For this type of cake only the pastry is baked.

Pastry
250 g (9 oz) unsalted butter
125 g (4½ oz) icing sugar
2 teaspoons vanilla sugar
2 egg yolks
375 g (13 oz) plain flour

Sieve the flour into a bowl. Make a well in the centre and place in the yolks, the sugar, vanilla sugar and diced butter. Work all the ingredients together with a knife and finally knead to a dough. Place in the refrigerator for 35–40 minutes. Divide the dough into two and evenly line the bottom of 2 greased baking tins (24 cm (10 in)). Prick with a fork a few times and bake at 210 °C (400 °F, gas mark 6) for about 20 minutes. Turn pastry cases out of the tins and cut one of them into 12 segments immediately. Leave to cool.

Filling
500 g (1 lb 2 oz) curd cheese
4–6 tablespoons milk or more (according to dryness of curd cheese)
200 g (7 oz) icing sugar
grated rind of 1 lemon
2 packets gelatine
4 tablespoons cold water
½ l (1 pt) whipping cream
8 teaspoons vanilla sugar

With an electric mixer beat the curd cheese adding milk, sugar and lemon rind. Mix the gelatine and the cold water and leave for 5–10 minutes. Then stand the dish with the gelatine in a saucepan of hot water and stir until dissolved. Add dissolved gelatine to curd cheese and mix well. Whip the cream with the vanilla sugar and add to the cheese mixture. Line a 5–7 cm (2–2¾ in) high spring-wire tin with greaseproof paper. Place the pastry base at the bottom of the tin and spread the curd cheese mixture on top. Cover with the 12 segments of the second pastry case. Leave to set in the refrigerator for 2–3 hours. When set carefully take out and dust with icing sugar.

Variation 1: Replace the pastry with a sponge mixture.
Variation 2: Mix the fruit from a small tin of mandarin oranges into the curd cheese filling.

BAKING WITH POTATOES
(Gebackenes aus Kartoffeln)

Potato dough is very suitable for the preparation of small cakes, gateaux and loaves. Potato baked products provide popular snacks with tea, coffee, beer and wine. East Germany, Hessen and Westphalia are areas where potato baking is popular.

Potato Pasties ***(Kartoffeltaschen—East Germany)***

500 g (1 lb 2 oz) boiled potatoes (cooled)
1 egg
¼ teaspoon salt
125 g (4½ oz) plain flour
jam, grated apple and nuts; or sweetened cream cheese
icing sugar

Grate the potatoes, add egg, salt and flour. Knead to a dough. Roll out to 5 mm (¼ in) thickness. Cut small squares of about 8–10 cm (3¼–4 in). Put 1 teaspoon jam, grated apple and nuts or sweetened cream cheese on each square. Fold over to a triangle. Press edges firmly together. Brush with milk or egg and bake on a greased tin in a pre-heated oven, 210 °C (400 °F, gas mark 6), for 10–20 minutes. Dust with icing sugar.

Potato Gateau (*Kartoffeltorte*)

375 g (13 oz) grated cooked potatoes
125 g (4½ oz) ground almonds
10 egg yolks
10 egg whites
250 g (9 oz) icing sugar
450 g (1 lb) cooked cherries
whipped cream

Mix the almonds and grated potatoes and gradually add yolks and sugar. Beat until mixture is creamy (use electric mixer). Beat egg whites until stiff. Add to the mixture and carefully stir in (do not use electric mixer). Fill into a greased 24-cm (10-in) continental cake tin lined with greaseproof paper. Bake for about 60 minutes at 190 °C (375 °F, gas mark 5). When cooled top with cooked cherries and whipped cream.

Sweet Potato Pancakes (*'Pickert'—Westphalia*)

In Westphalia 'Pickert' is served at coffee-time in the afternoon. The little cakes are eaten warm spread with fresh unsalted butter. Some Westphalians prefer them with liver sausage or jam.

500 g (1 lb 2 oz) plain flour
½ teaspoon salt
600 g (1 lb 6 oz) potatoes
¼ l (½ pt) lukewarm milk
4 eggs
30 g (1¼ oz) fresh yeast
2 teaspoons sugar
150 g (5 oz) raisins
vegetable oil for frying

Dissolve yeast and sugar in half the milk. Mix in a little flour and leave to rise, covered with a cloth in a warm place. Peel, wash and grate the potatoes and work with the rest of the ingredients and the risen yeast mixture to a dough. Leave to rise for 1½–2 hours. Heat oil in a frying pan and fry small cakes (about 10 cm (4 in) diameter) slowly until cooked on both sides.

Potato Bread
(Kartoffelkuchen—Westerwald and Hessen)

Potato bread tastes best when fresh, sliced and spread with unsalted butter. It is also delicious sliced and fried in butter.

1000 g (2¼ lb) plain flour
50 g (2 oz) fresh yeast
3–4 tablespoons lukewarm milk
1 level teaspoon sugar
6 medium-sized potatoes
1 level teaspoon salt
4 eggs
breadcrumbs

Dissolve the yeast and sugar in the milk. Sieve the flour and salt into a bowl. Make a well and pour in the yeast mixture. Mix with a little flour and leave to rise in a warm place for about 20 minutes. Peel and grate the potatoes and squeeze out some of the liquid. Mix all the ingredients to a dough. Grease two loaf tins and sprinkle with breadcrumbs. Divide the dough between the two tins. Cover and leave to rise in a warm place for about 1 hour. Bake in a pre-heated oven, 200 °C (400 °F, gas mark 6), for 50–60 minutes.

Savoury Potato Pancakes
(Kartoffelpfannkuchen—Rhineland and Berlin)

These small pancakes (about 12 × 8 cm (5 × 3 in)) are called Reibekuchen in the Rhineland and Kartoffelpuffer in Berlin. They are usually served with tinned fruit or stewed apple and hot coffee at lunch-time or for an evening meal.

1000 g (2¼ lb) peeled potatoes
1 large onion
2 eggs
1 level teaspoon salt
¼ level teaspoon ground black pepper
¼ level teaspoon ground nutmeg
50 g (2 oz) plain flour
vegetable oil for frying

Peel, wash and grate the potatoes and onion. Mix in all the other ingredients. Heat 1 tablespoon oil in a frying pan. Place 3 tablespoons of the potato mixture into the hot oil and with a spoon press out into 3 thin pancakes. Fry them on both sides until crisp and golden. Serve hot. The recipe makes about 25–30 pancakes, sufficient for 4 people.

Savoury Potato Pot Cake

(Topfkuchen—Rhineland)

2500 g (5¾ lb) potatoes
2 large onions
3 eggs
250 g (9 oz) diced lean smoked bacon
2–3 tablespoons plain flour
1 level teaspoon salt
½ level teaspoon ground black pepper
¼ level teaspoon ground nutmeg
2–3 tablespoons vegetable oil for baking

Peel, wash and grate potatoes. Peel and grate the onions. Add eggs, bacon, flour, salt, pepper and nutmeg. Mix well all together. Preheat oven at 250 °C (475 °F, gas mark 9). Pour the oil into a wide casserole pan (a cast-iron meat pan for pot-roasting is best). Let the oil get very hot in the oven. Pour the potato mixture into the pan and bake without a lid in the oven for 1½–2 hours until crisp and brown. Serve hot with stewed apple or tinned fruit and hot coffee. Any left-overs can be eaten cold or warmed up in the frying pan.

BREAD

(Brot)

Germans like to start the day with a substantial breakfast containing variety. Apart from filter coffee, boiled egg, jam, cheese and slices of smoked sausage, a choice of bread and fresh bread rolls are laid out on the family breakfast table. As working life begins at 8 o'clock in the morning, work in the bakeries starts early. Rolls (Brötchen or Semmel) for breakfast are only acceptable if baked the same day. Most bakeries offer their customers fresh rolls twice a day. In many areas bakeries still deliver bread rolls to the front door before 7 o'clock. Bread is also an essential part of the evening meal in Germany, when it is eaten with sliced smoked sausage or cheese.

Usually a German housewife keeps three or more kinds of bread in store to present her family with a choice at meal-times. It is not surprising then that there is a selection of two hundred different sorts of bread in Germany. In addition, some 1,200 kinds of small bakers' products (rolls and other non-sweet bakes of less than 250 g (9 oz) in weight) are available throughout the country. The milling and type of flour used in bread preparation, the way of baking the dough, the raising agent and the spices added all influence the final loaf. Whole grains are used as well as whole ground and refined flour. It is, however, not permitted to bleach flour in order to obtain a very white bread. Wheat is the main ingredient with rye supplying about one quarter. There is pure wheat bread, pure rye bread and a mixed wheat and rye bread. The higher the rye content, the darker and more moist is the bread, the heartier the taste and the longer it keeps. The use of rye requires the additional application of sour dough as a raising agent. Germany still has a large number of family bakeries in addition to the growing mass production of bread. One of the traditional ways of baking bread is maintained by producing stone oven bread (Steinofenbrot). In stone built ovens, which look like little huts, a wood fire is lit. This heats the stones. After some hours, the glowing fire is removed and the bread dough is placed in the space where the glow had been. Depending on the kind of wood, the bread crust takes on a very spicy taste. This method of baking is still carried out as a community activity in small villages and farms in the Rhineland. The crust and shape of a loaf also influences the taste. If loaves are baked 'free sitting' in the oven they produce a crisp crust all around. Setting them tightly side by side or baking them in a tin leaves the sides soft. Whole grain loaves which need a long baking time are cooked in steam to keep them moist.

Caraway seeds, linseed, aniseed, fennel seed, poppy seed, salt and onions are added to the dough or sprinkled on the crust to give an individual taste. In North Germany the outside of the bread is sometimes flamed before baking (Gersteln). This is supposed to seal in the flavour.

The original round shape of a loaf is still predominant in South Germany, whilst in the North the oblong shape prevails. On the whole Germans prefer a hearty tasting, spicy, darker bread to the loaf baked with white flour.

'Ready mix' packets for baking home-made bread make the preparation of genuine German bread very easy. All that is required, even for the preparation of sour-dough bread, is to add water to the ready mixture. These packets are also imported to the United Kingdom. The following recipes, however, give some guidance for do-it-yourself from the basic ingredients.

Sour Dough *(Sauerteig)*

This recipe is for the preparation of a sour-dough starter which is required when rye flour is used.

¼ l (½ pt) warm water
200 g (7 oz) plain wheat flour
2 teaspoons sugar
1 tablespoon dried yeast

Mix the ingredients and leave to ferment in an open bowl for 5 days. Stir daily. The starter is then ready for use. For further use it can be kept covered in the refrigerator or alternatively 40 g (1¾ oz) of the uncooked sour-dough bread mixture can be kept for the next loaf.

Rye Bread *(Roggenbrot)*

1600 g (3 lb 10 oz) wholemeal rye flour
10 tablespoons sour-dough starter (see above)
1 l (2 pt) lukewarm water
⅛ l (¼ pt) oil
30 g (1¼ oz) salt
15 g (½ oz) fresh yeast
1 teaspoon sugar
15 g (½ oz) caraway seeds

1st day, late afternoon: Mix 720 g (1 lb 10 oz) flour with the sour-dough starter and $\frac{7}{8}$ l (1$\frac{3}{4}$ pt) water. Leave overnight in an open bowl in a warm room.

2nd day, in the morning: Dissolve yeast and sugar in 4 tablespoons lukewarm water. Leave to rise for 30 minutes. Mix the rest of the flour with the salt. Add risen yeast, flour, caraway seeds and oil to the started dough. Beat well until dough comes away from bowl. Knead for 10 minutes. Add a little more flour if dough is too wet. Cover with a cloth and leave to rise in a warm place for 3–4 hours. Form into loaves and put into greased bread tins. Leave covered with a cloth in a warm place for 2–4 hours. Place in pre-heated oven, 220 °C (425 °F, gas mark 7), for 20 minutes. Brush with cold water. Reduce heat to 190 °C (375 °F, gas mark 5) and bake for 60 minutes. Brush with water again. Return to the oven for another 5 minutes.

Mixed Bread *(Mischbrot)*

375 g (13 oz) rye flour
375 g (13 oz) wheat flour
2–3 tablespoons sour-dough starter (page 261)
10–15 g ($\frac{1}{4}$–$\frac{1}{2}$ oz) fresh yeast
1 teaspoon sugar
15 g ($\frac{1}{2}$ oz) salt
15 g ($\frac{1}{2}$ oz) caraway seeds
lukewarm water or buttermilk

1st day, at night: Mix half the flour and half the sour dough with enough water to obtain a thick paste. Leave overnight.

2nd day, in the morning: Dissolve the yeast and sugar in 4 tablespoons lukewarm water; leave to rise for about 30 minutes. Mix the rest of the flour with the salt and caraway seeds. Add risen yeast and the flour mixture to the started dough. Add enough water to make a firm, not too dry dough. Knead well for 10 minutes. Cover with a cloth and leave to rise in a warm place for 3–4 hours. Knead and place in an oiled bread tin. Leave to rise for 2–4 hours. Bake as for rye bread (see previous recipe).

BREAD ROLLS *(Brötchen)*

Bread rolls are produced in many shapes, shades and combinations. The names are manifold according to ingredients and areas: Semmel and Weck in South Germany; Schrippe in Berlin; Rundstück in Hamburg; Röggelchen in the Rhineland. Bread rolls with slices of smoked sausage, smoked ham or cheese are a popular snack with wine and beer.

Wheat Bread Rolls *(Weizenbrötchen)*

500 g (1 lb 2 oz) plain wheat flour
20 g (¾ oz) fresh yeast
½ level teaspoon salt
¼ l (½ pt) lukewarm milk
50 g (2 oz) unsalted butter

Dissolve the yeast in the milk and mix immediately with all the other ingredients. Knead in a bowl for 10 minutes and leave to rise for 2–3 hours. Knead again, form rolls and leave to rise once more. Brush with water or milk and bake at 180 °C (350 °F, gas mark 4) for about 15–20 minutes until golden.

Variations: (1) Sprinkle with caraway seeds or poppy seeds before baking.

(2) Work fried onions and fried diced smoked bacon into the dough.

Rye Bread Rolls *(Roggenbrötchen—Rhineland and Berlin)*

400 g (14 oz) rye flour
200 g (7 oz) wheat flour
30 g (1¼ oz) yeast
1 teaspoon salt
⅜ l (¾ pt) lukewarm water

Prepare in the same way as wheat rolls (above). Rye rolls taste particularly good with cheese, accompanied by a beer.

Whole Grain Bread—Pumpernickel

(Vollkornbrot—Pumpernickel—Westphalia and Osnabrück)

Whilst the Westphalians claim the introduction of this very tasty bread, the inhabitants of the North German town Osnabrück insist that the recipe was created there during a famine around the year 1400. The argument about the origin of pumpernickel has therefore not been settled; the existence of the Pumpernickel Tower in Osnabrück, which it is claimed once housed the oven to bake the 'bonum paniculum' is not accepted by the Westphalians as proof that pumpernickel is not a Westphalian speciality. Another theory has it that the name given to the bread was due to its flatulent effect on the eater.

It is not an easy undertaking to home produce pumpernickel. The whole rye grains are used for the preparation of this slightly sweet tasting, very dark bread. It is baked with steam at low temperatures for 16–24 hours. The following recipe is only an attempt to produce the original.

200 g (7 oz) whole wheat grains (coarsely cracked)
200 g (7 oz) whole rye grains (coarsely cracked)
200 g (7 oz) wholemeal rye flour
1–2 teaspoons salt
2 tablespoons vegetable oil
2 tablespoons honey or molasses
⅜ l (¾ pt) boiling water
2 tablespoons sour-dough starter (page 261)

First day, in the morning: Pour the boiling water over the wheat and rye grains and leave to soak in a bowl.

First day, at night: Add rest of ingredients to the grains and water and leave overnight.

Second day: Place the dough in a greased tin. Cover with baking foil and bake at 95 °C (200 °F, gas mark ¼) on a low shelf for 4–5 hours. Put a dish filled with water at the bottom of the oven. Wrap the baked loaf in a moist cloth and keep in the refrigerator for a few days. Serve sliced and spread with unsalted butter with a slice of smoked ham or cheese.

Nuremberg 'Hutzelbread'

(Nürnberger Hutzelbrot—Bavaria)

This is a fruit bread which is prepared and eaten during Christmas time. Hutzelbrot is one of the traditional baked wares offered on the Nuremberg Christmas Market, a 300-year-old custom taking place during the four weeks before Christmas. Hutzel (dried fruit) is the main ingredient.

250 g (9 oz) dried pears
250 g (9 oz) dried prunes
60 g (2½ oz) chopped dried figs
30 g (1¼ oz) chopped dried dates
50 g (2 oz) raisins
50 g (2 oz) sultanas
60 g (2½ oz) chopped almonds
60 g (2½ oz) chopped nuts
50 g (2 oz) candied lemon and orange peel
grated rind of ½ lemon
pinch of salt, ground cloves, aniseed, cardamom
1 teaspoon cinnamon
50 g (2 oz) sugar
30 g (1¼ oz) icing sugar
2 teaspoons vanilla sugar
375 g (13 oz) plain flour
30 g (1¼ oz) yeast
½ l (1 pt) water
1–2 tablespoons Black Forest Kirschwasser or brandy

For decoration
whole peeled almonds

Soak the pears and prunes overnight. Simmer for 15–20 minutes over low heat the next day. Drain and leave to cool. Stone the prunes; chop the prunes and pears. Keep the juice from simmering the fruits. Dissolve the yeast with 1 teaspoon sugar in ⅛ l (¼ pt) of the lukewarm fruit juice. Add 1 dessertspoon flour and leave to rise in a warm place for about 30 minutes. Sieve flour into a warmed bowl. Add the risen yeast mixture to the flour. Mix in all the other ingredients and enough fruit juice to make a firm but easily kneadable dough (about ⅛ l (¼ pt)). Knead well for 10 minutes. Cover with a cloth and leave in a warm place to rise. Knead again; form small loaves and leave to rise on a greased, flour-dusted tin. Decorate with almonds, brush with fruit juice and bake at 210 °C (400 °F, gas mark 6) for 20–60 minutes (according to size). Take out of the oven and brush with fruit juice again.

Preserves

(*Eingemachtes*)

Rum Pot	Rumtopf
Sweet-Sour Plums	Süss-Saure Pflaumen
Sweet-Sour Grapes	Süss-Saure Trauben
Pears in Vinegar	Essigbirnen
Sweet-Sour Gherkins	Süss-Saure Gurken
Pickled Beetroot	Eingelegte Rote Beete
Sauerkraut	Sauerkraut

In spite of modern methods of preserving fruit and vegetables by freezing, the old-fashioned ways of preserving with salt, vinegar and alcohol are still used where the distinct taste of the end product is popular. In the Rhineland, with its numerous orchards, apples and pears are still processed into apple syrup (Apfelkraut) and pear syrup (Birnenkraut) by simmering the fruit in large containers for days. The fruit syrup is then used in sandwiches.

Rum Pot *(Rumtopf)*

This is a delicious—although rather expensive—way to catch the taste of summer and enjoy it throughout cold winter nights. For this preparation, fruit as it ripens from early summer to late autumn, is arranged in layers in a large cylindrical earthenware dish and covered with rum (around 60 per cent proof is ideal). The fruit must be sweet and ripe, but not mushy. Stalks and stones are removed; peaches and pears are peeled. The fruit to start the rum pot are strawberries, followed by cherries, peaches, apricots, plums, pears, etc. Avoid apples, blackberries and blackcurrants as they are too dry in taste.

An earthenware pot of about 30 cm (12 in) height and 18–20 cm (7–8 in) diameter is usually used, but smaller containers are possible. Wash and dry the fruit, with pears and plums and other larger fruit being cut into smaller pieces. It is important to dry the fruit thoroughly with kitchen paper. Mix with sugar—500 g (1 lb 2 oz) sugar for 500 g (1 lb 2 oz) fruit—and leave for 1 hour. Then place in the earthenware dish. Pour over enough rum so that all the fruit is covered. Weight with a plate or saucer to keep the fruit down. Cover the pot with cling film and keep in a cool place, preferably a cellar. After 3–4 weeks the rum pot is ready for the next layer of fruit. Wash, dry and sugar fruit again. Add to the fruit already in the dish and pour in enough rum to cover the fruit. The fruit soon starts to produce plenty of juice so that less rum than anticipated is required. Continue throughout the summer, adding layers of fruit. After adding fruit, and in between, stir fruit with a silver spoon. The rum pot is ready for eating at Christmas time.

Serving suggestions:

1. Serve in sundae dishes or glasses topped with whipped cream. (Beware of large portions!)
2. Serve with ice cream.
3. Serve with vanilla or chocolate flummery (page 192) or as a trifle base.
4. Serve with champagne in a shallow champagne bowl.

Sweet-Sour Plums (*Süss-Saure Pflaumen*)

1500 g (3½ lb) plums (the early smaller dark-purple type)
750 g (1¾ lb) sugar
¾ l (1½ pt) wine vinegar
1 piece of cinnamon bark
4 cloves
grated rind of ½ lemon

Wash and dry the plums with kitchen paper. Prick each fruit a few times with a needle. Place the plums in a porcelain, glass or earthenware dish. Bring the vinegar, sugar, rind and spices to the boil. Leave to cool a little and pour warm over the plums. Cover the dish with cling film or cellophane paper. After three days drain the fruit and put into jars. Bring the drained liquid to the boil and simmer for 5–10 minutes. Pour hot over the plums. Cover jars immediately with a lid or cellophane paper. After 4–6 weeks, the sweet-sour plums are ready for serving. They go well with beef, fried sausage and cold meat.

Sweet-Sour Grapes (*Süss-Saure Trauben—Rhineland*)

500 g (1 lb 2 oz) blue grapes
175 g (6 oz) sugar
⅜ l (¾ pt) wine vinegar
1 piece of cinnamon bark
2 cloves

Wash the grapes; pull off the stalks and dry with kitchen paper. Put into glass jars or earthenware dishes. Bring the vinegar, sugar and spices to the boil and simmer for 3–5 minutes. Leave to cool a little and pour lukewarm over the grapes. Pour off liquid after three days. Bring to the boil and pour hot over the grapes. Cover the jars immediately with cellophane. Serve with flummeries or use in fruit salads.

Pears in Vinegar (Essigbirnen)

750 g (1¾ lb) juicy pears
250 g (9 oz) sugar
⅛ l (¼ pt) water
⅛ l (¼ pt) wine vinegar
1 piece of cinnamon bark
3 cloves
grated rind of ¼ lemon

Peel, halve and core the pears. Bring the liquid, sugar, lemon rind and spices to the boil. Add the pears and bring to the boil again. Remove the pears and fill into glass jars. Simmer liquid for 5–10 minutes and pour over the pears. After three days, drain off the liquid; bring to the boil. Simmer for 5 minutes, pour back into glass jars and cover immediately.

Sweet-Sour Gherkins (Süss-Saure Gurken)

Gherkins and cucumbers, up to a size of 10 cm (4 in), can be preserved this way. Glass jars or large earthenware jars can be used as containers.

2500 g (5¾ lb) gherkins or small cucumbers
250 g (9 oz) small pickling onions
8 g (¼ oz) peppercorns
5 bay-leaves
5 sprigs of fresh dill or 3 teaspoons dried dill herb
2 teaspoons dill seeds
10 g (¼ oz) mustard seeds
1 l (2 pt) wine vinegar
1 l (2 pt) water
250 g (9 oz) sugar

Wash the gherkins and cover with cold salt water (200 g (7 oz) salt in 2½ l (4½ pt) water). Leave for 24 hours. Then rinse and brush the gherkins carefully and dry with kitchen paper. Put layers of gherkins into container, spreading each layer with onion, spices and herbs. Bring vinegar, water and sugar to the boil and pour hot over the gherkins. The gherkins must be covered with the liquid. Cover the container immediately with cellophane. Leave for 4 weeks before eating. Serve with salads and open sandwiches or use for beef olives.

Pickled Beetroot *(Eingelegte Rote Beete)*

cooked beetroot
onion rings
peppercorns
caraway seeds
dill seeds
fresh or dried dill leaves
bay-leaves
mustard seeds

Liquid
Use ½ l (1 pt) wine vinegar with ½ l (1 pt) water and 125 g (4½ oz) sugar

Peel and slice the beetroot. Put a layer of beetroot slices into an earthenware jar and spread with a few onion rings, 2 or 3 peppercorns, ¼ teaspoon of the spices and herbs and ½ bay-leaf. Put on another 3–4-cm (1–1½-in) thick layer of sliced beetroot and spices. Repeat until all the beetroot is used. Now prepare enough liquid to just cover the beetroot by bringing vinegar, water and sugar to the boil. Pour hot over the beetroot. Cover jar immediately with cellophane and keep in a cool place. The beetroot is ready for eating after about 4 weeks. Serve with salads, open sandwiches and cold meat.

Sauerkraut *(Sauerkraut)*

Sauerkraut is a vegetable preparation popular in all parts of Germany. It used to be a cheap way of preserving white cabbage. Berliners seem to be particularly fond of sour and salted food. This might have its origin in the salt monopoly of Frederick the Great. He forced his subjects to purchase more salt than they needed. In this way, preparations such as salted cucumbers, cured meat and Sauerkraut were encouraged. In raw condition (page 163) sauerkraut is rich in vitamin C, vitamin B, iron and calcium; low in calories and therefore very suitable to be included in slimming diets. In Germany it is sold in butchers' shops or grocers where it is offered by the pound from big barrels or in smaller tins. Most delicatessen shops and larger food stores in England stock Sauerkraut. Many German households still make their own according to the following recipe:

5000 g (11¼ lb) white cabbage
100 g (4 oz) salt
500 g (1 lb 2 oz) peeled, cored and finely sliced apples
1–2 tablespoons juniper berries
⅛ l (¼ pt) dry/sour Mosel wine

Cut the white cabbages in halves; remove the outer leaves and inner stalk. Finely shred the cabbage. Germans use a specially manufactured Sauerkraut shredder but a sharp long knife is just as useful. Put one layer of shredded cabbage into a deep earthenware pot. Sprinkle with salt. Then stamp the cabbage with a wooden stamper until juice forms and stands up to the level of the cabbage layer. Place a few juniper berries and apple slices on the top. Cover this with another layer of shredded cabbage, salt and a tablespoon of wine. Continue stamping until the juice rises. Carry on layer by layer until all the cabbage, salt, wine, juniper berries and apples are used. This is quite a tiring job and is best done as a joint family effort. After the last layer the juice level should be above the cabbage.

Place a clean cotton cloth directly on the cabbage and on the cloth a board or plate to approximately the shape and size of the pot. Weight with a clean, heavy, smooth stone (not brick!). Spread a cloth over the opening of the dish, secure with an elastic band and keep at about 20 °C (68 °F) for 6 weeks. During that time the cabbage will ferment. Every fortnight remove the scum (a velvety looking skin) from the top, wash the cloth and clean the plate and stone. If the liquid sinks below the top of the cabbage, add cold brine made by boiling ½ l (1 pt) water and 15 g (½ oz) salt.

Drinks

(*Getränke*)

Coffee	**Kaffee**
Pharisee Coffee	Pharisäer Kaffee
Iced Coffee	Eiskaffee
Prince's Coffee	Prinzen Kaffee
Milk	**Milch**
Milk Punch	Milchpunsch
Cocoa	Kakao
Prince's Cocoa	Prinzen Kakao
Iced Chocolate	Eisschokolade
Fruit Milk	Früchtemilch
Tea	**Tee**
East Fresian Tea	Ostfriesischer Tee
Iced Tea	Eistee
Tea Punch	Teepunsch
Soft Drinks	**Alkoholfreie Getränke**
Strawberry Mix	Erdbeermischgetränk
Lemonade	Limonade
Wine and Water	Schorle

Beer	**Bier**
Altbier Punch	Altbierbowle
Hot Beer	Heisses Bier
Warm Beer	Warmbier
Beer and Champagne	Bier und Sekt
Wine	**Wein**
Strawberry or Peach Bowle	Erdbeer- oder Pfirsichbowle
Orange Bowle	Apfelsinenbowle
Fire-tongs Punch	Feuerzangenbowle
Cold Duck	Kalte Ente
Mulled Wine	Glühwein
Spirits	**Spirituosen**
Grog	Grog
Bear's Liqueur	Bärenschnaps
Egg Punch	Eierpunsch
Egg Liqueur	Eierlikör

Drinking habits in Germany vary considerably from those of the United Kingdom. One would expect that in a major wine-growing country there would be a large consumption of wine, and in fact the statistics show the annual consumption of wine in Germany to be in excess of 20 litres per head of population. Many different types of liqueur are also produced and drunk in Germany.

The relative importance of tea, coffee and beer represents the most significant difference in drinking habits, since in Germany very little tea is drunk. Coffee is the standard breakfast and afternoon drink, and in other circumstances where tea is drunk in the United Kingdom, such as with a light evening meal or snack, this would be replaced in Germany by beer. According to the statistics beer consumption in Germany is roughly twice that of milk.

The collection of drink recipes in this chapter is intended to give assistance in selecting the appropriate drink for the occasion and to indicate the variety to choose from.

COFFEE

(Kaffee)

The most popular form of coffee drunk in Germany is the filtered variety. There are many coffee shops throughout the country selling freshly roasted beans for home consumption, and the cafés and Konditoreien cater for the German custom of late afternoon coffee and cake. The North German city of Bremen is regarded as a paradise for coffee drinkers on account of its many suppliers of coffee.

For the production of filter coffee the beans are finely ground and placed in a filter bag in a funnel on top of the pre-heated coffee pot. Boiling water is poured on to the coffee and passes into the pot which is then kept warm on a réchaud or in a bowl of hot water.

Coffee is always served with fresh single cream or evaporated milk since fresh milk is thought to dilute the coffee and remove some of its pleasant aroma and colour. Mocha is popular as a drink after dinner served in small cups and is made as above only twice as strong.

Pharisee Coffee

(Pharisäer Kaffee)

In the North German state of Schleswig-Holstein, the popularity of rum has influenced the way coffee is taken. The rum-enriched coffee, however, is hidden under a layer of whipped cream, so justifying its name.

Place 1 teaspoon sugar into a cup. Three-quarters fill the cup with hot filter coffee. Add 1 tablespoon rum and top with whipped cream.

Iced Coffee

(Eiskaffee)

During summer time all German cafés offer this drink which is very refreshing on a hot day. It is usually served in deep conical glasses.

Make a pot of strong, slightly sweetened filter coffee. Leave to cool; add single cream and place in the refrigerator for several hours until ice cold. Place one scoop of vanilla ice cream into a glass. Fill up with the ice-cold coffee; top with sweetened whipped cream and serve with a drinking straw, a long-handled coffee spoon and an ice wafer.

Prince's Coffee *(Prinzen Kaffee)*

3 cups strong coffee
4 egg yolks
4 dessertspoons brandy
4 tablespoons fresh single cream
2 dessertspoons honey

Pre-warm the cups with hot water and dry them. Combine the egg yolks, honey and brandy and whisk until frothy. Divide the froth between four cups. Add the cream and the very hot coffee. Serve immediately.

MILK *(Milch)*

Milk Punch *(Milchpunsch)*

¼ l (½ pt) milk
¼ l (½ pt) single cream
¼ l (½ pt) rum
½ vanilla pod
40 g (1¾ oz) sugar or 1 tablespoon honey
1 egg yolk
pinch of nutmeg

Heat milk, cream, sugar and vanilla pod. Then remove from the heat. Mix the yolk with the rum and stir into the cooled liquid. Reheat over low heat whisking all the time. Sprinkle with a little grated nutmeg and serve immediately.

Cocoa *(Kakao)*

½ l (1 pt) milk
3 cm (1¼ in) of a vanilla pod
20 g (¾ oz) cocoa
1–2 tablespoons cold water
25 g (1 oz) sugar
whipped cream

Mix the cocoa, sugar and cold water to a smooth paste. Bring the milk with the vanilla pod to the boil; add the cocoa mixture and whisk until boiling. Remove from the heat. Take out the vanilla pod. Pour into cups and serve topped with a tablespoon of whipped cream.

Prince's Cocoa *(Prinzen Kakao)*

Prepare in the same way as Prince's Coffee (page 276) using cocoa instead of coffee.

Iced Chocolate *(Eisschokolade)*

Prepare cocoa (see recipe above); leave to cool and keep in the refrigerator for at least 2 hours. Into a glass place one scoop of vanilla or chocolate ice cream. Fill the glass with the cold cocoa and serve with whipped cream and grated chocolate.

This is a refreshing drink welcomed by children on a hot summer's day.

Fruit Milk *(Früchtemilch)*

½ l (1 pt) ice cold milk
¼ l (½ pt) fruit purée (strawberries, raspberries, bananas, blackberries)
2 tablespoons icing sugar
grated rind of ¼ lemon

Mix the ingredients with a whisk or in the liquidizer. Serve ice cold with drinking straws.

TEA *(Tee)*

The level of consumption of tea in Germany is quite low and then during the winter months often reinforced with a spirit. In addition to the normal black tea (schwarzer Tee), there is available a choice of herb teas such as peppermint, rosehip or mallow. Black tea is normally served with fresh lemon juice, rum and sugar and is chiefly popular in the north of the country. It is said that more black tea is consumed in Ostfriesland—a northern coastal district—than in the rest of Germany, the habit originating from the discovery on the shore of a box of tea from a sunken English ship.

East Fresian Tea *(Ostfriesischer Tee)*

Put tea leaves—one teaspoon per cup and one for the pot—into a pre-warmed teapot. Pour over boiling water and leave for 5 minutes. Stir and strain into a second pre-warmed teapot. Serve immediately in cups in the following way: Place a piece of candy sugar (rock sugar) into a tea cup. Pour over the tea which will immediately cause a crackling sound. Add fresh single cream (*not* milk, as this would weaken the tea). Do not stir the tea but gradually proceed through the cream with the bitter tea to the sweet tea at the bottom of the cup. It is the Ostfriesian custom to have three cups and to keep the teapot on a réchaud.

Iced Tea *(Eistee)*

Prepare a strong tea and leave to cool. Place 2–3 ice cubes in a high tea-glass. Add 1 teaspoon icing sugar, ½ teaspoon lemon juice, 1 dessertspoon brandy and 1 dessertspoon orange liqueur. Fill the glass with the cold tea. Serve with a slice of orange.

Tea Punch *(Teepunsch)*

1½ l (3 pt) wine
1 l (2 pt) strong tea
300 g (11 oz) sugar
¼ l (½ pt) rum
juice from 2 lemons and 2 oranges
4 cloves
2 pieces of cinnamon bark
1 piece of washed orange peel
1 piece of washed lemon peel
1 tablespoon raisins
1 tablespoon pitted dates

Prepare the tea. In a saucepan heat the wine, sugar, raisins, dates, fruit juice, peel and spices. Leave covered over low heat for 10 minutes and strain. Then add the rum and tea. Serve hot in punch- or tea-glasses.

SOFT DRINKS *(Alkoholfreie Getränke)*

It is not common practice to drink tap water with a meal in Germany. Apart from beer and wine, fruit juices such as apple juice, grape juice or blackcurrant juice, are taken with a meal. If water is required, either on its own or to dilute fruit juice or wine, one of the many natural mineral waters would be served. Germany has a great many hot and cold mineral springs, such as Apollinaris, Sinziger, Emser, Selters and Tönnissteiner. A number of spring waters are bottled and more of the natural carbonic acid gas, which is already present in the water, is added to make it effervesce. These naturally carbonated beverages are very popular in Germany as they are refreshing and also recommended as an aid to digestion. Hotels, restaurants and cafés offer them and most private households keep a few bottles in stock. These mineral waters are also exported.

Strawberry Mix *(Erdbeermischgetränk)*

125 g (4½ oz) strawberries
1–2 tablespoons castor sugar
1 glass natural mineral water

Wash and sugar the strawberries and leave for 30 minutes. Pass through a liquidizer. Pour strawberry purée into a glass and fill with mineral water.

Lemonade *(Limonade)*

Mix the juice of a lemon, or orange, or a tablespoonful of fruit syrup (raspberry, currant, grape or others) with one glass of mineral water.

Wine and Water *(Schorle)*

To half a glass of 'new wine', cider or wine, add half a glass of mineral water.

BEER *(Bier)*

Over two thousand varieties of beer are brewed in Germany. South Germans like a 'quart from the barrel' (Mass vom Fass). North Germans brew a fairly strong beer which they drink with Schnaps or Korn, a strong clear spirit. One Schnaps precedes each glass of beer to 'warm the stomach'. The weakest beer is Malt beer (Malzbier) which is dark and sweet with a very low alcohol content. The Berlin White Beer (Berliner Weisse) is also low in alcohol content. It tastes slightly sour and is usually mixed with a dash of raspberry syrup (Weisse mit Schuss). People in Berlin also like to drink beer with Schnaps which is known there as Molle mit Strippe.

The South German town of Bamberg produces Smoked beer (Rauchbier) for which the malt is smoked beforehand. It is said to go particularly well with salt bretzels and roast sausage.

Export and Bock have the highest alcohol content. The first Bock was brewed in the thirteenth century in the north German village of Einbeck in Saxony to celebrate the arrival of spring. The name Einbeck became Beck and then Bock.

Altbier is the dark beer from the Westphalian city of Münster. In recent years beer with a reduced carbohydrate content has come on to the market. It is intended for people suffering from diabetes and slimmers on a low calorie diet.

The list of beers could be continued with names such as Kölsch (from Cologne), Münchner (from Munich), Dortmunder Union (from Dortmund) or Bitburger. But a description of all different kinds could never do justice, since it is said that the same recipe tastes different when prepared in different areas. The type of water used determines the taste of a beer.

Altbier Punch *(Altbierbowle)*

The recipe is for use with the original Altbier from the old university city of Münster, but English brown ale could also be used.

500–600 g (1 lb 2 oz–1 lb 6 oz) strawberries, apricots and peaches
75 g (3 oz) sugar
2½–3 l (4½–5½ pt) beer

Wash, dry and sugar the fruit. Put into a glass or earthenware punch dish. After 30 minutes add one litre of beer. Stir, cover and leave in a cool place for 3–4 hours. Just before serving add the rest of the beer.

Hot Beer *(Heisses Bier)*

1 l (2 pt) beer
75 g (3 oz) sugar
juice of 1 lemon
grated rind of ½ lemon
1 vanilla pod
1 piece of cinnamon bark

Heat the beer with the sugar and lemon juice (do not boil!). Remove from the hot plate. Add the rest of the ingredients and leave for 5–10 minutes. Take out the vanilla pod and cinnamon bark. Re-heat if necessary and serve in heatproof glasses or tea-glasses.

Warm Beer *(Warmbier—East Germany)*

½ l (1 pt) beer
½ l (1 pt) milk
50 g (2 oz) sugar
2 egg yolks
1 dessertspoon cornflour
grated rind of ½ lemon
pinch of cinnamon
1 tablespoon rum

Heat the beer with the sugar, lemon rind and cinnamon and remove from heat. Mix the cornflour with 4 tablespoons cold milk; whisk in the egg yolks. Bring the rest of the milk to the boil. Remove from the hot plate and stir in the egg mixture. Return to heat and bring to the boil, whisking continuously. Then remove from heat and gradually whisk in the beer and rum. Serve hot in heatproof glasses as an accompanying drink with open sandwiches.

Beer and Champagne *(Bier und Sekt)*

Fill a beer glass half with beer and top with champagne.

WINE *(Wein)*

Germany is the most northerly of the major wine-growing countries. Cultivation was started by the Romans who planted the first vines along the Rhine valley 2,000 years ago. From there wine growing spread into nearby areas and today there are eleven wine-growing regions in Germany (see map).

Good climatic conditions and favourable soil are important in the growing of wine. Most German wine regions are along the Rhine and its side rivers. The sunny south-west-facing banks in these sheltered valleys provide the warmth and humidity which is necessary for the growth of the vine. Most of the soil in the Rhineland Palatinate contains volcanic sand and slate which store the warmth of the sun. The vineyards along these river banks are arranged in terraces. Those along the Mosel and Ahr valleys are

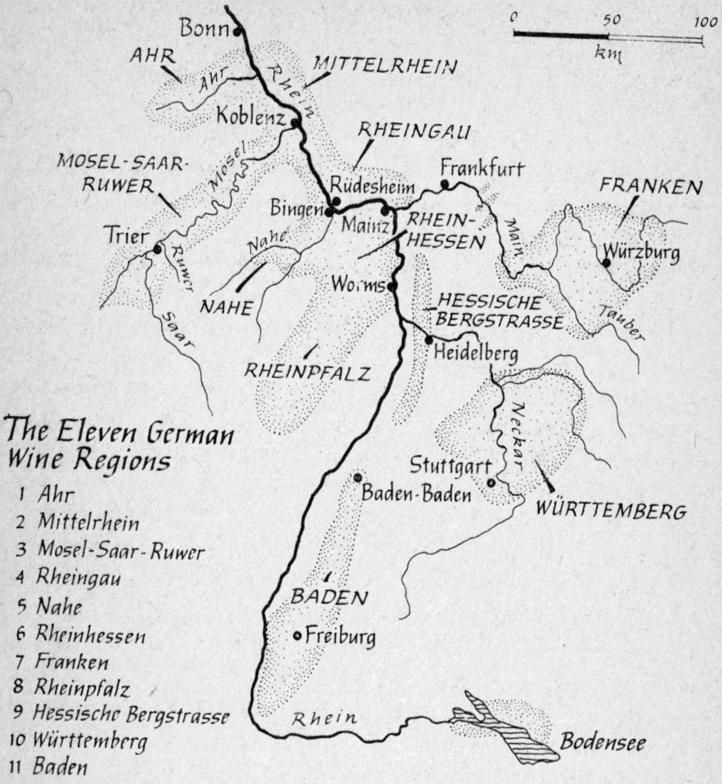

particularly steep and make it necessary for most of the arduous work to be carried out by hand. Rheinhessen and the Rheinpfalz have vineyards in level field-like plantations.

Green as well as black grapes are grown in Germany, but the green predominate. The main green varieties are:

1. Riesling: a very light grape, predominantly grown in the Mittelrhein, along the Mosel, in the Rheingau and along the Hessische Bergstrasse.
2. Silvaner: a slightly bronze-coloured grape, predominantly grown in the Rheinpfalz, in Rheinhessen and along the Nahe.

3. Müller-Thurgau: a slightly pink grape, being a cross between Riesling and Silvaner; it is found mainly in Franken, Baden, in the Rheinpfalz, in Rheinhessen and along the Nahe.

The main red vines grown in Germany are:

1. Burgunder: a dark blue grape which was originally introduced into Germany from Burgundy in France. It is the main type of vine in the Ahr Valley, the most northern wine region; it is also found in Baden.
2. Trollinger: lighter than Burgunder. Mainly grown in Württemberg.

Germany produces three types of wine. White wine is made from green grape juice, whilst red wine is produced from mashed black grapes. Fermentation is started with the grape pulp, which includes the grape skins to achieve the dark red colour of the wine. Rosé wine is also made from black grapes but in this case the grape juice is fermented without any grape skins.

German wines are dry and low in alcohol content compared with wines produced in other countries. By measuring the sugar content of the must the alcohol content of a wine can be calculated in advance. The sugar content is measured in Öchsle with an instrument introduced during the nineteenth century by the chemist and wine lover Ferdinand Öchsle from Pforzheim. Grape harvest in Germany lasts from September to December. The fermentation of the grape juice takes several weeks and produces the so-called 'new wine', a milky-looking drink, high in CO_2, which is also called Federweisser. In South Germany the Federweisser is served as a local speciality, with fresh sweet chestnuts in the Palatinate, or onion cake (Zwiebelkuchen) in Baden. The 'new wine' still needs several months to allow impurities to settle and to ripen before it is bottled. Traditionally, Rhine wine is bottled in brown bottles, whilst Mosel wine comes in green bottles. In Baden the wine is bottled in Bocksbeutel with their distinctive short-necked shape.

According to German wine law, wines are graded in three different classes. The class gives an indication of the individual wine's quality and has to appear on the label.

1. Table wine (Tafelwein) must come from one of the four main

German wine areas: Rhine/Mosel, Neckar, Main or Upper Rhine.

2. Quality wine (Qualitätswein) must be from only one of the eleven wine regions, which has to be specified.
3. Graded Quality Wine (Qualitätswein mit Prädikat) is divided into five grades in ascending order of sweetness and quality. The grade depends on the natural sugar content of the must. No sugar may be added to the juice.
   (a) Kabinett: a dry wine produced from grapes harvested in October.
   (b) Spätlese: wine produced from grapes harvested later than the normal time.
   (c) Auslese: wine produced from specially selected fully matured grapes.
   (d) Trockenbeerenauslese: wine made from raisin-like grapes which are dried as a result of 'noble rot' (Edelfäule).
   (e) Eiswein: wine produced from grapes harvested after the first frost. They are particularly sweet.

Quality wines and graded quality wines must also show the official examination number on the label.

There are no fixed rules for selection of a wine to accompany a particular meal. The combination depends on one's taste. A general rule indicates that white wine is appropriate with fish, chicken and veal, whilst red wine is associated with beef, game, goose and turkey. Table wine, Quality wine and Kabinett are suitable to be served with meals, whilst the higher grade wines of Spätlese, and Auslese are usually drunk on their own for entertaining friends in the evening. Trockenbeerenauslese and Eiswein are usually reserved for special occasions.

The ideal temperature for serving white and rosé wine is 10–12 °C (50–54 °F) with the wine being cooled under running water. Red wine should be at a temperature of 18 °C (64 °F) when served. The bottle should be de-corked 2–3 hours before serving and left in a warm room. It should not be placed on a radiator or a hot plate! Before uncorking a bottle, the top part of the metal capsule which covers the cork must be cut away.

The assessment of wine involves the sequence of looking, smelling and tasting and is an ability developed from considerable experience.

BOWLEN

Bowlen time begins in May and lasts throughout the summer. Bowle is a refreshing drink made from cold wine, fruit or the woodruff herb (Waldmeister) and is served during summer evenings.

A May-Bowle is made by immersing a small bunch of woodruff herbs (before flowers appear) in a litre of wine. Two slices of orange and 75 g (3 oz) sugar are added. After 30–40 minutes the herbs are removed. A bottle of champagne or mineral water is added and the well-cooled Bowle is served.

Bowlen are prepared in a Bowle dish—a large glass dish with a lid. Always start a Bowle with wine at room temperature. The wine which is added later should be well cooled. Bowle is cooled by suspending a separate container of ice cubes into it. Never add ice cubes directly to the Bowle as it would dilute it.

Strawberry or Peach Bowle
(Erdbeer-oder Pfirsichbowle)

500 g (1 lb 2 oz) strawberries or peeled and quartered peaches
60 g (2½ oz) sugar
1½ l (3 pt) white wine
1 bottle of champagne or mineral water

Wash and sugar the fruit. Place into the Bowle dish with ½ l (1 pt) wine and leave covered for 2–3 hours. Then add the rest of the wine. Just before serving add the champagne.

Orange Bowle
(Apfelsinenbowle)

5 oranges
10 sugar lumps
50 g (2 oz) sugar
1½ l (3 pt) white wine
1 bottle of champagne or mineral water

Wash and dry 2 oranges. Grate their skin on the sugar lumps. Peel all the oranges; cut them into small pieces and remove pips. Mix with the sugar and sugar lumps. Leave covered for 1 hour. Then add ½ l (1 pt) wine and leave for another 2 hours. Add the rest of the cooled wine. Just before serving, pour in the champagne.

Fire-tongs Punch *(Feuerzangenbowle)*

Preparing a Feuerzangenbowle is an interesting event on a cold winter evening. The following utensils are needed: a réchaud; a copper or enamel pan for the Bowle; a sugar-cone holder (Zange) which is laid across the top of the pan to hold the sugar-cone (Zuckerhut).

In Germany special Feuerzangenbowle sets are popular. But it is possible to use a fondue pan with réchaud and to purchase just the sugar-cone and holder. The sugar-cones are made from pressed sugar by German sugar manufacturers and are about 15 cm (6 in) high.

2–3 l (3¾–5¾ pt) red wine
juice from 1 lemon
grated rind from ¼ lemon
5 cloves
1 piece of cinnamon bark
½ l (1 pt) rum (about 55 per cent proof)
juice from 3 oranges

Heat the red wine with the cloves, cinnamon bark and lemon rind. Do not boil. Add the fruit juice. Pour the heated wine into the copper pan over the réchaud. Place the sugar-cone on the holder across the opening of the pan. Spoon the rum over the sugar-cone until the cone is soaked in it. Light the sugar-cone. The sugar will melt and drip into the wine. From time to time, when the flame dies down, add a little more rum with a spoon (keep the bottle away from the flame!), until all the sugar is melted. Stir the wine and serve in heatproof glasses or tea-glasses.

Cold Duck *(Kalte Ente)*

1 lemon
1 l (2 pt) wine
1 tablespoon brandy or orange liqueur
75 g (3 oz) sugar
½ bottle champagne or a small bottle of mineral water

Wash and dry the lemon. Cut into thin slices and place in the Bowle dish. Cover with sugar. Add the brandy and the wine. Leave covered for about 2 hours. Just before serving, pour in the champagne.

Mulled Wine *(Glühwein)*

This is a very warming red wine drink which is served on cold winter evenings. For its preparation it is best to use an enamel or stainless steel saucepan.

1 l (2 pt) red wine
¼ l (½ pt) water
50 g (2 oz) sugar
1 piece of cinnamon bark
5 cloves
grated rind of ½ lemon
1 vanilla pod

Heat all the ingredients, but do *not* boil. Leave to stand over low heat for 20–30 minutes. Remove the vanilla, cinnamon bark and cloves. Serve very hot in heatproof glasses or mugs.

SPIRITS *(Spirituosen)*

Apart from brandy, which is produced from wine, Germany offers a variety of other spirits, commonly called Schnaps. In the North the clear Korn produced from cereals is popular. A well-known brand is the East Fresian Dornkaat. Brandy is also made from fruit. The well-known Steinhäger, a clear juniper brandy, comes from Steinhagen in Westphalia. The Black Forest distillery Schladerer prepares clear fruit brandies from wild Black Forest raspberries (Himbeergeist) and cherries (Kirschwasser).

Other fruit brandies in Baden (South Germany) are prepared from plums (Zwetschgenwasser) and pears (Birnenwasser). Fruit brandies are *not* sweet as is sometimes wrongly assumed. They have a comparatively high alcohol content (45–50 per cent) and are said to assist the digestion after a rich meal. Especially composed to promote the well-being of the stomach is the range of bitter aromatic liqueurs prepared from herb and root extracts such as Jägermeister, Sechsämtertropfen, Underberg and Boonekamp.

Grog *(Grog)*

Grog is a hot rum and water drink which is very warming and particularly appreciated in the North of Germany. A well-known saying may be translated: 'Rum is necessary and water may also be used.' Fill a glass two-thirds with hot water. Add 1–2 teaspoons of sugar to taste. Fill the last third of the glass with rum. Some rum producers in Germany (for example Pott), supply individual small bottles which are just the right size to prepare one glass of Grog.

Bear's Liqueur *(Bärenschnaps—East Germany)*

¾ l (1½ pt) rum
500 g (1 lb 2 oz) honey
4 cloves

Add the honey and cloves to the rum in a saucepan and bring to the boil. Leave to cool and put into bottles. Care should be taken over fermentation whilst storing the bottles.

Egg Punch (*Eierpunsch*)

350 g (12 oz) sugar
2 eggs
4 egg yolks
1 lemon
½ l (1 pt) white wine
½ l (1 pt) water
⅜ l (¾ pt) rum

Whisk the eggs, egg yolks and sugar. Add the wine, water, juice and grated rind of the lemon. Whisk continuously over low heat until the mixture thickens. Then add the rum. Remove from hot plate and carry on whisking for a while. Serve hot in warmed glasses.

Egg Liqueur (*Eierlikör*)

6–7 egg yolks
150 g (5 oz) icing sugar
core of a vanilla pod
½ l (1 pt) brandy

Whisk the egg yolks and the sugar with an electric mixer until creamy. Gradually stir in the brandy. Add the vanilla and put into bottles. Shake the bottle before serving.

Index

Lists of recipes, in German and English, will be found at the beginning of each chapter